COLLECTED WHEEL PUBLICATIONS

VOLUME 18

NUMBERS 265 – 280

BPE

BPS Pariyatti Editions

BPS Pariyatti Editions
An imprint of Pariyatti Publishing
www.pariyatti.org

Although this is an American edition, we have left any British spelling of words unchanged.

First BPS Pariyatti Edition, 2025
ISBN: 978-1-68172-192-7 (Print)
ISBN: 978-1-68172-193-4 (PDF)
ISBN: 978-1-68172-194-1 (ePub)
ISBN: 978-1-68172-195-8 (Mobi)
LCCN: 2018940050

Contents

WH 265 Buddhism and Society
Heinz Bechert 1

WH 266 & 267 Wayfaring
Bhikkhu Sobin S. Namto 15

WH 268 The Second Discourse of the Buddha
Dr. N. K. G. Mendis 49

WH 269 The Exposition of Non-Conflict
Bhikkhu Ñāṇamoli 65

WH 270 Three Symbolic Ways of Life
Carlo Gragnani 85

WH 271 & 272 Bag of Bones
Bhikkhu Khantipālo 103

WH 273 & 274 Ānanda
Hellmuth Hecker 159

WH 275 & 276 Buddhism and Christianity: A Positive Approach
M. O' C. Walshe 215

WH 277 & 278 Transcendental Dependent Arising
Bhikkhu Bodhi 253

WH 279 Inspiration from the Dhammapada
Dr. N. K. G. Mendis 305

WH 280 The Position of Women in Buddhism
Dr. (Mrs.) L.S. Dewaraja 333

Key to Abbreviations

A	Aṅguttara Nikāya	Paṭis	Paṭisambhidamagga
Ap	Apadāna	Peṭ	Peṭakopadesa
Bv	Buddhavaṃsa	S	Saṃyutta Nikāya
Cp	Cariyāpiṭaka	Sn	Suttanipāta
D	Dīgha Nikāya	Th	Theragātha
Dhp	Dhammapada	Thī	Therigātha
Dhs	Dhammasaṅgaṇī	Ud	Udāna
It	Itivuttaka	Vibh	Vibhaṅga
Ja	Jātaka verses and commentary	Vin	Vinaya-piṭaka
Khp	Khuddakapāṭha	Vism	Visuddhimagga
M	Majjhima Nikāya	Vism-mhṭ	Visuddhimagga Sub-commentary
Mil	Milindapañha	Vv	Vimānavatthu
Nett	Nettipakaraṇa	Nidd	Niddesa

The above is the abbreviation scheme of the Pali Text Society (PTS) as given in *A Dictionary of Pali* by Margaret Cone.

The commentaries, *aṭṭhakathā*, are abbreviated by using a hyphen and an "a" ("-a") following the abbreviation of the text, e.g., *Dīgha Nikāya Aṭṭhakathā* = D-a. Likewise the sub-commentaries are abbreviated by a "ṭ" ("-ṭ") following the abbreviation of the text.

The sutta reference abbreviation system for the four Nikāyas, as is used in Bhikkhu Bodhi's translations is:

AN	Aṅguttara Nikāya	DN	Dīgha Nikāya
MN	Majjhima Nikāya	Sn	Saṃyutta Nikāya
J	Jātaka story	Mv	Mahāvagga (Vinaya Piṭaka)
Cv	Cullavagga (Vinaya Piṭaka)	SVibh	Suttavibhaṅga (Vinaya Piṭaka)

Buddhism and Society

by

Heinz Bechert

Professor of Indian and Buddhist Studies,
University of Göttingen

Lecture delivered at Max Müller Bhavans, Poona,
Bangalore and Madras, in April 1978

WHEEL PUBLICATION NO. 265

Buddhism and Society

If we consider the contribution of India to world culture and to the civilization of mankind, Buddhism holds a key position indeed. On the one hand, Buddhism as a philosophy is one of the greatest achievements of human thought. On the other hand, the Buddhist religion has also served as a vehicle for spreading Indian culture far beyond the limits of the subcontinent, to Sri Lanka, to the whole of Central Asia, to Southeast Asia and to East Asia. It was mainly as a Buddhist culture that Indian culture has been accepted and assimilated in countries like Sri Lanka, Burma, Thailand etc., and that it has become the basis for the national cultures of these peoples. India and Buddhism seem so much interrelated to most western observers that many Europeans tend to overlook the fact that Buddhism had almost completely disappeared from India after the Muslim conquest of the northern plains and of Bengal. In recent times, however, we have witnessed a renaissance of interest in Buddhist thought not only in the Buddhist countries of South and Southeast Asia but also in the country of its origin.

In my studies of the interrelation of Buddhism and society, as published in three volumes on *Buddhism, State and Society* (1966–73), I have proposed to distinguish three different forms of Buddhism to be dealt with, viz. early Buddhism, traditional Buddhism and modernistic Buddhism. I may add here that I shall confine myself to the discussion of the relation of Buddhism and society in the so-called Hīnayāna Buddhism. Therefore I shall not enter into a discussion of the changes that have taken place in the other schools of Buddhist thought such as in Mahāyāna and Vajrayāna. Hīnayāna Buddhism may be characterized as the earlier school of Buddhism, and it has survived to the present day in one particular form only, viz. in the form of Theravada Buddhism. The sacred scriptures of the Theravada Buddhists are written in the Pali language.

Thus, we can derive information on the relation of Buddhism and society in the earliest period of the Buddhist Dharma from the Pali scriptures of Theravada Buddhism which may be described as the conservative form of the Buddha's religion. There can be no doubt that originally it was the only objective of the Buddha's

Dharma to show the way to final salvation to mankind, i.e. the way to Nibbāna. The doctrine of *saṃsāra* and rebirth as well as the doctrine of the law of karma were already known in India at that time. The way to Nibbāna as taught by the Buddha is, however, different from the early Upanishadic teachings which had spread at that time, as well as from the way to salvation which was taught by other contemporary ascetic schools like by the Jains and the Ājīvakas. The Buddha did not accept the concept of an eternal soul or an *ātman* nor did he approve of the extreme ascetic practices as prescribed by Mahāvīra, the founder of the Jain religion. The Buddhist concept of the universe may best be described as the concept of a constant and continuous "process" which is being governed by eternal and unchangeable laws, in short by Dharma. This is the Dharma which is fully known to the Buddha and which was taught by the Buddha.

There exists, however, no permanent substance nor an eternal soul nor an almighty god nor anything else which could escape from the law of impermanence. Again, from this impermanence, it follows that everything is subject to the law of suffering. And because there is no eternal "self" which could escape from impermanence and suffering, we must realize that there are three *lakkhaṇas*, i.e. the three basic characteristics of everything that exists, viz. suffering (*dukkhatā*), impermanence (*aniccatā*) and being not the self (*anattatā*). It is only with the realization of this true nature of the universe that we may escape from the endless cycle of rebirth or *saṃsāra* and may attain to Nibbāna. Nibbāna, however, cannot be described simply as "nothingness." Nibbāna is totally different from anything that we could describe as extant or by any other categories accessible to our ways of thinking.

I shall not deal with more details of Buddhist philosophy here, but I should like to draw your attention to the consequences of this particular way of thinking. If salvation can be reached only by non-involvement in worldly affairs and by deep meditation, it is obvious that the early Buddhist community tended to be an elitist movement, oriented towards nothing else than salvation. It was elitist in the sense of being accepted by a spiritual elite, not elitist in the sense of being open only to particular sections of the people as the Vedic tradition has been. On the contrary, the Buddhist Saṅgha or monastic order was open to anybody irrespectively of his caste, and all members of the Saṅgha had equal rights and obligations. In this sense, the early Buddhist Saṅgha can be characterized as egalitarian. Some modern authors have even described it as democratic, but the term "democracy" means the "rule of the people." In the early Buddhist Saṅgha, however, there was no question of anybody ruling over anybody. The laws for the Saṅgha were issued by the Buddha, and the Buddha declined to appoint any successor. Only *Dharma*, i.e. the Buddhist law as taught by the Enlightened One, was to govern the Saṅgha, and all bhikkhus were expected to follow the Dharma.

It is easy to understand why the early Buddhist community was conceived as a strictly non-political religious movement. Any entanglement of the Saṅgha in worldly affairs would have contravened the main goal of the religious life itself, viz. reaching Nibbāna. At the same time, the then prevailing political order in Northern India made it advisable for all ascetic groups to avoid any misunderstandings as to their political neutrality, because there existed no continuous political authority, but various rather small and often instable states only at that time. The Buddha gave, of course, instructions to kings that they should practise righteousness and observe peace. He also commented upon a given situation in political life in his famous remarks concerning the Vajjis as handed down in the Sutras, but this was not meant to be an instruction on political matters, but it was the background for advice given to the Saṅgha as we learn from the textual evidence. We would be wrong to say that there is no teaching of early Buddhism on state and politics, but we may describe this as nothing else than an application of the *gihivinaya*, i.e. the layman's code of ethical conduct as taught by the Buddha, to public life. The principle of non-violation of all beings (*ahiṃsa*) must be recognized as the superior principle of Buddhist ethics in all spheres of life inclusive of political and communal life.

A new situation arose after the Mauryan empire had been created. Emperor Asoka was the first Indian ruler to elaborate a well-defined religious policy in an great Indian Empire. And it was during his reign that Buddhism emerged as a leading spiritual force under the protection of a great political authority all over India and even beyond the borders of the Mauryan empire. Asoka, though personally a follower of the Buddhist religion, did not yet make Buddhism the religion of the state. The state was to further all great religious movements, as we can see from Asoka's famous rock edicts and other inscriptions which he ordered to be engraved in all parts of his empire. Incidentally, these inscriptions are still the earliest exactly dated written records from India. Asoka did not explicitly propagate Buddhism in his edicts, but he propagated an understanding of Dharma which was based on Buddhist thought, but remained equally acceptable by other important religious communities of India. Non-violation of living beings, i.e. *ahiṃsa*, is being declared to be an ethical principle binding for the individual citizen as well as for the political power. The king no longer strives to achieve the *digvijaya*, i.e. the rule over the world by force of his army, but he aims at the *digvijaya* of the Dharma, the principle of morality which is to replace the power struggle as it was provided for by secular political theory. The king also decided to send out missionaries to all neighbouring countries to spread Dharma all over the world. Within his empire, he accepted full responsibility of ruler and state for the well-being of all his subjects. Asoka's rule as described in his inscriptions may be characterized as the first welfare state in history. Building hospitals and many other forms of social responsibility for welfare and relief of the people were declared to be the main task of the ruler.

At the same time, Asoka also developed a new religious policy which was designed to protect the religious institutions of Buddhism. In this context, his reform of the Buddhist Saṅgha by excluding unworthy elements from the monastic order must be mentioned. This reform is recorded by inscriptions as well as by the chroniclers of Sri Lanka. Until then, the institutions of the Buddhist order had no formal relation with the state or with the ruler. Pious kings would offer donations to the monks and they would provide land for the establishment of monasteries, but questions of the administration of the internal affairs of the Saṅgha until then had remained outside the scope of interest of the state. Now, Asoka appointed particular state officers to look after the religious institutions and to provide for public protection of these institutions. Unworthy elements were to be excluded from the Saṅgha and the king's religious officers were ordered to ensure the observation of the monastic laws in accordance with the regulations of Vinaya (Buddhist ecclesiastical law).

If we compare Asokan Buddhism with original Buddhism, we do not find any contradiction, but we observe the introduction of a new goal, viz. the aim to build up a society which is modelled on Buddhist ideals. As we have seen before, the Buddha had already given instructions to rulers to follow the code of Buddhist ethics for laymen, but we cannot trace a separate Buddhist political theory in the, earliest period. From Asoka's times onwards, however, Buddhist states were established, i.e. states where Buddhism had become the national and the state religion. The first country to accept Buddhism as a result of Asoka's missions was Sri Lanka or Ceylon. Almost simultaneously, the Dharma was also introduced to the people of Suvaṇṇabhūmi, i.e. the Mon people of Lower Burma. Since then, Theravada Buddhism has become the national religion of the Sinhala people in Sri Lanka, and in the course of time it has spread over most parts of mainland Southeast Asia. In all these countries, the Buddhist Saṅgha has played an essential role as a vehicle for the spread of advanced cultural achievements from India to these then still underdeveloped regions.

As mentioned before, Theravada Buddhists made a continuous effort to preserve the ancient interpretation of Lord Buddha's teachings. We may add, however, that some of the most noteworthy innovations or supplementary traditions observed in Theravada of Ceylon and Southeast Asia may be identified as the particular ways in which Buddhist thought has influenced society in these countries. In the course of time, a rather complex political theory based on the acceptance of Buddhism was worked out. We may term this system of traditions and beliefs as "traditional Buddhism."

The political teachings of traditional Buddhism were not handed down in a compendium which could be compared with the *Arthaśāstra*, the hand-book of secular Indian statecraft. The Buddhists choose another form of propagating their concepts of social and political thought which is known from India too, viz. that of giving examples. This type of literature is commonly known as *nīti* literature. There is, however, one basic difference between all other types of *nīti* literature and the literature which I have in mind now. This difference consists in the fact that the Buddhists of Ceylon and Southeast Asia decided to use the vehicle of history in order to teach the concepts of state and society that a Buddhist should follow. Thus, from the time of king Duṭṭhagāmaṇi in the 2nd century B.C., onwards, history was written in Sri Lanka with the particular aim to serve didactic purposes. Thereby the earliest historical records known from South Asian tradition came into existence. Based on these early accounts, the *Dīpavaṃsa* or "Chronicle of the Island" of Ceylon was composed in the 4th or 5th century A.D. and Mahānāma wrote the *Mahāvaṃsa*, the "Great Chronicle" of the island, during the first part of the 6th century.

As early as in these works, we can trace the political theory of traditional Theravada Buddhism. The ideas known from Asoka's inscriptions were further elaborated now: The political authority should fulfil the aim to build up a welfare-state where such abundance is to be produced that there is sufficient wealth not only for providing for the welfare of the poor and the disabled, but also for securing the opportunity of leading the religious life of a bhikkhu to as many people as possible. In addition, the king is required not only to make provision for the material welfare of the Saṅgha, but also to supervise the monastic institutions in order to ensure that they fulfil their duties and observe the monastic rules. During this so-called mediaeval period, regulations for the Saṅgha were formulated by Saṅgha assemblies and ceremonially promulgated by the king of Sri Lanka. Such documents are known as *katikāvattas*. Several of these texts have been preserved and translated into English recently.

In this way, the state was transformed into an institution with religious legitimation. The Buddhist religion now constituted the essential factor to build up the identity and the legitimation of political authority, and, at the same time, it became a factor restricting the use and preventing the misuse of political power. Simultaneously the relation of Saṅgha and society radically changed as a consequence of the above-mentioned responsibility of the Saṅgha for spreading cultural achievements. In early Northern India, the Buddhist monk's role was restricted to practising and teaching the way to Nibbāna. It did not yet extend to the task of spreading or preserving traditional literary culture. True enough, beginning with the Maurya period, the Buddhists of India established their own particular literature including Buddhist *kavyas*, philosophical works etc., but the Buddhist monks of India have never assumed responsibility for preserving literature and science as such. They only contributed towards its development in competition with other groups. However, in Sri Lanka as well as in Buddhist Burma, the task of preserving the literary heritage of the national culture has been entrusted to the Buddhist Saṅgha.

In this context, we should not forget the role which the Saṅgha has played for nation-building. It is a widespread misunderstanding of modern historians to claim that "nationalism" was a new feature of 19th century. In fact, nationalism can be traced back many centuries, not only in European, but also in Asian history. This is also the case with Sri Lanka and Burma. Buddhism became the national religion of the Sinhala nation when it was introduced in the 3rd century B.C., whereas the Buddha's followers had coexisted side by side with several other religious communities wherever the Dharma had spread in mainland India. Therefore, along with the language factor, Buddhism may be identified to have been the essential factor of nation building allowing the Sinhala nation to develop a marked and continuous sense of identity which lasts until today. Within these political and social structures of the Buddhist kingdoms of Ceylon and Southeast Asia, the Saṅgha guaranteed for the continuity of most cultural traditions and educational values as well as for the application of Buddhist ideals in communal life. The claims in this respect were clearly formulated in the ancient chronicles as well as by later Buddhist authors.

This traditional role of the Saṅgha in social and in political life was embedded in a firmly established system of state-Saṅgha relations and it formed part of a particular structure of political authority which derives its legitimation from religious values. The underlying ideas are formulated in inscriptions and in other documents from mediaeval Ceylon and Burma. Several concepts of different origin have merged together in this system of traditional Buddhist politics. Firstly, the ruler is described as a *cakravartin*, i.e. as the ideal world-ruler who governs the world without falling back upon the use of force. The *cakravartin* ideal is found in the early Buddhist scriptures as well as in many other religious traditions of India, and it is related to the belief that there was a golden age in the past and that, in the cyclic evolution of the world, there will be a golden age in the future again.

Cakravartin has become an official title of Buddhist kings since many centuries. Secondly, we find the concept of the *devarāja*. The concept of divine kingships originated in Hindu India, and it survived in Nepal until very recently. In the Khmer kingdom of mediaeval Cambodia, it reached its most powerful and magnificent representation. The Buddhist kings also adopted the *devarāja* concept, but in a more mitigated way. It was still valid in Thailand at the beginning of our century. For ceremonies at the royal court, therefore, brahmin priests were employed by the Buddhist kings. Still another element of legitimation was the identification of the king as a *bodhisattva*, i.e. as a future Buddha. It originated from an undercurrent of Mahayanistic influence in mediaeval Sri Lanka and in Southeast Asia which was finally superseded by Theravada orthodoxy. Another element of the legitimation of authority was the *Dharmarāja* concept. Here, Hindu and Buddhist thought have merged in a rather syncretistic way. The *rājadharmas* of Buddhist tradition are enumerated and described in the Jātakas, i.e., the Buddhist birth stories, whereas those of Hindu thought were elaborated in Purāṇas and related works.

In the purely Buddhist tradition as represented by the Buddhist chronicles, Asoka has remained the model king whom to follow is the highest aim of a ruler. The king is expected to support the *Sāsana*, i.e. the institutions of the Buddhist religion, not only by donations to the Saṅgha, but also by exercising his patronage over all religious institutions. Following the advice given by himself and by the example of Asoka, not only Buddhist but also non-Buddhist religious institutions are to be supported by the king. Patronizing the Saṅgha implies that the king takes the necessary steps for a reform of the Saṅgha if necessary. This is termed "Sāsana reform." Thus, there is an intimate interrelation of Saṅgha and state. Though the Saṅgha is entrusted with the goal of ensuring that the religious and ethical values should be upheld in the country, the bhikkhus were expected not to indulge in any activities which fall into the realm of the secular power, e.g. in political activities as such.

The relation between Saṅgha and laity was an equally close one on the lower level of village religion. Here, the main religious activities consisted of "merit-making" and participation in "merit-making" (*puñña* and *pattānumodanā*). This aim, of course, was far away from the original goal of Buddhism, because it was directed towards good karmic results like good rebirth etc. Performing meritorious deeds did not, however, in any way conflict with genuine Buddhist ideals, though it represented a much lower level of spiritual progress than that to be achieved by meditation as taught in the Buddhist scriptures. If considered as an end in itself, however, merit making could even be described as a diversion from the way to Nibbāna, but it was always accepted as a great value for those on the lower stages of the way to salvation. The Saṅgha is the "highest field of merit," and the participation of the bhikkhus in the traditional merit-producing ceremonies forms the most important occasions of community life. At the same time, the monks, being the guardians of higher civilization in the villages, were the teachers in the rural areas where the village youth studied under their guidance. It is well known that the majority of the Buddhist population in Ceylon and in Southeast Asia were literate since an early period. As late as in early 19th century, the percentage of illiterates was higher in England than in Ceylon at the same time.

From these remarks, we may conclude in which manifold ways the Buddhist Saṅgha interacted with society in traditional Buddhism. Theoretically, Buddhism had remained rather unchanged in the Theravada tradition. Innovations as propagated by the adherents of Mahāyana were rejected; and the scriptures along with the ancient commentaries continued to be viewed as the only valid sources of the true Dharma. On the other hand, as we have seen, Buddhism had become part of a complicated system of traditions and beliefs which included elements of the so-called "Little Tradition" as well as of the "Great Tradition." of the sophisticated elite. To sum up, Buddhism never has influenced political and social developments as a purely religious theory, but always as in its actual manifestation, i.e. as a part of the totality of a structured system of traditions including notions and beliefs of Buddhist as well as of non-Buddhist origin. In this way, Buddhism was accommodated to serve the needs of the times, and such accommodations were tacitly agreed, not discussed theoretically.

This system of state-Saṅgha relations which was built up in the mediaeval Buddhist kingdoms was destroyed during the colonial age. This breakdown was effected by the strict separation of Saṅgha and state, which was termed the "disestablishment" of Buddhism. The institutions of Buddhism were now converted into private institutions, and state patronage as well as state supervision ceased to be exercised. There were predictions made in early 19th century that Buddhism would gradually disappear in Ceylon and in Burma because of its disestablishment. But the opposite happened to be the case. Buddhism was so deeply rooted in the culture of Ceylon and Burma that it became the starting point for the resurgence of national identity. For the newly emerging urban and semi-urban population of the colonial period, Buddhism now served as the symbol of their own cultural heritage and thus it became an integral element in their struggle for freedom from foreign domination.

An idealistic image of life as it was supposed to have been in the precolonial period was pictured by the writers of the independence movement, and these writings were widely read by the new middle class.

In this modern period, the third of the forms of Buddhism mentioned in my introduction came into existence, viz. Buddhist modernism. Buddhist modernism has originated as a reaction against foreign cultural domination and as a revival of the heritage of the ancient national culture. We can draw parallels between Neo-Hinduism and Buddhist modernism. The earliest Neo-Hindu movement was the Brahma-Samaj which was founded by Ram Mohan Roy in 1828, but the Brahma Samaj has remained a very small movement. It was only with the Arys Samaj that Neo-Hinduism became a really influential reform movement in India. It was established in 1875 by Dayanand Sarasvati.

Buddhist modernism was initiated about the same time. The public debates or *vādas* between Buddhist monks and Christian missionaries are considered as the turning-point at which the decline of Buddhism was arrested. The first of these public debates was held as early as in 1865, but the most successful defence of Buddhism was considered to have been produced by Mohotivattē Guṇānanda Thera in the *vāda* of Pānadura in 1873. The text of this debate was translated into English. It was then read by Colonel Olcott who came to Ceylon to help in the Buddhist revival. The most influential of the reformers was, of course, the Anāgārika Dharmapāla who lived from 1864 to 1933. He is well known in all Buddhist countries as the founder of the Mahā Bodhi movement.

This Buddhist resurgence was not simply a revival of traditional Buddhist ideals. It is characterized by the emergence of new concepts, by a response to the challenge presented by Western cultural influence. The modernists argue that Buddhism is by far superior to Christianity. Buddhism is the religion of reason, rejecting blind belief. The philosophy of Buddhism is in full accordance with modern science. "Buddhism and Science" has remained one of the main arguments of Buddhist modernism until today.

To be able to present this argumentation, modern Buddhists began to look back to the original sources of Buddhism with the objective to distinguish between the essential teachings of Buddhism and mythological additions.

In their search for an exact understanding of the original teachings of the Buddha, Buddhist modernists from the East and Western scholars have closely cooperated. As is well known, until the middle of the 19th century, many Western scholars have doubted the historicity of the Buddha. The famous French scholar Emile Senart, e.g., has described the life of the Buddha as a sun myth. It was the German scholar Hermann Oldenberg who first gave a detailed reliable account of the Buddha, his life, his doctrine and his Saṅgha, for the Western world in 1881 in his famous work "Buddha."

Buddhist modernism was started as a movement of a small elite in the Buddhist countries as well as in mainland India. It was first accepted by the highly educated classes only. However, in the course of time, more and more sections of the Buddhist Saṅgha came to know about the new ideas and concepts, and these monks began to disseminate such concepts in the villages. In this way modernistic ideas reached the masses of the population in Buddhist Ceylon and in Burma. It was, of course, a popularized form of these ideas, but it was highly effective to bring about the awakening of a new religio-political consciousness. Thus, the centuries-old intrinsic interrelation of Saṅgha and laity resulted in a sort of mass politicization of the Buddhist population which helped in the necessary process of political and social modernization of the Buddhist countries.

By this development, the concepts of Buddhist modernism were, of course, changed. Traditional beliefs and myths combined with rationalistic elements. New literary traditions and new forms of a mythology which is quite different from the traditional one may be observed. Let me mention two examples only. The Anāgārika Dharmapāla and later Buddhist leaders including Dr. Ambedkar of India have proposed the claim that democracy is an essentially Buddhist concept. Their argument is based on the observation of the structure of the Buddhist Saṅgha. In the Saṅgha equal rights are given to all monks, and the resolutions of the Saṅgha must be passed unanimously for most matters. In some cases, resolutions by a majority of votes are allowable. In this way, basic rules of democracy are virtually identical with basic regulations of the Saṅgha. Therefore, the modernists could claim that the Saṅgha was a model for the democratic organisation of human society: though this may not be correct from an historical point of view, because the Buddha's Dharma was not concerned with the discussion of a political system, yet it proved a very valuable contribution towards political modernization indeed. Another example is the Buddhist justification of the teachings of modern socialism. In a justification of socialist policies in a Buddhist country, the Burmese politician U Ba Swe in 1952 has described socialism as the "lower truth" which may be used to build up a society of affluence which gives opportunity to as many human beings as possible to live a religious life in order to realize the highest truth, i.e. the Dharma of the Buddha. There is a vast literature of Buddhist socialism which is based on this and similar concepts of different levels of thinking. Buddhists, however, should always follow the middle Path and avoid any form of extremism.

Wayfaring

A Manual for Insight Meditators

by

Bhikkhu Sobin S. Namto

WHEEL PUBLICATION NO. 266/267

Foreword

The instruction in this manual is that given by the Venerable P.M. Sobin Namto, our teacher (*achan*), a Buddhist monk and meditation teacher from Thailand. Selected portions were chosen from taped conversations with Achan, recorded in an informal atmosphere. An interview section, slightly edited, is provided for the meditator as general guidance in the initial phases of meditation practice. The instruction is in no sense definitive, as each meditator's experience differs; however, similar problems manifest under different guises. Our frustrations, anxieties and conflicts appear to have a common genesis: all spring from the root-base of greed, hatred and confusion.

The material presented in this digest presumes the reader's acquaintance with the techniques of Vipassanā (Insight Meditation) and fundamental knowledge of the Dharma. The text is not highly polished; some repetition is inevitable. But if a glint of the brilliance of the Crown Jewel of the Dhamma—the way of mindfulness—is reflected within the mind of the reader, these writings will have served their purpose.

Wat Buddhawararam of Denver
4801 Julian Street
Denver, Colorado 80221, U.S.A.

Introduction by Achan Sobin

As a novice, I carefully studied the Buddhist teaching and diligently applied myself to the study of philosophy, scripture, history and language. I could explain the most abstruse points of Buddhist philosophy and speak on the field of Buddhist meditation. My mind was packed to overflowing with facts. Only when I decided to put the books away and actually entered meditation training myself, did I begin to understand truly what I had studied and what I had been taught.

I sincerely hope that each reader is encouraged to pursue the training with ever-greater determination, to search for the truth—to discover the *dharma* not found in books.

May you all persevere on the path.

Achan Sobin

Provisions For the Journey

The arising of Insight-knowledge occurs spontaneously and intuitively. This realization of truth differs, however, from knowledge born of focusing on painful physical and mental phenomena. The Noble Truth of Suffering is not restricted solely to negative conditions of body and mind, nor to the readily observable facts of birth, sickness, old age and death. The suffering, which the Buddha, repeatedly emphasized, concerned the profound truth of the lack of stability of all phenomena in the mental and physical world ... the primal insecurity.

The acknowledgement of this particular aspect of suffering is the gateway to deeper levels of Insight-knowledge. All unliberated beings have this original dis-ease, for we have not penetrated fully the profound magnitude and significance of suffering. The root causes of pain—craving and attachment—have not been completely exposed. By entering training in Insight-development, the meditator experientially discovers the Dharma. The truth becomes a living reality.

The great majority of Buddhists content themselves with superficial knowledge of the teachings, convinced that spiritual evolution is quite beyond their capacity. Let us not be so sceptical of our potential for development! Neglecting to take advantage of our good fortune to practice Insight Meditation is to have wasted the finest opportunity for growth afforded a human being.

The Buddha-Dharma pulses with life. Even the distance of 2,500 years has not obscured the way for the earnest seeker. The path is clearly marked. Why delay any longer?

Novice meditators often enter Vipassanā (Insight) meditation practice with keen expectations of experiencing blissful or mystical states of mind; in fact, occasionally meditators seek training specifically to develop supernormal powers. If we believe the purpose of training is gauged specifically to yield altered states of consciousness, we seriously misunderstand Insight Meditation training. The purpose of training in Vipassana is to *know* the mind, in its actual condition, *moment-to-moment*. Training is undertaken to establish the true power of the mind. Its only purpose is the realization of enlightenment.

The calm and spiritual ease born of Insight is that knowledge giving clear vision of the true nature of existence. We awake to see the illusory nature of the ego concept. The misery-making defilements of the mind are finally totally exposed in the powerful beam of mindfulness. And as we grow watchful and alert, their ability to delude the mind is gradually weakened. This is the coolness that quenches the burning ... the unshakeable calm born of seeing things as they are. It is the refuge giving protection amidst the diffuseness of the world.

Insight training builds mindful awareness. It develops clarity of mind that is strong and precise. Meditation is not our goal, but rather serves as the tool enabling the unfolding of Insight into the real nature of the world.

Meditators are often discouraged during the early stages of practice to discover they are experiencing greater mental and physical pain than ever before. Becoming disheartened and lacking proper guidance, many abandon training, or continue "meditating" in a haphazard, unproductive manner, with little or no discernible progress. This unfortunate situation may prevail for some years. And it is not uncommon to see serious mental disorders result from such mismanaged practice. *Mind development should be cultivated with emphasis on careful progression.*

Initial resistance to training the mind is a normal occurrence, and when the rope of mindfulness is finally applied, the struggle for freedom is intense and searing. Applied too tightly, strain is bound to result; applied too loosely, the mind drifts away. It is at this crucial stage that meditators who are experiencing difficulty should seek all possible means to seek proper guidance.

Meditation training follows the same principles governing the mastery of any skill. Step-by-step training assures steady, sure progress. The perfection of the mind requires the utmost determination and a most decidedly courageous attitude to pursue training through the inevitable confusion, the boredom and restlessness, the physical discomforts and the desire to escape the necessity of disciplining the mind. The desire to run away is strong. But how can we run, shackled as we are by greed, hatred and delusion? The weight of the deluded, unknowing mind is oppressive. We can drop that weight and be free, *now*!

Beginning meditation instruction is simplicity itself: when bodily calmness is present, focus is naturally centered on the breath, an easily discernible object. This main object of mindfulness (the breath) is temporarily averted any time there is awareness of seeing, hearing, smelling, tasting, touching or thinking. The mind is then brought back gently to the breathing.

Lapses in attention are a normal occurrence in the early phases of practice. As concentration is stabilized and the mind is calmed, mindfulness is naturally sharpened. The meditator learns to observe the mind objectively. All feeling-tones, desires, memories, etc. are exposed and scrutinized—gently and non-judgmentally. We learn to look closely at what is *actually present.*

Newcomers to training often feel that meditation is "not going well." Surrendering to depression and impatience, they often wish to terminate practice. The correct procedure to follow is to maintain the position of an observer, simply acknowledging all feelings which arise in consciousness in a calm, detached manner. Nothing is suppressed. We should try to train calmly, patiently, sincerely ... not yearning for quick results.

Training should not be deferred until some nebulous "future time." No certainty exists to guarantee that our mental and physical capabilities will be sufficient to the task. The Buddha had many lay and ordained disciples who made the resolution to practice under the most trying circumstances. Occasionally the ocean of suffering was crossed at the cost of life itself. They felt it was the proper decision, preferable to continuing to live a meaningless existence—a life of desolation and emptiness.

It is not difficult to compose an assortment of a myriad of rationalizations to justify putting off training to another day. Sometimes, as we approach the moment of commitment, hesitation causes us to retreat ... fear is awakened, for we are approaching unknown territory and we wonder if perhaps it isn't better to continue as we are ... we might miss something. And why, after all, should we embark on such difficult training? Immersing ourselves in the normal round is, after all, so easy.

Ultimately, the great incentive for training is our growing sensitivity to suffering and the vacuous, insipid nature of life. It is not really a question of renunciation of the so-called pleasures of life, but rather of interest dying naturally—the allurements fade and grow dim. Until such time as we are stirred by our own unrest, the mind will be uncertain, wavering and full of doubt.

It is crucial that we become aware of our internal drives and the impulse to remain in the world. The most fatal of attachments can be the clinging to suffering itself: the fear of "letting go," the fear of freedom. So we go on clutching suffering to our hearts. Perhaps that is the only thing we have, and we are afraid. The time may come when we realize there is no need to suffer at all, no need to fear the unknown.

One may speak of the spiritual journey as leaping to the "Other Shore"—to Nibbāna. Leaping here signifies dedicating the mind to the task completely, committing ourselves with the same determination as the first astronaut who jumped from the space capsule onto the moon.

When a woman or man reaches awakening, deluded ways of thinking are abandoned. Though life continues rather normally, the mind is free and luminous. It is an immutable condition, impossible to fully relate to others—as is the astronaut's experience not wholly communicable to earth-bound people. *No matter what our circumstances in life, each one of us can attempt this journey.*

The birth of Insight is not very far from us, especially when cultivation of the mind is continuous and resolution is present. There is a saying in Thailand that enlightenment is right under one's nose! So continue breathing mindfully!

Clarity and radiance appear in the minds of the Liberated Ones. The unenlightened mind is dark. Worldly people do not have a crystalline pure, unfettered mind. If we did, there would be no need to practice.

Sights Along the Way

Strange mental phenomena appearing during training is a natural event in the course of Insight practice. Do not permit imagination to create two kinds of understanding. Attention given to any vision or peculiar occurrence only serves to hamper progress. Watch closely and see what is happening. Be the good audience of the drama, but remain unattached to the passing show. Mindfulness will be undermined if interest or curiosity is aroused. Students—use your intelligence! Attention must protect the mind at all times. The unguarded mind permits any weakness to easily gain control.

Do not waste time. If there is confusion regarding practice or fears which cannot be resolved by you, consult your instructor for corrective action.

The student of mental training should understand well the differences between *samādhi*, or concentration-type meditation, and Insight meditation. The mind in higher stages of *samādhi* is temporarily restrained with regard to the mental hindrances. *The highly tranquilized mind cannot gain wisdom.* The flux of phenomena cannot be observed, for consciousness is fixed.

Certainly, no Insight develops without concentration. In Vipassana training, a sufficient level of momentary concentration is developed to do the work of *knowing* the arising and passing away of phenomena.

A meditator may have particular fears of uncomfortable memories half-buried in the shadows of consciousness and suddenly, without warning, the difficulty is encountered in practice. Armed with courage and the attitude of not succumbing in the face of anxiety, the meditator will be able to successfully confront any obstruction. *Focus mindfulness on any disturbing mental state.* Be calm, strong and patient. If fear is permitted to hold sway over the meditator's practice, it will gain in strength and return repeatedly to test the endurance of the meditator. When the obstacle has been faced and the way cleared, training can be resumed. Indeed, the *Dhamma* protects those who practice it.

When one truly understands the urgency to cultivate the mind, the student realizes that training continues everywhere. To "break training" or "return to training" does not arise in the mind of the meditator who fully comprehends the implications of mind-development. Meditators are often confused regarding practice, and actually believe that meditation only occurs when seated cross-legged with eyes closed! Whenever the eyes see a form, the ears hear a sound, the nose senses a smell, the tongue experiences a taste, the body knows touch, or the mind recognizes an idea, one is aware of it. *That is meditation.* We try to remain awake, at all times. If we do not grasp at anything or have attachment, then there is no suffering.

The mastery of the mind increases with devoted practice. We should ask ourselves simple questions and test our understanding daily. Do we feel differently about life? Are we aware of mental defilements when they arise? How soon are we able to remove the nourishment-giving support to these peace-robbing mental stains?

When understanding matures, everything we do in life will be meaningful. When we do any kind of work with attention and clarity, ignorance and defilements cannot enter the guarded mind.

After we have trained in meditation for some time, if there is no improvement in our daily life we may be certain that a particular understanding is lacking. Do we know how to rectify the situation?

Usually a meditator will realize some level of Insight after continuous practice of Vipassana training for seven days, seven weeks or seven months. If no higher knowledge has been realized during these periods, it will be reached during other stages of practice.

A student who wishes to terminate an intensive period of practice and resume training at a later time will continue from the level of development attained. The awakened condition of mind does not have to manifest at any particular moment; in fact, if the goal of liberation is not attained within this lifetime, one can proceed in the next life. Firm intention and high motivation, however, must be present to walk the path.

As meditation practice develops, the student will have experiences never encountered in ordinary life. The body will seem to disappear and no "self" can be found to exist. Its "ownerlessness" becomes clearer. The physical body will be perceived solely as an accumulation of aggregates of form, feeling, perception, mental formations and consciousness, conditionally existent and ever-disposed to suffering. Memories and all thoughts will be seen to appear and disappear in lightening-quick flashes. Awakening is approaching when we perceive these truths for ourselves. Our doubts will be completely resolved. Our questions no longer pertain. A calm, unshakeable certainty is born. We simply *know.*

During periods of intensive retreat, it is difficult for the meditator to evaluate progress during certain stages of practice. The major thrust of attention is directed toward keeping mindfulness on all activities, making self-evaluation practically impossible.

Feedback is an essential element in meditation training, and it is the duty of the teacher to be aware of the increasing strength of a student's practice. After the trainee has been practicing for some time, an appraisal should be made so the meditator can be aware of the significance of training. This is especially necessary when the student feels that meditation has not been going well. The meditator may, in some instances, actually be progressing.

Meditation training should not proceed blindly or unthinkingly.

If we could focus precisely on the present moment when following the mindful walking exercise, then the idea of "my" leg would not arise. There would be no "I" involvement and no "practice." Similarly, the eye would not be able to identify objects coming into the area of perception. Sound, which merely has the function of entering the eardrum and causing it to vibrate, would not be concretized as speech or music, etc. In fact, it is possible to focus on the split-second between hearing sound and recognizing it in the conventional manner.

Conventional interpretation of sense data is necessary, of course, for functioning in the mundane world. In Vipassana training, however, the meditator exposes the reality behind all appearances. It is our usual way of interpreting sense perception which leads us astray, compounding the error by superimposing negative and positive qualities on bare cognitive reception.

The Enlightened Ones can see so-called beautiful or ugly physical forms and view them objectively, with equanimity, i.e., without the discriminating mind giving rise to attraction or repulsion. Everything is seen as it really is: impermanent, possessing the potentiality of suffering or dissatisfaction, and ownerless. The man or woman who truly comprehends the nature of the world does not cling to appearances or conceptions. The ordinary person and the person of Insight can remain in society but the latter truly knows the world as it is. There is no possibility of deception, of having the mind shift off-center.

This is the truth about our physical and mental world. Each meditator can verify it personally. Rapid progress can then be made toward awakening.

Any time when we can gather together all our meditative energies into one unique, powerful force—specifically the concentrated power of the Eightfold Path—the groundwork has been prepared which has the strength, endurance and direction to enable the realization of a higher level of Insight.

After some skill has been acquired in training, meditators should be able to more easily detect the instant when mindfulness is weakening. Focus well on every activity and mindfulness will resume its strength.

The meditator may, in fact, be able to detect that developed mindfulness carries a comfortable, alert feeling; when it decreases, a subtle sluggishness can be sensed. In all circumstances, try to be aware of the strength of mindfulness.

In all stages of training, Insight can occur in the presence of so-called "good" or "bad" states of mind. In Vipassana practice, we discover such negative or positive conditions are *equally unstable*—both states rise and fall away. The deeper the level of truth realized, the more profound will be our understanding of life.

Meditators may find detailed information regarding the development of Insight in the section relating to the Stages of Purification as presented in *The Path of Purification* (*Visuddhimagga*), by Buddhaghosa.

Training which does not proceed through stages of Insight remains training in the worldly sphere and will not lead to the end of suffering and confusion. One's practice merely remains a practice.

An erratic stop-and-start pattern of meditation practice delays progress. Nevertheless, students should be aware of their zeal for training and not proceed if faith in the practice has weakened. Further progress in the development of Insight meditation can proceed only when confidence, earnestness and powerful mindfulness are equally matched.

There is an initial stage of Insight which leaves the meditator experiencing a strange depression and restlessness. This uneasiness is peculiar to the dawning of Insight and has no parallel with worldly mental states of distress. A sense of amazement appears, as though one has seen for the first time the impermanent, suffering and impersonal nature of the world. These facts of existence were known before, of course, but seen only with worldly understanding—until now.

A loneliness suddenly descends. There is nothing in the world in which we can place our trust. A nauseating desolation, sometimes approaching oceanic proportions, may be acute for a time. And one feels isolated from the rest of the world.

The meditator who is not aware of the basis of these feelings very likely may develop pronounced feelings of anxiety and agitation. Rebellion at this stage is a frequent response to this melancholic condition. The meditator may feel training is useless and that it is preferable to leave practice rather than endure such trials. During this crisis a teacher can direct attention to the source of this most stressful condition. The student will understand that these feelings appear as a phase in practice and the disquiet emanates from his own mind. The temptation to abandon practice will be put to rest and training can be resumed.

When first entering practice, trainees have to contend with the hindrances of sensuous desire, ill-will, laziness, restlessness and sceptical doubt. When the student progresses beyond that point, even more subtle defilements appear to test the endurance of the meditator. These tests along the path are called Defects or Defilements of Insight. There are ten Imperfections: effulgence of light, rapture, tranquility, happiness, faith, exertion or energy, mindfulness, knowledge, equanimity, and gratification. Each category can be further enlarged as to the particular variety of Imperfection the meditator may experience. *Please understand they are not in themselves defilements, but may become the basis for subtle feelings of pride.* In fact, many meditators experiencing one or the other may feel they have reached enlightenment! Some practitioners of Vipassanā meditation reach a plateau where total peace and emptiness prevails and they think that Nibbāna has been realized. They ask their teacher to release them from practice. Others take great pride in believing themselves to be good meditators. It is extremely easy to grasp at any one of these stages. Inability to progress further in practice is often linked to attachment at this stage. It is the rare person indeed who can self-monitor practice at this point. The inexperienced student will hardly realize that attachments are being formed.

Our feelings therefore can cause us many difficulties. It is the mind which is fooling us, playing games. The mind has been enslaved by defilements for so long that it will not relinquish its hold without a death struggle.

Continue your practice steadfastly. Above all, don't let your feelings be your teachers.

The Way Clears

Correct practice of Vipassanā Meditation is the highest cultivation of The Noble Eightfold Path. Correct practice of The Eightfold Path means living constantly with mindfulness. Mindfulness is our only protection from delusion and suffering in the world.

Only when realizing the first stage of deliverance can the precepts for wholesome living or morality be firmly established. Until that attainment, ordinary human beings will experience fluctuations in observing the requisites for harmless living.

According to Buddhist tradition, the Stream-Winner (*Sotāpanna*) is one who has realized the first liberation. He or she has perfected the Five Precepts of basic morality which arise spontaneously and never disappear. No necessity exists for formally taking the precepts. The Once-Returner (*Sakadāgāmi*) also has the Five Precepts which appear automatically. The Never-Returner (*Anāgāmi*) spontaneously observes the Eight Precepts at all times. Though they may live at home, they have truly given up attachment to their families. The Buddhas and Enlightened Saints have established natural morality permanently. It is true morality of the purest kind, for the Awakened Ones always have mindfulness. The specific development of spontaneously-arising morality for living in the world belongs exclusively to those Noble Persons who have entered the path to Nibbāna.

The type of virtuous conduct or morality maintained during periods of meditation retreat is observed by those disciples who are committed to walking the path to liberation. The requisites for correct living are fulfilled when mindfulness rules all activities of thought, word and deed. No delusion or suffering can gain entry into the protected mind.

It should be noted that the blameless conduct born of following the Five, Eight or Ten Precepts of the Buddhist lay devotee, or the many disciplinary rules governing the monk or nun, are essential for the orderly functioning of the lay or religious life. The observance of these worldly rules permits the follower, lay or clergy, entrance into the heavenly worlds alone. Not even the most rigid adherence to these precepts, however, will permit the realization of Nibbāna if penetration into the true nature of life is lacking. *The discovery of truth is gained only by insight, which is inextricably linked with the development of concentration and morality.*

When attachment to the world begins to wane, there arises a deeper penetration of the world as it is. A natural compassion and sympathy begins to flow to all creatures; their suffering is seen sharply. Life moves on and for the person of growing Insight, life tends to appear as rather normal in most respects—but there is a difference. When something in the worldly sphere is not obtained, no disappointment arises. There is the understanding that nothing in the world is actually "mine," that nothing really belongs to one. This awareness allows us to live more at ease than the person who lives with grasping, who does not see the world clearly.

The Buddhist texts say that the person with clear spiritual vision sees the world as a grand, gorgeous play, forever rolling on and on, one act following another. A play. A dream. Buddhist scripture also tells of a glittering chariot belonging to a king. His subjects were so entranced by this splendid vehicle that its true purpose was all but forgotten. Our true purpose in this world is to end suffering—to go home, to realize Nibbāna.

The Buddha and his disciples, of course, wished to help suffering humanity. They lived in the same physical world with other beings. They were, however, enlightened, free beings. They knew the magnitude of suffering and looked upon this sorrowful world with utmost compassion. In their wisdom, however, they knew that human beings differ in their capacity for understanding the truth. There were people who had difficulty understanding the truth and could not follow the path at all. Others listened, but had no desire to change their life. Only those people who had been taught the lessons that suffering so amply provides could benefit at all from the teaching. At least they were willing to change the direction of their lives.

The Buddha used the simile of a lotus to describe the spiritual ascension of the human being. The lotus begins its journey to the sun from an underwater bed of mud. No one knows exactly when—or if—the lotus will bloom. When the bud finally does open, the plant may be healthy or rotten. As the bud pushes its way to the surface, it may be snapped away by a sea animal. Some flowers will indeed be hovering above the surface of the water, and when the sun warms the petals, they bloom—and receive the light.

The life of the individual is no different with regard to understanding. Some may not come in contact with the path in this lifetime, others will meet it and, depending on their understanding, develop the path to a lesser or greater degree. And, of course, others may turn to another direction.

When it is possible we should try to help others. There are many different ways we can aid each other, but it is extremely difficult to help others skillfully. We do not know their past history or their tendencies. Sometimes we can help by doing nothing at all. If we can maintain a balanced mind then we can aid others in the very best way, without becoming entangled in suffering ourselves. To ensnare ourselves in suffering is of no help to anyone at any time.

In the first and final analysis, we should rely on ourselves alone in the development of the spiritual life. The Buddha cautioned that the truth was to be our Supreme Teacher, the only refuge. The Buddha cannot cleanse our defilements, for it is *our* mind which is steeped in confusion. The Buddha and his teachings give the proper direction to follow, but neither he, the teaching, nor the Buddhist clergy possess any power in themselves to lead anyone to Awakening. It depends entirely on our own determination to end suffering. No one can do our work. Similarly, the Good Friend, the meditation teacher, can only offer instruction, pointing the way and helping clear obstacles from the path.

The Buddha always encouraged monks, nuns and laity to constantly develop mindfulness. The Enlightened Ones have freedom from ignorance and do not, therefore, have to develop mindfulness as a practice or training. For various reasons, laypeople have a tendency to curtail training. We should, therefore, be aware of the great gift of the Dharma bestowed on us and apply ourselves diligently to the practice of mindfulness.

There are only a few guiding principles to be emphasized for all-round practice of mindfulness in our everyday life:

1. Try to cultivate mindfulness at all times.
2. Have only a single thought—that of staying in the middle path, and not falling into the trap of liking and disliking.
3. We only have this day, this hour, this moment. Continue training until finished.

The Teacher

For many meditators, the association with an experienced teacher can be the pivotal experience influencing the maturation process leading to Insight-knowledge. Perhaps months or years of nearly fruitless meditative efforts may be corrected by merely the briefest hint from a teacher. As the meditator ascends to higher stages of Insight, the obstacles strewn along the path grow so subtle that often the lack of proper guidance precludes further advancement.

The relationship of meditation teacher and student is a delicate, intense and intricate one. Most of us need guidance to integrate our understanding into daily life. Until the day comes when we are "on our own," cut loose from delusion and neurotic attachments, the Good Friend, the meditation teacher, can be the helpful companion during much of that long journey.

The Preparation

The personal interview is the basic communication link between teacher and student. Inquiry is made regarding previous meditation experience and basic knowledge of Dharma. Instruction is given in the theory and practice of Vipassana meditation. Careful watch is made of the student's progress. New instructions are given on the basis of the meditator's stage of knowledge or awareness realized.

The Interview

The meditation interviews which follow trace the practice of two students, commencing on the seventh day of training. Though both students had previous meditation experience, this retreat marked the initial introduction to intensive practice. Quite often questions overlapped and responses are grouped together. The reader is reminded again that instructions are given solely as guidelines for the serious meditator who may not have access to qualified instruction. No written statement, however, can replace the personal guidance of a skilled teacher in assessing the step-by-step progress of a student.

Interview with Student A

Seventh Day

Achan: Now that your mindfulness (*sati*) is stronger, have you noticed anything about your breathing?

Student A: Yes, there is space between the rising and falling of each breath, and the next round of breathing.

Achan: Good. The fact that you perceive space means *sati* is following the breathing well. When the meditator is clearly aware of space in the breathing in-and-out cycle, it is necessary to find additional objects of attention to "spoon-feed" the mind, as you would a child. If attention is placed only on acknowledging breathing and sitting, the mind may find the opportunity to stray. We have to give it more work to do.

I would like you to focus on breathing in ... out ... sitting ... and, now, touching. By "touching" I mean mental touching, not physical impact as such. Actually, they are the same reality for it is the *mind* which focuses on the point of touch, and it is the mind which knows the perception of touch. Focus on the touching point as being a small circle. Place your attention on that point, while mentally acknowledging touching. After you have acknowledged touching, I want to see if you can move your mind and have it "touch" a different area of your body. Choose one point which is most distinct to you: your knee, buttocks, shoulder, etc. Whatever body part is chosen, focus attention there until I have another interview with you and tell you to go ahead and change the point of observation. Since your *sati* is strong now, I want to increase your level of concentration (*samādhi*) as a balancing factor. If you change the point of focus too often, *samādhi* will not arise.

I would like you also to test your *sati* by walking slowly and walking almost normally. Please report the results tomorrow.

Eighth Day

Achan: How is your mindfulness today?

Student B: In this morning's practice, mindfulness was not good at all. Nothing seemed to go right, and my practice was falling apart. I was thoroughly depressed. In the afternoon, however, practice was a good deal better.

Achan: At this stage of training, it is not unusual to have such a varied day. Meditators become extremely sensitive to altering conditions of mind and become easily upset, depressed or worried. They often veer to the other extreme and feel elated by a period of steady mindfulness. Trainees often make judgments: this is good practice; this is bad practice.

Both depression and elation are forms of clinging. One will inevitably suffer when conditions change. Most of us usually wish an unpleasant condition to change and, of course, we want a happy state to remain. You are making too much effort, and strain naturally leads to discouragement and depression which, in turn, drains mindfulness. Elation, as well, pulls you off-center and similarly hampers development. The variance in your practice is proof of the fact of impermanence. Everything in life is uncertain. Though we should certainly try to use our intelligence and act skillfully in the mundane world, the truth is that we really cannot control events as much as we think we can. Most of us dimly perceive this truth, but it makes us uneasy to admit it. We are experts in submerging this fact of life most of the time.

What you have experienced first-hand proves many of the teachings of the Buddha. Suffering happens all the time, by itself. It is the suffering inherent in the worldly condition. Though we cannot fully control a given situation, we can learn to watch the mind. We can give up attachments and unrealistic expectations for ourselves and others. Enough clarity of mind must be present, however, to do this. This is one of the reasons we train in meditation. We can learn from every situation that presents itself. Disappointments arising in life have their value as teaching experience. We should learn the profound truth that disappointments carry: that life is truly uncertain. We should not, however, grow cynical, but rather try to be deeply aware at all times that life is change.

Ninth Day

Achan: Are you able to clearly focus in-out breathing, sitting and touching?

Student A: Yes, every meditation object is quite clear now.

Achan: Fine. I want you to work at making each object of attention as clear as all other objects which rise in consciousness. They are of *equal value*; they all rise and fall away. Each phase of attention should be clear: the contraction and expansion of the abdomen, the sitting, and the touching. When walking mindfully, you should be able to clearly know the lifting of the heel, the rising of the foot, and the placing of the foot on the ground. The word "clear" means focusing on the present moment; noticing precisely how each of these movements arises, stays momentarily, and then falls away.

The clarity that I wish you to develop can be compared to standing by a lake and watching raindrops slowly fall into the water ... watching each drop fall, the rising of the bubbles and circles ... and its spreading out into nothingness. It is like walking in the bright sunlight and seeing spots appear before your eyes—rising and falling away. It is with this precise clarity that each object should be known.

Yesterday, I asked you to test *sati* by walking slowly and walking faster. Were they different? Can you follow mindful walking?

Student A: Both the slow and faster walking were clear most of the time.

Achan: Slow walking is a training exercise in mindfulness. If you can keep mindfulness when walking normally, then do so. It is like riding a bicycle. At first you must exercise great care and hold on with both hands. As skill develops you can relax and even let go with one hand ... or you might let go with both hands. But you must know what you are doing!

Walking faster helps to prevent laziness which often occurs with only slow movements. But I do not want you to walk in a natural gait for a long period. It is easy to become careless in practice and to "forget" mindfulness. I think your *sati* has ability, but I want you to take good care of it—to make sure it is constant.

When you first entered practice, your *samādhi* was much too strong, which is often the case when meditators work alone or are not guided properly. When *samādhi* levels are elevated, it often causes the meditator to feel drowsy, heavy, dull or simply peaceful. Mindfulness is weak when concentration levels are raised. This is important for the student to know.

Testing mindfulness was a way of correcting your overbalance of concentration. From now on, I have to carefully watch the progress of your meditation and closely control your practice. The way to build your *samādhi* now—to balance *sati*—is to have you sit for longer periods of time. Be constantly mindful and *samādhi* will arise of its own volition.

At the present time, there is no other work to do except to watch the appearing and fading of bodily and mental states.

Interview with Student B

Achan: Can you focus equally well on all phases of mindful breathing, sitting and touching?

Student B: The breathing in-and-out is always clearer than the touching.

Achan: Usually the perception of breathing is always clearer. Breathing is a natural activity. It is constantly there, whether we focus on it or not. Our focusing on touching is done less naturally; it is more artificial. But mental "touching" is most important. If a thought were to arise to "touch" the mind, the meditator will be able to know or be aware of the thought. When you are aware of thinking, you will know: "I am thinking," and you can observe how thoughts rise and fall away. We use our mind in the same way that we use it to focus on touching. And when there is awareness of thoughts rising and falling, no grasping occurs—and there is no suffering. I would like you to focus mindfulness on touching until the perception of touching is as clear as the perception of breathing. Do you have any questions?

Student B: Yesterday I experienced a tremendous sense of impermanence. It was overpowering and it was much stronger than anything I have ever experienced. Today it has recurred, but not to such an intense degree. Will it return again to its original strength?

Achan: If you would like it to recur because of curiosity or ego involvement, it will not reappear. In fact, the desire to have it return will actually decrease the power of mindfulness. It will return naturally if you relax and do not think about past experiences. Just continue to develop mindfulness. Do not feel that something is being lost. You are not losing anything at all. Keep to the middle way. There is resistance occasionally to moderating our feelings. We think we will miss certain experiences. With the cultivation of our practice, the natural development of higher stages of Insight will help loosen this particular attachment.

Tenth Day

Student A: I have physical pain now almost all the time. I decided to rest most of the day, and I wonder now if it was correct to surrender so easily to discomfort.

Achan: Of course it is correct that you rested; it is a physical necessity. The problem arises, however, that you had to temporarily break your schedule, slowing you down.

Student A: Yes. It took me two hours of walking practice for mindfulness to resume its previous strength.

Achan: Yes. It is as if one were paddling in a boat, confronting the waves. Stop for an instant and the waves push you back all the time. Similarly, the meditator has to use considerable effort to regain lost territory. Physical problems arising in the course of meditation practice are a normal occurrence, and handling them is a test of progress in mind-development. Pain is one kind of opponent or obstacle the meditator has to face and conquer. After all, we enter meditation training to understand the root cause of suffering. Certainly, bodily pain is one of the most obvious forms of suffering. Physical obstacles are preferable, however, to mental defilements: sometimes we battle with the mind—and lose. When a physical problem arises, rest will usually relieve the discomfort, and practice can be resumed.

Student A: When mindfulness is keen, I can sometimes just look at the discomfort and see it as pure pain, without an emotional overlay ... but usually I cannot be so objective.

Achan: The man or woman who enters the first stage of liberation, the *Sotāpanna*, no longer identifies the physical form as being the self. No degree of intellectual affirmation can substitute for the experiential realization of this truth.

We usually learn more about the constructs of clinging when we are ill than in periods of good health. Indeed, good health is only a relative condition. We need to pay particular attention to bodily pain, as this is the body's natural condition, though we are usually not aware of this truth, for distractions in everyday life cover this awareness. In Vipassana practice, however, we see the true nature of the body.

The meditator should try to understand the arising of physical feelings and emotional states associated with physical discomfort. I am not recommending that the meditator withstand torture—pain for pain's sake—but the more pain experienced at a certain point in practice, the more suffering will be perceived. Normally we all fear pain, and so it is imperative that we observe pain and confront our fears. It is one of the objectives of Vipassana practice to deeply penetrate the truth of suffering. *Every Buddha and enlightened saint has to realize suffering and perceive its significance clearly in order to see the falling away of suffering.*

We find instances in the Buddhist scriptures where enlightenment was realized at a moment of extreme physical pain. The mind was primed and ready for deliverance, and at that moment the greatest possible focus and penetration occurred. I know it is difficult for you now, but we should not be unduly concerned with physical discomfort at this point. We should rather content ourselves and make deliberate haste to practice so that suffering can be escaped for all time. If training is halted now, we will be born again with the five groups of clinging—with corporeality, feeling, perception, mental formations and consciousness—and experience suffering again and again. Confidence and commitment to our training will support us during any period of crisis.

There is another kind of physical pain, pain which arises specifically in Insight practice. It appears to make us tired of pain, all pain, tired of revolving in the cycle of birth-and-death. The understanding of this kind of pain strengthens our determination and we resolve to escape suffering once and for all.

The Buddha taught a method of spiritual development which can be termed non-violent practice. It refers to "killing oneself," and it is also applicable to meditation training, that is, to bearing the various gradations of pain, frustration and other trials which beset a meditator walking the path.

Visualize an angry person who insults you. Receiving his insults are better than him striking you. If he hits you, it is far better than him killing you. If he kills you, it is better than you "killing yourself." In this context, "killing yourself" refers to the decision to fight and you killing the other person. Our defilements would follow us into future lives. When applied to mind-development, neither flee from pain nor torture yourself, thereby "killing" your training and wasting the opportunity to realize Insight. If we can make the effort to bear this discomfort now, we can move forward with training.

In practical application, regardless of how many times you must mindfully change position to relieve any discomfort, you should still resolutely continue your practice and not break the flow of mindfulness and concentration.

Interview with Student B

Student B: I injured my leg slightly before practice. When I focus on pain, it reduces a bit but never really goes away.

Achan: The mind is exaggerating the pain, concentrating its force in a weakened area. There are basically two ways to handle pain. Continue to meditate and mindfully change position when necessary. The second method, however, requires well-developed *sati* and *samādhi*. One continues to meditate on the discomfort until the feeling of pain separates from the mind. It may be called a way of separating mental images. If the meditator has sufficient power of mind, one can take the mind away from the body. Focus attention on the pain itself and you will see it rise and fall. If the pain does not disappear, then observe the mind itself rising and falling. When your mindfulness is strong there will be nothing which "sees" the pain and it will disappear.

I have noticed that your *sati* is stronger in the morning than in the afternoon or evening. I recommend that you save some of your strength by changing position and walking in the morning.

This reservoir of strength will aid in overcoming the discomfort in the latter part of the day. When you first entered practice, your mindfulness was unevenly balanced. If you were making a retreat of indefinite length, this imbalance would he resolved and *sati* would equalize throughout the day and night. Do not let this pain weaken mindfulness.

Eleventh Day

Student A: In yesterday's practice, I began to experience hallucinations and sensory distortion. What is happening?

Achan: Strange phenomena appearing in practice occurs to almost every meditator. It arises when mindfulness increases in strength. This is a crucial stage in your practice. If these visions do not appear at this level, you will confront them at another time.

You are moving through one stage and approaching a higher level of meditation. The gap between these two levels is too wide and the mind now has an opportunity to play games. The meditator may be so upset or shaken by these experiences that it may be very difficult to focus mindfulness. The student must clearly understand that these strange phenomena arise from one's own mind. They are temptations born to lure the meditator from practice. When external phenomena are no longer distracting to the meditator, then imagination begins its attack by creating pictures or other distortions. If you cling to these visions, most assuredly mindfulness will be weakened or even destroyed. This is also a test for you—to determine if you have sufficient understanding or control of your mind. Weird phenomena may arise at any point in practice when *sati* strengthens, but visions occur most frequently during the sitting exercise, for this is a most concentrated position. If you "see" pictures when your eyes are closed and fear or agitation arises, practice by opening your eyes until you feel stronger. Relax and do not strain. Overexertion will only increase tension and create more pictures. If pictures keep flooding your mind and mindfulness cannot keep pace, try to take longer breaths. When walking, if you encounter sensory distortion, increase your pace. If you do not follow this method of coping with visions, you will have a most difficult time re-establishing mindfulness.

Your attention should be directed toward your practice, that is, focusing mindfulness on all phenomena arising in consciousness, and then letting them go. Even if you see the Buddha or Christ, do not let anything whatsoever divert your attention. Do not think about previous meditation experiences. You will be distracted again. They have come and gone.

It is crucial that the meditator understands the reasons for strange phenomena appearing. It is equally important that instructions given by the teacher be followed carefully. Many meditators who do not have competent guidance entirely abandon practice when they encounter these visions. They fear the past and they fear the future.

When I was teaching in Thailand, meditators who reached this stage would often visualize ghosts or people threatening them with knives. They would completely lose control of themselves. Becoming hysterical, they would run away from the temple. I would have to find them and try to persuade them to re-enter practice. If they did not resume training, they would have surrendered to their anxiety.

When the student of mind-development gains the skill of cutting off external disturbances by watching the rise and fall of phenomena, soon internal temptations will also be "cut off"— and when you cut off everything, freedom appears.

The student who is familiar with every step in training will know how to approach any problem. When mindfulness is strong and skillfully applied, no disturbance will be too bothersome. Whenever one sees, hears, touches, tastes, smells or thinks, the skilled and mindful meditator will be able to detect its rise and fall and not be attached to any situation.

Twelfth Day

Student A: My breathing is very shallow now and sometimes I can hardly catch my breath. I become frightened. I am not sure if I can continue to practice.

Achan: This is a normal occurrence in the last moment before you make a final decision to enter deep meditation. When the mind begins to separate from the idea of identifying the body as the self, it is natural to experience these unsettling conditions of mind.

As the power of the mind gradually strengthens and reaches higher stages, many different kinds of fear will appear to the meditator. Meditators feel that everything seems to be out of control ... that something is being lost. The breath becomes almost imperceptible, and one naturally may panic and think: "I want to breathe." When fear occurs, immediately collect yourself and focus accurately on the feeling and it will disappear.

If you stop practice now you will meet these same difficulties any time training is resumed. You should try to continue with your training even when mindfulness is not very clear. Everyone has the same feelings. It is an inevitable part of practice.

[Same student, late evening]

Achan: You look anxious.

Student A: I feel afraid so much of the time now. It is a strange kind of fear ... an unnamed fear. I sometimes find myself weeping and I have all the symptoms of anxiety. It is very difficult to practice.

Achan: Our person is composed of five groups of clinging. They are sometimes called Mara, or opponents. Once awakened, they are ever-ready to assault the meditator and to destroy all efforts in meditation. Many aspects of Mara will appear in your consciousness. Some of these disturbances are necessary tests in the development of Insight. Defilements, often in the form of hatred, impatience and boredom, may rise sharply to test the power and endurance of the meditator. Anxiety, too, is a way of testing the strength of mindfulness. It is a pitched battle between that part of the mind wishing to continue practice and the opposing force tempting you to abandon training. The latter is giving you great feelings of anxiety. You have to be victorious over these temptations. Do you feel you can conquer your fears?

Student A: Sometimes I think I am not strong enough to face these difficulties ...

Achan: Before you entered practice you made a commitment to follow the path of the Buddha—that is, you dedicated yourself to the quest for enlightenment. This is the one and only reason for entering Vipassana training. It is a serious commitment and not for the weak-hearted. You can be confident and put your heart at ease that the Buddha's teachings can guide you, and the Dharma is protecting you from harm. If you have good intentions and are willing to place confidence in the truth of the Buddhist teaching as the path to end all suffering, you need have no cause to fear.

To the best of my ability, I will help you solve any problems which may appear in your practice. I have even seen cases where meditators had nervous breakdowns. Fortunately, they were willing to cooperate—to make the effort to continue training. Working together, their problems were solved.

Although it is uncomfortable for you now, it is really a sign of your progress. Some meditators practice for an entire month and do not have problems of fear arise. These difficulties are not monumental. I, myself, have experienced them and many of my students, as well.

I asked you before to come and see me at once if you were afraid or shocked by some experience and could not resolve the problem yourself. You should have actually told me immediately, rather than spend needless time worrying. But it is all right. Don't push too hard. Relax.

If you can pass through this particular period, you will not encounter these particular disturbances again. Resolve to go ahead with your practice. It is fear that is causing you to hesitate. It is fear that will keep you from progressing. There are many difficulties. The Future Buddha himself almost lost to Mara. Do you understand? Are you all right?

Student A: Yes. I am reassured. Thank you.

Thirteenth Day

Achan: I feel that your concentration and mindfulness are strong now, and that all the conditions have been prepared for both of you to make a special effort in your practice. This test is a natural part of the strengthening process, a natural development in ascertaining how well any skill is being developed. Do you both feel confident enough in your training to make this effort?

Student A: Yes.

Student B: Yes.

Achan: These are my instructions to you. Place focus, as accurately as possible, on acknowledging the rising and falling of phenomena. Using the analogy of the high jumper preparing to leap, the meditator similarly consolidates all his or her energies into a singular effort. The high jumper places his energy into his legs and body, establishes his will, makes a commitment and runs fast.

Just work naturally, in a relaxed manner. If a higher stage of awareness is born it will be a natural result of your practice; if it does not manifest at this time, it will do so in the future with continued practice. After the trainee begins to practice, there is no way of predicting when these experiences will begin. It may take five minutes, a few hours, or nothing may happen. Remember, if you wish for something to happen, it is an ego-play. Do not weaken your *sati* by wishing for an "experience." Other meditators feel so happy at this stage they become careless. Be watchful. Use your intelligence. Stay as even-minded as possible.

It is best to forewarn you, however, that occurrences of an unexpected nature may well appear in your meditation at this time. The meditator, as with the athlete, may suddenly be distracted and find his mind pulling him back. You must be willing to stand firm. You must be willing to "die"; in fact, you should think of yourself as being dead. If you do not already think of yourself in these terms, a particular confrontation at this point may be devastating. You will find yourself running away. But if you feel your whole life is over—really over and empty— you will be able to face any situation. This mind, again, will often make an all-out attack, hoping to remove you from your place of meditation.

In order to prepare you for handling any problem which might occur, I will tell you what has happened to other meditators. I tell you these incidences not to frighten you, but to prepare you. Of course, do not think that you will experience exactly the same phenomena. Whatever happens, happens. Just be wide-awake and alert at all times. Do not lose mindfulness.

Many meditators report at this stage of practice the appearance of strange, even terrifying, phenomena. They report fearing their heart will stop beating; or their breath, as it becomes lighter and lighter, will disappear. Others have reported actually believing they were about to drown. Or they see a dead body begin to decay in front of their eyes. Alarmed and losing control, meditators often leave practice abruptly.

If you experience fear or other emotions which cannot be controlled, stop practice immediately and see me for further instructions. If you feel you are going to "die," then let everything go. You will "die" for a time, and will then return to normal consciousness. When you return to your normal state you will experience a particular understanding and joy which will suffuse body and mind. It cannot be described ... it will never be forgotten.

This "dying" is a normal condition of body-and-mind which appears when one focuses precisely on the rising and falling away of phenomena. As focusing becomes more powerful, the momentum quickens until rising and falling appear to "stop." One's practice begins to mature at this stage.

This is a crucial stage in your training. Give up the idea, however, of gaining anything. Just work naturally. Stay in the middle path.

Fourteenth Day

Achan: I asked you both to make a special effort yesterday in your practice. Do you have anything to report?

Student A: I noticed a very bright, white light—as if someone had opened the door. It stayed for quite a while, and then gradually faded. Last night, faces of dying people flashed into my mind. This morning, I felt my body to be extremely fragile, like glass, and a deep sense of dissolution appeared. The only other awareness is that I seem to have dropped naming everything: this is good; this is bad. I am just aware of seeing, or hearing, etc. Nothing else happened.

Student B: I had a strange meditation lasting about an hour. At first I felt engulfed in absolute silence, and then I found myself encased in clouds. There was a sensation of movement, and I seemed to forget my body. Colors changed from brown to gray to white. I felt as if I was in a space found inside an arena, not that I could see one ... and then, suddenly, a battle started in my head ... I could feel my face going through all kinds of contortions. My head began swinging around, being pulled in every direction, as though two adversaries were fighting for control. I could not stop the battle or the movement. A few times I felt as though I was going to die. My eyes suddenly switched shut and then ... a flash of light ... and I would be back again in the battleground. The flash occurred again ... and then everything finally died away. After that episode, I was completely exhausted. I could not focus *sati*. Samadhi was impossible ... nothing worked. I felt very tired and only now am I regaining my strength.

Achan (to Student B): You are not moving through the entire stage. If all the factors of energy, confidence, *samādhi*, *sati* and wisdom were concentrated into one force, it would have carried you through to the next level. You were exhausted because the power of *sati* was not sufficiently developed at this time. This experiment has been a useful test of your *sati*. It serves to demonstrate what still remains to be done in your practice. Be confident that if you continue to practice as diligently and single-mindedly as you have done, you will accomplish this stage.

The flash of light you experienced—and the immediate return to the battleground—suggests that you hit something, and it prevented you from going to the next stage. If you continue to practice, these flashes of light will occur more frequently. As I mentioned previously, when *sati* is powerful, you will feel that suddenly something "turns off." At first this experience may last for only a few seconds. Some meditators who practice constantly may be in this state for twenty-four hours, or even longer. It is as if one died and then returned to life. The longer one "dies" the more profound the understanding of this particular experience when you return to normal consciousness.

Practicing Insight meditation is like walking in the dark. The meaning of darkness here signifies being surrounded by greed, hatred and confusion. One often feels during practice that no good exits in the world at all. All the defilements seem to engulf the meditator. When these flashes first occur, and remain only an instant, nothing can be "seen" or understood very clearly. But if you continue your training, the flashing becomes brighter. As your mind brightens you will be able to reach out of the darkness. And when the mind begins to brighten, you will begin to understand, and begin to see things as they truly are. You will start making your ascent to higher levels of Insight.

Student A: I recall seeing bright flashes of light during an illness. It was accompanied by a high fever and I was semi-conscious ... I really thought I was dying. Other people, too, have recounted similar experiences during a moment of great pain. People who have been clinically dead for a time report seeing a great light.

Achan: Yes. Any time when a person feels utterly helpless, during serious illness, for example, when death seems imminent, *sati* is automatically focused on that experience.

There is a story which illustrates such an experience. The young son of a wealthy merchant was desperately ill. The father, being more concerned about his wealth, barred all visitors from seeing his son inside the mansion, for he did not want strangers to see his great estate. He placed the boy's bed on the balcony. His son slowly grew worse. The lad lay on the balcony, his face turned toward the wall, and resigned himself to death. Day after day passed, but he did not die. One day the Buddha came near the mansion on his alms round. Seeing one enduring such suffering, the Buddha focused all his compassion towards the dying youth. The boy noticed a very bright light cast on the wall and wondered if the sun was shining. He turned around and saw the radiant form of the Enlightened One. In that very moment he placed his faith in the Buddha and, smiling, died peacefully. Some see the light and end their life; others see the light but recover from illness.

Now that this intensive period of meditation is drawing to a close, I want you to continue with your training as much as possible. Do not depend on the special circumstances and environment found in a meditation center, but try to practice everywhere. Be ever-mindful. Test yourself daily, all the time. Make mindfulness first in your life—everything will naturally follow.

Mindfulness is the only protection in the world. Insight is the special understanding which will transform your life. It is the end of birth and death. It is the end of craving. It is the emancipation from all attachments, from all bondage, and is the realization of the highest happiness.

It is the end of the journey.

Biography of Achan Sobin S. Namto

The Venerable Phra Maha Sobin S. Namto was born in Thailand in 1931. At sixteen, he became a novice at Wat Mahadhatu temple in Bangkok and was ordained a *bhikkhu* (monk) in 1953. While still a novice, he completed his training in both Dharma and Pali studies, and then chose to pursue studies in Abhidharma and Vipassana meditation. Over a twelve-year period he had four Dharma teachers, six Pali professors, three Abhidharma teachers and five Vipassana instructors. He studied in Burma with three meditation masters, as well as training at the temple of the famed meditation master, Mahasi Sayadaw.

In order to cultivate his own practice of meditation preparatory to teaching, he then entered into periods of retreat, living in total seclusion for seven, three and four months, respectively. He then became an instructor in Dharma, Abhidharma and Vipassana meditation at Wat Mahadhatu, as well as teaching in other temples.

Achan Sobin was invited by the Saṅgha of Laos to be an instructor in Vipassana meditation from 1960 to 1962. Returning to Thailand, he became the founder-principal and instructor in Abhidharma and Vipassana meditation at Abhidhamma Vidyakorn School in Phuket Province.

In 1972, the Venerable Phra Dhammakosacharn, head of the First Division of Missionary Activities, with the approval of the Saṅgha Council of Thailand, selected him to be Chief Incumbent of Wat Thai, the first Thai temple in America. The Saṅgha, sensing the growing interest in Buddhism and meditation in America, confirmed his appointment as a monk highly competent in both knowledge and ability to effectively represent Buddha-Dharma in the United States.

Achan Sobin is the author of a number of books on Vipassana meditation, Abhidharma psychology, and devotional and ceremonial literature.

The Second Discourse of the Buddha

On the No-Self Characteristic
(*Anattalakkhaṇa Sutta*)

Pali Text and Translation
With an Introduction by
Dr. N. K. G. Mendis

WHEEL PUBLICATION NO. 268

The Second Discourse of the Buddha on the No-Self Characteristic

Introduction

Seven weeks after the recluse Siddhartha Gotama attained supreme enlightenment and came to be known as the Buddha, he gave his first discourse to the group of five ascetics with whom he had been associated six years earlier. These five ascetics were: Kondañña, Bhaddiya, Vappa, Mahānāma and Assaji. By the first discourse the Buddha set in motion the Wheel of the Law. He explained to the five ascetics why he had discarded the two extremes of indulgence and mortification; he declared that he had discovered the Middle Way which is the Noble Eightfold Path leading to Enlightenment; he expounded the Four Noble Truths and convinced the five ascetics that he had attained supreme enlightenment.

At the end of the first discourse the "spotless, immaculate vision of the *Dhamma*" arose in Kondañña thus: "all that is subject to arising is subject to cessation." The Venerable Kondañña then told the Buddha that he wished to go forth under the Blessed One and asked for full admission, which he received. With further instruction by the Buddha the "spotless, immaculate vision of the *Dhamma*" arose in the Venerable Vappa, the Venerable Bhaddiya, the Venerable Mahānāma and the Venerable Assaji in this order. They too knew thus: "all that is subject to arising is subject to cessation." These four ascetics too expressed their wish to go forth under the Blessed One and asked for full admission, which they received.

At this stage, then, the first five disciples of the Buddha had insight only into the impermanence of anything which had a conditioned origin. It was at this stage that the Buddha gave his second discourse. Between the first and second discourses the Buddha had, in his instructions to the five disciples, analysed the sentient being into five aggregates. These five were material form, feeling, perceptions, volitional states (or mental formations) and consciousness. The Buddha showed that the sentient being was made up of these five aggregates only. The disciples had to have this knowledge to follow the second discourse. Having thus instructed the five disciples the Buddha gave the discourse on the no-self characteristic of existence. No-self is one of the three characteristics of existence, the other two being impermanence and unsatisfactoriness. These three are interrelated and one cannot be taken apart from the other two. They are found only in the teaching of the Buddha.

Impermanence (*anicca*) may appear obvious to some who see the gross origin and disappearance of animate and inanimate entities. However, the Buddha's teaching goes beyond the gross and obvious and extends also to the mind, including its most subtle and sublime level. He taught that anything which has an origin exists only for a fleeting moment and that what appears to be compact and stable, both animate and inanimate, is from moment to moment arising and perishing. This fact can be experienced by one who follows the Noble Eightfold Path.

Unsatisfactoriness (*dukkha*) is a fact of life regardless of whether those critical of the Buddha's teaching label this as pessimism or not. The first Noble Truth explains why this existence is essentially unsatisfactory. Some do not accept this view because, for the time being, all appears to be going well for them; some see it in others but do not give it much thought because it does not affect them; some are unable to see this unsatisfactoriness due to mental impairment or gross ignorance; some would accept that life has its suffering and resign themselves to it, stating that it is all due to "original sin." The Buddha did not hesitate to focus full attention on this characteristic of existence and did so because he was aware of its cause and knew that others too could realize this for themselves. The cause of this unsatisfactoriness is found in the other two characteristics of existence.

No-self (*anattā*) means that there is no permanent, unchanging entity in anything animate or inanimate. With regard to the animate, this implies the absence of a soul which either emanated from a divine source or was created by a divine being. Biblical religions bless only the human being in the whole of the animal kingdom with this soul. The no-self doctrine is found only in the teaching of the Buddha. At least an intellectual grasp of this characteristic of existence is needed to appreciate the Buddha's teaching. It is only when insight is gained in this respect that progress can be made along the Path to full enlightenment.

The second discourse can be analysed into the following parts:

1. Introduction: A statement is made by the *Arahat* Ānanda to the first council of five hundred arahats who met at Rājagaha two months after the Buddha's *Parinibbāna* for the purpose of rehearsing the Law and the Discipline as expounded by the Buddha.

2. A categorical statement is made by the Buddha with reference to each of the five aggregates, namely the material form and the mental components which are feeling, perception, volitional states and consciousness. The Buddha also explains in this section of the discourse the reasons for his statements.

3. The Buddha questions the five disciples as to whether each of the five aggregates is permanent or impermanent. The disciples agree that the aggregates are impermanent. Then, on further questioning, they agree that what is impermanent is unsatisfactory. Going on to the next logical conclusion they agree that what is impermanent, unsatisfactory and changing cannot really belong to anyone nor can it be said that these aggregates form an abiding essence in a sentient being.

4. Conclusions are drawn from the foregoing analysis in respect of each of the aggregates in any form whatsoever.

5. The result of this analysis is insight into the true nature of a sentient being, which leads to initial disenchantment with the aggregates, then detachment and equanimity and final emancipation.

6. The five disciples were delighted with the Buddha's discourse and all attained enlightenment so that at the end of this discourse there were six arahats in this world.

There is an implication here that unless one gains insight into the no-self characteristic of existence it is not possible to start on the path to enlightenment. Of the ten fetters that bind us down to wanderings in *saṃsāra*, belief in a soul is the first to be broken. Hence the profound importance of this discourse.

This second discourse was on a discovery which was revolutionary in human thought. Before the Buddha's time and even after, religious teachers emphasised the existence of an abiding soul. A sceptic would say that this soul-less doctrine is one of hopelessness and despair and equates a sentient being to an automaton. On the contrary, the no-self doctrine gives the sentient being the highest sense of responsibility, the greatest amount of encouragement, the highest measure of hope, and is conducive to contentment which will be reflected in the disciple's attitude to other fellow beings which is the only way to put an end to all the strife on this earth.

Can we verify for ourselves the truth of this aspect of the Buddha's teaching? The Buddha urged his disciples to investigate the *Dhamma*. In fact, this investigation is the second of the seven enlightenment factors. In order to convince ourselves about the truth of this doctrine we have to follow the Noble Eightfold Path. By constant mindfulness and insight meditation we will know whether this teaching is true or not. The bodily form is subject to disease, decay and death over which we have no ultimate control. The body does not decide to move, stand, sit or lie down. These movements are always preceded by a mental directive. So the ultimate truth is that we cannot state that "the body is mine" or "I am the body." We do, however, use these terms but this usage is only a conventional expression. The mental components arise, exist for a moment and then perish. They arise dependent on conditions; so, here again, according to the ultimate truth we cannot state that the "mental components are mine" or "I am the mental components."

Now, according to this teaching of no-self, wherein lies the responsibility, the hope and the possibility of enlightenment? As regards bodily form we have no ultimate control over it. Even the Buddha and the Arahats suffered bodily afflictions. Disease, decay and death cannot be prevented. The young die through accident or disease. Living brings in its trail all the signs of decay. *Kamma* alone decides the fate of this bodily form. All we can do in this present existence is to avoid the two extremes which the Buddha discarded, namely indulgence and mortification. The rest will happen to the bodily form regardless of our interference. This does not mean that when the body is afflicted by accident or disease no attempt should be made to alleviate such affliction if ways and means are available. A negative attitude in this respect would amount to one of the extremes, namely mortification. The Buddha too had a physician and his name was Jīvaka. On the other hand it is different with the mental components. These arise dependent on conditions which are intimately connected with what are called the "roots" which are either unwholesome or wholesome, found in various combinations and degrees in all worldlings, that is in those who have not reached sainthood. The unwholesome roots are:

1. Greed (*lobha*) in various forms and degrees.
2. Hatred or anger (*dosa*) in various forms and degrees.
3. Delusion (*moha*) or ignorance (*avijjā*), particularly with reference to the true nature of phenomena.

In a person tainted with greed and lust the mental components will be predominantly those associated with greed and lust. As a result, volition will produce actions, bodily, verbal and mental, which will reflect these taints and bring in their trail unpleasant consequences in accordance with the law of action and reaction (*kamma*). The same applies to the other two roots of an unwholesome nature. Even though our past unwholesome volitions are resulting now in painful and unpleasant feelings, perceptions and consciousness, we can accept these with wisdom and set out on a favourable course by replacing the unwholesome roots by wholesome ones, that is:

1. Greed and lust by greedlessness, lustlessness and generosity (*alobha*).
2. Hate and anger by hatelessness (*adosa*) and by kindness and goodwill (*mettā*).
3. Delusions by undeludedness (*amoha*) and by wisdom (*paññā*).

In the discourse the Buddha said that, with reference to any of the aggregates, because there is no self ("soul") the possibility does not exist whereby it could be said "may my form be thus" and "may my form not be thus," etc. The conclusion to be drawn from this is that it is futile to expect returns from prayer, appeal, entreaty or offering to an outside source or by wishing and just hoping for the best. The Buddhist teaching is that we have to make the effort ourselves. Help we may get from outside in the form of salutary advice and association with the wise but, in the final analysis, as stated in verse 276 of the Dhammapada "striving should be done by yourselves, the *Tathāgatas* are only teachers." How do we strive? It is by following the Eightfold Path. The unwholesome roots are replaced by wholesome ones; as progress is made and the end of the Path is reached the saints have neither unwholesome nor wholesome roots, their actions are kammically inoperative and this is the *summum bonum* of the Dhamma.

This striving is by no means easy. The Buddha was realistic about this. In verse 239 of the Dhammapada it is stated: "By degrees, little by little, from time to time, a wise person should remove his own impurities, as a smith removes (the dross) of silver" (both Dhammapada translations are by Venerable Nārada). Confidence in the Threefold Refuge, diligent application and patience will take the disciple along the Path.

What then is the cause of this delusion that a self or soul exists? It is purely subjective, born of ignorance and nourished by the roots, both unwholesome and wholesome. It is lack of insight into the most profound statement ever made that "bare phenomena roll on." There is no doer but only the action, there is no speaker but only the utterance, there is no thinker but only the thought.

The no-self doctrine leads to harmlessness, contentment and peace. In contrast, it would be pertinent to refer briefly to some of the repercussions of the self or soul doctrine. Even in very ancient times the sentient being, as a result of stimuli from the senses in different forms, had the subjective impression that there was something abiding in himself, which may be called the self or soul. He also had the notion that this entity had the capacity to possess and own animate and inanimate objects. His survival depended on protecting this self. Apart from his own efforts towards this end, when the situation seemed to be beyond his control, or when events occurred that he could not understand, he looked for someone outside of himself for protection and to provide an answer to the mysterious. This outside source had to be someone better than any of his fellow beings. It had to be supernatural.

In times of calamity he looked up to the supernatural for help to ward off the danger. At times, he also made bargains with the supernatural to improve his lot, perhaps in comparison with that of his fellow beings. Even at this so-called primitive stage, repercussions of the self view were harmful. He would resort to anything to preserve the self and its possessions and, obviously, for his own gain, he had to please his protector usually by making sacrifices of innocent animals or even humans. Then there started arriving on the scene different individuals of mystic temperaments who claimed that they had revelations of the supernatural. They not only made this claim but also said they had a message for mankind from the supernatural. They said that the soul was created by the supernatural being or emanated from that source and that this soul must be purified so that at the termination of this existence on earth the soul will live in everlasting happiness in communion with the supernatural. As a result of the appearance of these intermediaries between the supernatural and the mortal being, organised theistic religion started. The message these intermediaries brought was not necessarily mild and peaceful. It doomed to eternal damnation anyone who did not believe the message; it exhorted the believer to spread the message even by force; it brooked no questioning regarding the validity of the message; it gave no explanation for the diversities, incongruities and misfortunes seen in this existence except to say that it was the will of the supernatural. Each group of believers insisted that its intermediary was the only genuine one and, from a sense of loyalty, fear or self-interest or a combination of all, bloody conflicts arose between the followers of the different theistic religions and they continue even to this day.

Mention must also be made of another section of mankind, of relatively recent origin, who, reacting violently to the social evils of theism, went to the other extreme and have abandoned all spiritual values, are not concerned with a life here-after and devote all their energy and skill to further the material aspects of existence. In pursuit of this they have caused and are still causing considerable suffering among fellow beings. They are as pernicious as anyone else who forcibly imposes views and philosophies on others. Progress on the material side alone is not enough. True happiness and contentment result from an emancipated mind and from nothing else.

The discourse is given in full, given first in Pali, followed by a literal English translation. By including the Pali it is hoped that it will stimulate some to study this inspiring language. What appears to be repetitions are, in fact, not so. One must bear in mind that the discourse contains a pronouncement that is the most lofty and revealing in human thought that has ever been made. Like present-day legal documents nothing was taken for granted and nothing unnecessary was said (*amogha vacana*). When the bodily form is afflicted the relevant part of the discourse can be recalled to one's mind and the same could be applied when feelings, perceptions, volitional states and consciousness arise and fall. It is hoped that reproduction of the discourse in full will be of benefit to the Buddha's disciples.

Gratitude is expressed to the Venerable D. Piyananda Mahānayaka Thera of the Washington Buddhist Vihāra, Washington, D.C. for his advice and for scrutinizing the translation of the *sutta* for inaccuracies. Also to Mr. R. Abeyasekera, Hony. Gen. Secretary of the Buddhist Publication Society, Kandy for arranging with a kind bhikkhu in Sri Lanka to send to the writer of this article a copy of the *sutta* in Sinhala script.

Dr. N. K. G. Mendis
Isaac's Harbour, Nova Scotia, Canada

Anattalakkhaṇa Sutta (Saṃyutta-Nikāya 22:59)

Evaṃ me sutaṃ, ekaṃ samayaṃ bhagavā bārāṇasiyaṃ viharati, isipatane migadāye. Tatra kho bhagavā pañcavaggiya bhikkhū āmantesi.

Rūpaṃ bhikkhave anattā. Rūpaṃ ca h'idaṃ bhikkhave attā abhavissa nayidaṃ rūpaṃ ābādhāya saṃvatteyya; labbhetha ca rūpe: evaṃ me rūpaṃ hotu, evaṃ me rūpaṃ mā ahosī ti. Yasmā ca kho bhikkhave rūpaṃ anattā, tasmā rūpaṃ ābādhāya saṃvaṭṭati; na ca labbhati rūpe: evaṃ me rūpaṃ hotu, evaṃ me rūpaṃ mā ahosī ti.

Vedanā bhikkhave anattā. Vedanā ca h'idaṃ bhikkhave attā abhavissa nayidaṃ vedanā ābādhāya saṃvatteyya labbhetha ca vedanāya: evaṃ me vedanā hotu, evaṃ me vedanā mā ahosī ti. Yasmā ca kho bhikkhave vedanā anattā tasmā vedanā ābādhāya saṃvaṭṭati na ca labbhati vedanāya: evaṃ me vedanā hotu evaṃ me vedanā mā ahosī ti.

Saññā bhikkhave anattā. Saññā ca h'idaṃ bhikkhave attā abhavissa, nayidaṃ saññā ābādhāya saṃvatteyya; labbhetha ca saññāya: evaṃ me saññā hotu evaṃ me saññā mā ahosī ti. Yasmā ca kho bhikkhave saññā anattā, tasmā saññā ābādhāya saṃvaṭṭati; na ca labbhati saññāya: evaṃ me saññā hotu evaṃ me saññā mā ahosī ti.

Saṅkhārā bhikkhave anattā. Saṅkhārā ca h'idaṃ bhikkhave attā abhavissaṃsu, na ime saṅkhārā ābādhāya saṃvatteyyuṃ; labbhetha ca saṅkhāresu: evaṃ me saṅkhārā hontu, evaṃ me saṅkhārā mā ahesuṃ ti. Yasmā ca kho bhikkhave saṅkhārā anattā, tasmā saṅkhārā ābādhāya saṃvattanti; na ca labbhati saṅkhāresu: evaṃ me saṅkhārā hontu, evaṃ me saṅkhārā mā ahesuṃ ti.

Viññāṇaṃ bhikkhave anattā. Viññāṇaṃ h'idaṃ bhikkhave attā abhavissa, nayidaṃ viññāṇaṃ ābādhāya saṃvatteyya; labbhetha ca viññāṇe: evaṃ me viññāṇaṃ hotu, evaṃ me viññāṇaṃ mā ahosī ti. Yasmā ca kho bhikkhave viññāṇaṃ anattā, tasmā viññāṇaṃ ābādhāya saṃvaṭṭati; na ca labbhati viññāṇe: evaṃ me viññāṇaṃ hotu, evaṃ me viññāṇaṃ me ahosī ti.

Taṃ kiṃ maññatha bhikkhave? Rūpaṃ niccaṃ vā aniccaṃ vā ti. Aniccaṃ bhante. Yaṃ pan' aniccaṃ, dukkhaṃ vā taṃ sukhaṃ vā ti? Dukkhaṃ bhante. Yaṃ pan' aniccaṃ dukkhaṃ vipariṇāma-

dhammaṃ, kallaṃ nu taṃ samanupassituṃ: etaṃ mama, eso 'haṃ asmi, eso me attā ti? No h' etaṃ bhante.

Taṃ kiṃ maññatha bhikkhave? Vedanā niccā vā aniccā vā ti? Aniccā bhante. Yā pan' aniccā, dukkhā vā sā sukhā vā ti? Dukkhā ti bhante. Yā pan' aniccā dukkhā vipariṇāma-dhammā, kallaṃ nu taṃ samanupassituṃ: etaṃ mama, eso 'haṃ asmi, eso me attā ti? No h' etaṃ bhante.

Taṃ kiṃ maññatha bhikkhave? Saññā niccā vā aniccā vā ti? Aniccā bhante. Yā pan' aniccā dukkhā vā sā sukhā vā ti? Dukkhā bhante. Yā pan' aniccā dukkhā vipariṇāma-dhammā, kallaṃ nu taṃ samanupassituṃ: etaṃ mama, eso 'haṃ asmi, eso me attā ti? No h' etaṃ bhante.

Taṃ kiṃ maññatha bhikkhave? Saṅkhārā niccā vā aniccā vā ti? Aniccā bhante. Yā pan' aniccā dukkhā vā sā sukhā vā ti? Dukkhā bhante. Yā pan' aniccā dukkhā vipariṇāma-dhammā, kallaṃ nu taṃ samanupassituṃ: etaṃ mama, eso 'haṃ asmi, eso me attā ti? No h' etaṃ bhante.

Taṃ kiṃ maññatha bhikkhave? Viññāṇaṃ niccaṃ vā aniccaṃ vā ti? Aniccaṃ bhante. Yaṃ pan' aniccaṃ, dukkhaṃ vā taṃ sukhaṃ vā ti. dukkhaṃ bhante. yaṃ pan' aniccaṃ dukkhaṃ vipariṇāma-dhammaṃ kallaṃ nu taṃ samanupassituṃ: etaṃ mama, eso 'haṃ asmi, eso me attā ti. No h' etaṃ bhante.

Tasmātiha bhikkhave, yaṃ kiñci rūpaṃ atītānāgata-paccuppannaṃ, ajjhattaṃ vā bahiddhā vā, olārikaṃ vā sukhumaṃ vā, hīnaṃ vā paṇītaṃ vā, yaṃ dūre vā santike vā, sabbaṃ taṃ rūpaṃ: n' etaṃ mama, n' eso 'haṃ asmi, na m' eso attā ti. Evaṃ etaṃ yathābhūtaṃ sammappaññāya daṭṭhabbaṃ.

Tasmātiha bhikkhave, yā kāci vedanā atītānāgatapaccuppannā, ajjhattā vā bahiddhā vā, olārikā vā sukhumā vā, hīnā vā paṇītā vā, yā dūre vā santike vā, sabbā sā vedanā: n' etaṃ mama, n' eso 'haṃ asmi, na m' eso attā ti. Evaṃ etaṃ yathābhūtaṃ sammappaññāya daṭṭhabbaṃ.

Tasmātiha bhikkhave, yā kāci saññā atītānāgatapaccuppannā, ajjhattā vā bahiddhā vā, olārikā vā sukhumā vā, hīnā vā paṇīta vā, yā dūre vā santike vā, sabbā sā saññā: n' etaṃ mama, n' eso 'haṃ asmi, na m' eso attā ti. Evaṃ etaṃ yathābhūtaṃ sammappaññāya daṭṭhabbaṃ.

Tasmātiha bhikkhave, ye keci saṅkhārā atītānāgatapaccuppannā, ajjhattā vā bahiddhā vā, olārikā vā sukhumā vā, hīnā vā paṇītā vā, ye dūre vā santike vā, sabbe te saṅkhārā: n' ete mama, n' eso 'haṃ asmi, na m' eso attā ti. Evaṃ etaṃ yathābhūtaṃ sammappaññāya daṭṭhabbaṃ.

Tasmātiha bhikkhave, yaṃ kiñci viññāṇaṃ atītānāgata-paccuppannaṃ, ajjhattaṃ vā bahiddhā vā, olārikaṃ vā sukhumaṃ vā, hīnaṃ vā paṇītaṃ vā, yaṃ dūre vā santike vā, sabbaṃ taṃ viññāṇaṃ, n' etaṃ mama, n' eso 'haṃ asmi, na m' eso attā ti. Evaṃ etaṃ yathābhūtaṃ sammappaññāya daṭṭhabbaṃ.

Evaṃ passaṃ bhikkhave sutavā ariyasāvako rūpasmiṃ pi nibbindati, vedanāya pi nibbindati, saññāya pi nibbindati, saṅkhāresu pi nibbindati, viññāṇasmiṃ pi nibbindati; nibbindaṃ virajjati, virāgā vimuccati, vimuttasmiṃ vimuttaṃ ti ñāṇaṃ hoti: khīṇā jāti, vusitaṃ brahmacariyaṃ, kataṃ karaṇīyaṃ, nāparaṃ itthattāyā ti pajānāti.

Idaṃ avoca bhagavā. Attamanā pañcavaggiyā bhikkhū bhagavato bhāsitaṃ abhinandun-ti. Imasmiṃ ca pana veyyākaraṇasmiṃ bhaññamāne pañcavaggiyānaṃ bhikkhūnaṃ anupādāya āsavehi cittāni vimucciṃsu.

Tena kho pana samayena cha loke arahanto hontī ti.

On the No-Self Characteristic
The Sermon

Thus it was heard by me. At one time the Blessed One was living in the deer park of Isipatana near Benares. There, indeed, the Blessed One addressed the group of five monks:

"Form, O monks, is not-self; if form were self, then form would not lead to affliction and it should obtain regarding form: 'May my form be thus, may my form not be thus;' and indeed, O monks, since form is not-self, therefore form leads to affliction and it does not obtain regarding form: 'May my form be thus, may my form not be thus.'

"Feeling, O monks, is not-self; if feeling were self, then feeling would not lead to affliction and it should obtain regarding feeling: 'May my feeling be thus, may my feeling not be thus;' and indeed, O monks, since feeling is not-self, therefore feeling leads to affliction and it does not obtain regarding feeling: 'May my feeling be thus, may my feeling not be thus.'

"Perception, O monks, is not-self; if perception were self, then perception would not lead to affliction and it should obtain regarding perception: 'May my perception be thus, may my perception not be thus;' and indeed, O monks, since perception is not-self, therefore, perception leads to affliction and it does not obtain regarding perception: 'May my perception be thus, may my perception not be thus.'

"Mental formations, O monks, are not-self; if mental formations were self, then mental formations would not lead to affliction and it should obtain regarding mental formations: 'May my mental formations be thus, may my mental formations not be thus;' and indeed, O monks, since mental formations are not-self, therefore, mental formations lead to affliction and it does not obtain regarding mental formations: 'May my mental formations be thus, may my mental formations not be thus.'

"Consciousness, O monks, is not-self; if consciousness were self, then consciousness would not lead to affliction and it should obtain regarding consciousness: 'May my consciousness be thus, may my consciousness not be thus;' and indeed, O monks, since consciousness is not-self, therefore, consciousness leads to affliction and it does not obtain regarding consciousness: 'May my consciousness be thus, may my consciousness not be thus.'

"What do you think of this, O monks? Is form permanent or impermanent?"—"Impermanent, O Lord."—"Now, that which is impermanent, is it "unsatisfactory or satisfactory?"—Unsatisfactory, O Lord."—"Now, that which is impermanent, unsatisfactory, subject to change, is it proper to regard that as: 'This is mine, this I am, this is my self.'?"—"Indeed, not that, O Lord."

"What do you think of this, O monks? Is feeling permanent or impermanent?"—"Impermanent, O Lord."—"Now that which is impermanent, is it unsatisfactory or satisfactory?"—"Unsatisfactory, O Lord."—"Now, that which is impermanent, unsatisfactory, subject to change, is it proper to regard that as: 'This is mine, this I am, this is my self.'?"—"Indeed, not that, O Lord."

"What do you think of this, O monks? Is perception permanent or impermanent?"—"Impermanent, O Lord."—"Now, what is impermanent, is it unsatisfactory or satisfactory?"—"Unsatisfactory, O Lord."—"Now, that which is impermanent, unsatisfactory, subject to change, is it proper to regard that as: 'This is mine, this I am, this is my self.'?"—"Indeed, not that, O Lord."

"What do you think of this, O monks? Are mental formations permanent or impermanent?"—"Impermanent, O Lord."—"Now, those that are impermanent are they unsatisfactory or satisfactory?"—"Unsatisfactory, O Lord."—"Now, those that are impermanent, unsatisfactory, subject to change, is it proper to regard them as: 'They are mine, this I am, this is my self.'?"—"Indeed, not that, O Lord."

"Now what do you think of this, O monks? Is consciousness permanent or impermanent?"—"Impermanent, O Lord."—Now, what is impermanent, is that unsatisfactory or satisfactory?"—"Unsatisfactory, O Lord."—"Now, what is impermanent, unsatisfactory, subject to change, is it proper to regard it as: 'This is mine, this I am, this is my self.'?"—"Indeed, not that, O Lord."

"Therefore, surely, O monks, whatever form, past, future or present, internal or external, coarse or fine, low or lofty, far or near, all that form must be regarded with proper wisdom, according to reality, thus: 'This is not mine, this I am not, this is not my self.'

"Therefore, surely, O monks, whatever feeling, past, future or present, internal or external, coarse or fine, low or lofty, far or near, all that feeling must be regarded with proper wisdom, according to reality, thus: 'This is not mine, this I am not, this is not my self.'

"Therefore, surely, O monks, whatever perception, past, future or present, internal or external, coarse or fine, low or lofty, far or near, all that conception must be regarded with proper wisdom, according to reality, thus: 'This is not mine, this I am not, this is not my self.'

"Therefore, surely O monks, whatever mental formations, past, future or present, internal or external, coarse or fine, low or lofty, far or near, all those mental formations must be regarded with proper wisdom, according to reality, thus: 'These are not mine, this I am not, this is not my self.'

"Therefore, surely, O monks, whatever consciousness, past, future or present, internal or external, coarse or fine, low or lofty, far or near, all that consciousness must be regarded with proper wisdom, according to reality, thus: 'This is not mine, this I am not, this is not my self.'

"O monks, the well-instructed noble disciple, seeing thus, gets wearied of form, gets wearied of feeling, gets wearied of perception, gets wearied of mental formations, gets wearied of consciousness. Being wearied he becomes passion-free. In his freedom from passion he is emancipated. Being emancipated there is the knowledge that he is emancipated. He knows: birth is exhausted, lived is the holy life, what had to be done is done, there is nothing more of this becoming."

This the Blessed One said. Pleased, the group of five monks were delighted with the exposition of the Blessed One; moreover, as this exposition was being spoken the minds of the group of five monks were freed of defilements, without attachment.

Indeed, at that time there were six Arahants in the world.

The Exposition of Non-Conflict

Araṇavibhaṅga Sutta
Majjhima Nikāya No. 139
A Discourse of the Buddha

Translated by

Bhikkhu Ñāṇamoli

WHEEL PUBLICATION NO. 269

The Exposition of Non-Conflict
Araṇavibhaṅga Sutta

Translated by Bhikkhu Ñāṇamoli

1. Thus I heard.

On one occasion the Blessed One was living at Sāvatthī in Jeta's Grove, Anāthapiṇḍika's Park. There the Blessed One addressed the bhikkhus thus: "Bhikkhus." "Venerable Sir" they replied. The Blessed One said this:

2. "Bhikkhus, I shall give you an exposition of the state of non-conflict. Listen and heed well what I shall say."

"Even so, Venerable Sir" the bhikkhus replied. The Blessed One said this:

3. "A man should not pursue sensual desires which are low, vulgar, coarse, ignoble and connected with harm; and he should not pursue self-mortification, which is painful, ignoble and connected with harm.

The Middle Way avoiding both these extremes has been discovered by the Perfect One (*Tathāgata*) giving sight, giving knowledge, which leads to peace, to direct knowledge, to enlightenment, to Nibbāna.

A man should know what it is to over-rate and what it is to under-rate and knowing both, he should neither over-rate nor under-rate but should speak only Dhamma.

He should know how to define pleasure,[1] and knowing that, he should pursue his own pleasure.

He should not utter covert speech, and he should not utter overt sharp speech.

He should speak unhurriedly, not hurriedly.

He should not insist on local language, and he should not override normal usage."

This is the summary of the Exposition of the State of Non-Conflict.

---

1. *Sukha*; alternative rendering: 'happiness.'

4. "'A man should not pursue sensual desires, which are low, vulgar, coarse, ignoble, and connected with harm; and he should not pursue self-mortification, which is painful, ignoble and connected with harm.' So it was said. And with reference to what was this said?

Such pursuit of enjoyment of one whose pleasure is linked to sensual desires, low, vulgar, coarse, ignoble and connected with harm is a state[2] beset by pain, by vexation, by despair and by fever, and it is the wrong way. Disengagement from such pursuit of enjoyment of one whose pleasure is linked to sensual desires, low, vulgar, coarse, ignoble, and connected with harm is a state without pain, without vexation, without despair and without fever, and it is the right way.

Such pursuit of self-mortification, painful, ignoble and connected with pain, is a state beset by pain, by vexation, by despair and by fever, and it is the wrong way. Disengagement from such pursuit of self-mortification, painful, ignoble and connected with harm, is a state without pain, without vexation, without despair and without fever, and it is the right way.

So it was with reference to this that it was said, 'A man should not pursue sensual desires which are low, vulgar, coarse, ignoble and connected with harm; and he should not pursue self-mortification which is painful, ignoble and connected with harm.'

5. "'The Middle Way avoiding both these extremes has been discovered by the Perfect One (*Tathāgata*), giving sight, giving knowledge, which leads to peace, to direct knowledge, to enlightenment, to Nibbāna.' So it was said, and with reference to what was this said?

It is precisely this Noble Eightfold Path—that is to say: right view, right intention, right speech, right action, right livelihood, right effort, right mindfulness, right concentration.

So it was with reference to this that it was said 'The Middle Way ... to Nibbāna.'

6. "'A man should know what it is to over-rate what it is to underrate[3] and knowing both, he should neither over-rate nor

2. The *Pāli* term used here is Dhamma in the sense of 'thing,' 'circumstance.'
3. Other translations proposed by the Venerable Ñāṇamoli: commend,

under-rate but should speak only Dhamma.' So it was said. And with reference to what was this said?

7. "So, bhikkhus, how does there come to be over-rating and under-rating and failure to speak only Dhamma?

When a man says 'All those engaged in such pursuit of enjoyment, which pleasure is linked to sensual desires, low, vulgar, coarse, ignoble and connected with harm, beset by pain, by vexation, by despair and by fever, and they have entered upon the wrong way,' he thus under-rates some.

When a man says, 'All those not engaged in such pursuit of enjoyment which pleasure is linked to sensual desires, low, vulgar, coarse, ignoble and connected with harm, are without pain, without vexation without despair, and without fever, and they have entered upon the right way,' he thus over-rates some.

When a man says, 'All those engaged in such pursuit of self-mortification, painful, ignoble, and connected with harm, are beset by pain, by vexation, by despair and by fever, and they have entered upon the wrong way,' then he under-rates some.

When a man says 'All those not engaged in such pursuit of self-mortification, painful, ignoble and connected with harm, are without pain, without vexation, without despair and without fever, and they have entered upon the right way,' he thus over-rates some.

When a man says, 'All those who have not abandoned the fetter of being[4] are beset by pain, by vexation, by despair and by fever, and have entered upon the wrong way,' he thus under-rates some.

When a man says, 'All those who have abandoned the fetter of being are without pain, without vexation, without despair, and without fever, and have entered upon the right way,' he thus over-rates some.

---

over-praise, condemn, detract.

4. *Bhava-saṃyojana*. The fetter which binds to "being" or existence, is craving (*taṇhā*).

This is how there comes to be overrating and underrating[5] and failure to speak only Dhamma.[6]

8. "And, bhikkhus, how does there come to be neither overrating nor underrating but speaking only Dhamma?

When a man does not say, 'All those engaged in such pursuit of self-mortification, painful, ignoble, and connected with harm, are beset by pain, by vexation, by despair and by fever, and they have entered upon the wrong way,' and says instead, 'It is the "being engaged" that is a state beset by pain, by vexation, by despair and by fever, and it is the wrong way,' then he speaks only Dhamma.

When a man does not say, 'All those not engaged in such pursuit of self-mortification, painful, ignoble, and connected with harm, are without pain, without vexation, without despair and without fever, and they have entered upon the right way,' and says instead, 'It is the *not* being engaged that is a state without pain, without vexation, without despair and without fever, and it is the right way,' then he speaks only Dhamma.

When a man does not say, 'All those who have not abandoned the fetter of being are beset by pain, by vexation, by despair and by fever, and have entered upon the wrong way,' and says instead 'As long as the fetter of being is "unabandoned," being is "unabandoned,"' then he speaks only Dhamma.

When a man does not say, 'All those who have abandoned the fetter of being are without pain, without vexation, without despair and without fever, and have entered upon the right way,' and says instead, 'When the fetter of being has been abandoned, being is abandoned,' then he speaks only Dhamma.

5. The Discourse illustrates "overrating and underrating" by mentioning sweeping statements about ideas. But it can be assumed that this warning of the Buddha also extends to exaggerated favourable or unfavourable opinions about persons, which is quite frequently a source of conflict. This application of the two terms is implied in the connotations of the two Pāli words as given in the footnote to §6 of the Discourse. It is also implied in the following commentarial remarks, of which we give here a free and expanded version:

6. *Speak only* Dhamma—The commentators explain: one should speak only factually (*sabhāvaṃ eva*), as things actually are (*yathābhūta-sabhāvaṃ eva*), without personal prejudices (*kassaci puggalassa anādesa-karaṇa-vasena*).

So it was with reference to this that it was said, 'A man should know what it is to over-rate and what it is to under-rate and knowing both, be should neither over-rate nor under-rate but should speak only Dhamma.'

9. "'He should know how to define pleasure, and knowing that, he should pursue his own pleasure.' So it was said. And with reference to what was this said?

Bhikkhus, there are these five cords of sensual desire. What are the five?

Forms, cognizable through the eye, that are wished for, desired, agreeable and likeable, connected with sensual desire and provocative of lust.

Sounds cognizable through the ear, that are wished for, desired, agreeable and likeable, connected with sensual desire and provocative of lust.

Odours cognizable through the nose, that are wished for, desired, agreeable and likeable, connected with sensual desire and provocative of lust.

Flavours cognizable through the tongue, that are wished for, desired, agreeable and likeable, connected with sensual desire and provocative of lust.

Tangibles, cognizable through the body, that are wished for, desired, agreeable and likeable, connected with sensual desire and provocative of lust.

These are the five cords of sensual desire.

Now, the pleasure and joy that arise owing to these five cords of sensual desire are called pleasure in sensual desire, which is pleasure in filth, coarse pleasure, ignoble pleasure. I say of this kind of pleasure that it should not be cultivated, that it should not be developed, that it should not be repeatedly practised, and that it should be feared.

Now, bhikkhus, quite secluded from sensual desires, secluded from unprofitable Dhammas, I entered upon and abode in the first *jhāna* which is accompanied by initial and sustained application, with happiness and (bodily) pleasure born of seclusion.

With the stilling of initial and sustained application, I entered upon and abode in the second *jhāna*, which has self-confidence and singleness of mind, without initial application and without sustained application, with happiness and pleasure born of concentration.

With the fading as well of happiness I abode in equanimity, mindful and fully aware, still feeling pleasure with the body, I entered upon and abode in the third *jhāna*, on which account Noble Ones announce, 'He has pleasure abiding who has equanimity and is mindful.'

With the abandoning of (bodily) pleasure and pain and with the previous disappearance of (mental) joy and grief I entered upon and abode in the fourth *jhāna*, which has neither pain nor pleasure and has purity of mindfulness due to equanimity.

This is called the pleasure of renunciation, which is pleasure of seclusion, pleasure of peace, pleasure of enlightenment. I say of this kind of pleasure that it should be cultivated, that it should be developed, that it should be repeatedly practised and that it should not be feared.

So it was with reference to this that it was said, 'He should know how to define pleasure, and knowing that, he should pursue his own pleasure.'

10. "'He should not utter covert speech, and he should not utter overt, harsh speech.' So it was said. And with reference to what was this said?

Here, bhikkhus, when a man knows covert speech to be untrue, incorrect and harmful, he should on no account utter it. When he knows covert speech to be true, correct and harmful, he should try not to utter it. But when he knows covert speech to be true, correct and beneficial, he may utter it, knowing the time to do so.

Here, bhikkhus, when a man knows overt, sharp speech to be untrue, incorrect and harmful, he should on no account utter it. When he knows overt, sharp speech to be true, correct and harmful, he should try not to utter it. But when be knows overt, sharp speech to be true, correct and beneficial, he may utter it, knowing the time to do so.

So it was with reference to this that it was said, 'He should not utter covert speech. He should not utter overt, sharp speech.'

11. "'He should speak unhurriedly, not hurriedly.' So it was said. And with reference to what was this said? Here, bhikkhus, when

a man speaks hurriedly, his body gets tired, his mind excited, his voice strained, and his throat hoarse, and the speech of one who speaks hurriedly is indistinct and hard to apprehend.

Here, bhikkhus, when a man speaks unhurriedly, his body does not get tired, or his mind excited, or his voice strained, or his throat hoarse, and the speech of one who speaks unhurriedly is distinct and easy to apprehend.

So it was with reference to this that it was said, 'He should speak unhurriedly, not hurriedly.'

12. "'He should not insist on local language.[7] He should not override normal usage.' So it was said. And with reference to what was this said?

And how does there come to be insistence on local language and overriding of normal usage?

Here, bhikkhus, in different localities they call the same thing a 'dish' (*pāti*) or they call it a 'bowl' (*patta*) or they call it a 'vessel' (*vittha*) or they call it a 'saucer' (*sarava*) or they call it a 'pan' (*dhāropa*) or they call it a 'pot' (*poṇa*) or they call it a 'mug' (*hana*) or they call it a 'basin' (*pisīla*). So whatever they call it in such and such a locality, he speaks accordingly, firmly adhering to and insisting on that, 'Only this is true, anything else is wrong.' This is how there comes to be insistence on local language and overriding of normal usage.

And how does there come to be non-insistence on local language and non-overriding of normal usage?

Here, bhikkhus, in different localities ... they call it a 'basin' (*pisīla*). So whatever they call it in such and such a locality, he speaks accordingly without adhering, (thus): 'These Venerable Ones, it seems, are speaking with reference to this.' This is how there comes to be non-insistence on local language and non-overriding of normal usage.

So it was with reference to this that it was said, 'He should not insist on local language. He should not override normal usage.'

13. "Here, bhikkhus, such pursuit of the enjoyment of one whose pleasure is linked to sensual desires—low, vulgar, coarse, ignoble and connected with harm—is a state beset by pain, by vexation,

---

7. That is, dialect.

by despair, and by fever, and it is the wrong way; therefore it is a state with conflict.

Here, bhikkhus, not being engaged in such pursuit of the enjoyment of one whose pleasure is linked to sensual desires—low, vulgar, coarse, ignoble and connected with harm—is a state without pain, without vexation, without despair and without fever, and it is the right way; therefore it is a state without conflict.

Here, bhikkhus, such pursuit of self-mortification—painful, ignoble and connected with harm—is a state beset by pain ... and it is the wrong way; therefore it is a state with conflict.

Here, bhikkhus, not being engaged in such pursuit of self-mortification—painful, ignoble and connected with harm—is a state without pain ... and it is the right way; therefore it is a state without conflict.

Here, bhikkhus, the Middle Way discovered by the Tathāgata, giving sight, giving knowledge, which leads to peace, to direct knowledge, to enlightenment, to Nibbāna, is a state without pain ... and it is the right way: therefore it is a state without conflict.

Here, bhikkhus, over-rating and under-rating and failure to speak Dhamma is a state beset by pain and it is the wrong way; therefore it is a state with conflict.

Here, bhikkhus, not over-rating nor under-rating and speaking only Dhamma is a state without pain ... and it is the right way; therefore it is a state without conflict.

Here, bhikkhus, the pleasure of sensual desires, which is pleasure in filth, coarse pleasure, ignoble pleasure, is a state beset by pain ... and it is the wrong way; therefore it is a state with conflict.

Here, bhikkhus, the pleasure of renunciation, which is pleasure of seclusion, pleasure of peace, pleasure of enlightenment, is a state without pain ... and it is the right way; therefore it is a state without conflict.

Here, bhikkhus, covert speech that is untrue, incorrect and harmful ... is a state with conflict.

Here, covert speech that is true, correct and harmful is a state with conflict.

Here, covert speech that is true, correct and beneficial ... is a state without conflict.

Here, overt, sharp speech that is untrue, incorrect and harmful is a state with conflict.

Here, overt, sharp speech that is true, correct and harmful is a state with conflict.

Here, overt, sharp speech that is true, correct and beneficial ... is a state without conflict.

Here, bhikkhus, the speech of one that hurries is a state beset by pain ... with conflict.

Here, bhikkhus, the speech of one who does not hurry is a state without pain ... without conflict.

Here, bhikkhus, insistence on local language and overriding normal usage is a state beset by pain ... with conflict.

Here, bhikkhus, non-insistence on local language and non-overriding of normal usage is a state without pain without vexation, without despair and without fever, and it is the right way; therefore it is a state without conflict.

So, bhikkhus, you should train thus: we shall know the state with conflict and we shall know the state without conflict, and knowing these, we shall enter upon the way without conflict.

Now, bhikkhus, Subhūti is a clansman who has entered upon the way without conflict."[8]

This is what the Blessed One said. The bhikkhus were delighted and they rejoiced in the Blessed One's words.

Majjhima Nikāya, Sutta 139

8. *Commentary and Sub-Commentary*: The Buddha, the Venerable Sāriputta and other disciples, in their instructions, sometimes commended or censured a monk for the sake of guiding and disciplining him. But the Venerable Subhūti refrained in his Dhamma talks from such personal references, limiting himself to saying that, "This is the wrong path" and "That is the right path." Therefore the Buddha singled out Subhūti by declaring him to be "the foremost of those dwelling in non-conflict (*araṇavihārinaṃ*)" (AN 1). Also at the end of the present Discourse, he speaks of him as one who "has entered the practice-path of non-conflict" (*araṇa-paṭipadā*).

Some Thoughts on Non-Conflict

Bhikkhu Khantipālo

Who does not wish to live without conflict? But wishes are not enough. If we desire the maximum peace here in this life and the minimum discord then we have to set up the conditions producing it. Peacefulness or non-conflict is not a situation which can arise without appropriate conditions. It is true that it may "by chance" occur but then it fades away again, usually rather quickly—and we are back with our conflicts again. Of course, it was not "by chance" that it occurred for a time in our lives, but as to *why* it happened we are no wiser and so cannot repeat the situation.

One has to try to think in terms of *cause-and-effect* (*hetu-phala*), which, one would think, should not be too difficult. After all, this is the foundation of all modern science and of a thousand ordinary things which we are inclined to take for granted. We press a switch and an engine roars into life. All— cause and effect. But though we apply cause-effect thinking to outside things quite well, we are less successful in applying the same principle to our "own" minds. We are greedy, envious, quarrelsome or whatever, and yet expect to be happy.

Now, happiness is an effect. For it to occur, the necessary causes must be present. This is largely what the Buddha's Teaching is all about. You like pain, grief, despair? No? Then do not produce the causes of them. You want peace, happiness, non-conflict? Of course! Then take good note of the conditions which produce them, listed by the Buddha at the beginning of the Araṇavibhaṅga Sutta.

A quick glance through this list seems to show a rather miscellaneous collection but they are all united in one matter: when practised, non-conflict is the result.

What follows here is some reflection upon, and explanation of, these factors, why they bring about non-conflict and why the absence of them and presence of their opposites leaves us open to all kinds of troubles and difficulties.

In this type of Sutta giving an "exposition" (*vibhaṅga*), a summary comes first of the contents which are afterwards described at length. The first item is nearly the same as the opening of the Buddha's first discourse, "Setting in Motion the Wheel of Dhamma," but there is one significant difference. In that discourse addressed to the five ascetics who would afterwards become the first Bhikkhus, the Buddha spoke of "two extremes which those who go forth should not practise." Here, however, the Buddha though addressing Bhikkhus just says "A man should not pursue sensual desires ..."

Now lay people will find this a bit difficult because much of the pleasure of their lives comes from the gratification of sensual desires. One likes to see beautiful forms and sights, one enjoys beautiful music, one delights in fragrance and craves for fine tastes while one seeks for pleasant tangibles as well. When one gets them, that is the *gratification* of sensual desires. But there is the *danger*, in them too—that one does not get what one wants (*dukkha*) or one gets what one does not want (*dukkha*), because then instead of pleasure arising, aversion and anger are liable to manifest. And there is more *danger* in them; they are all impermanent, transient, and subject to arising and passing away and so not satisfactory (*dukkha*). When one relies on them for happiness then one should realize their inherent nature, otherwise one suffers too the *disappointment* of sensual desires (*dukkha*). They are always glittering there before one's eyes, rich in promise of complete satisfaction, yet when one has obtained or enjoyed them and they are finished, one finds them just tinsel, just glitter.

So the pursuit of sensual desires does not lead to internal peace, but then neither does it make for peace in society. If everyone were to go all out for each one of their desires, chaos would reign. And as it is, with the "fulfilment" of desires encouraged commercially and psychologically, there is trouble enough. Desires, in fact mean conflicts. My desires and your desires may be quite different and we are each one of us quite sure that our own desires are the "right" ones, so there is bound to be conflict. The more desires people have, the more conflict is produced in society, as the developed countries of this world show so clearly. Non-conflict then, goes with the way of renunciation and giving up—not with the way of getting and gain. But how can this apply to a lay person's life? Desires which will cause the strengthening of unwholesome mental states should be gradually given up by the power of Dhamma-practice. Desires, which are really unnecessary for life, just extravagance or showiness, should be abandoned as soon as one is aware of their real purpose. But those desires for necessary things which are moderate and reasonable cannot be sacrificed while the household life is lived. This leaves a good deal for individual judgement, of course, but almost everyone has some desires in which they could well cease to indulge. Renunciation of these things becomes easy as one matures in Dhamma, just as giving up playing at mud-pies becomes quite natural as children grow up. Therefore renunciation should not be forced or unnatural which would be one extreme, nor should one just let things slide, which is the other.

Some people instead of growing into renunciation perform a violent about-face. In the past they had been very indulgent sensualists and then, because of sudden "conversion" or guilt, they suddenly swing over to self mortification. This is the reason why this topic follows in the Sutta upon the pursuit of sensual desires.

There are many accounts of this change, notably among "Saints" of the Christian Churches, who seem to have had little psychological insight as to the true nature of their change of life. When sensual desires are pursued, the evil root of greed directs the heart, but with the sudden conversion experiences (in which such ingredients as fear of God's Wrath, everlasting hellish torment and guilt and remorse all play their part), the evil root of aversion takes charge. This manifests as hatred of pleasure—in others as well as in oneself, hatred of oneself—as a sinner who will be damned, and hatred of beauty—which tempts one's now virtuous and straightened self.

All this is very unwholesome indeed. In many ways it is better to be an indulgent sensualist rather than a destructive self-hater. The former, however selfish he is, at least has some pleasure and may not cause others too much misery, but the latter neither enjoys himself nor permits others to do so. *Greed* can be accompanied by pleasure but aversion always goes along with *dukkha*.

But whether a person is ruled by greed or aversion, bad *kamma* is made. And bad, unwholesome *kamma* in time bears the fruits of *dukkha*, mental and physical. Therefore, both these courses are labelled in the Sutta "the wrong way." Immediately after this section, follows "The Middle Way avoiding both these extremes ..." In what sense is it the middle? Does this mean halfway between greed and aversion, a sort of neutral compromise? The term "Middle Way" is used for the Buddha's Noble Eightfold Path because it transcends all extremes—of views, of mental development and of moral conduct. Due to the presence of various defilements in the mind it is easy to go to extremes and difficult to hold to a perfectly balanced course which does not depart from truth. The Noble Eightfold Path is such a perfectly balanced course and it can be tested in every aspect to see whether or not it adheres to truth. But this is a whole subject in itself for which we have no space here.[9]

Now we come to the subject of over-rating, under-rating and speaking only Dhamma. This long section is upon the use of correct terminology. The Dhamma is precise, it is the precision associated nowadays with technical and scientific subjects. It is in fact a technical and precise study of the mind and its workings, and how actions of body and speech arise dependently. Therefore, the formulation of Dhamma is important and words should be used carefully if a correct account of Dhamma is to be given. In particular, loose or ambiguous statements should be avoided, as the Buddha himself does. None of his words are hazy or admit of many interpretations, a great contrast to other religious "Classics" such as the *Tao Te King*, the *Bhagavad Gīta* or the *New Testament.*

Paragraph seven of the *Sutta* gives us examples of loose generalities in which there is under-rating or over-rating, which is a form of going to extremes and so, a failure to speak what is Dhamma or Truth. Sweeping statements always very popular with people, certainly cause conflicts. People take exception to such wide generalities which are not true when closely examined, or only true, given certain conditions. If one wants to live without conflict, therefore, these types of statements should be avoided.

It is not for sweeping statements that the Buddha is famous, but for his analytic procedure. He was known as a *vibhajjavādī*, one who taught analytically, as illustrated in the present *Sutta*

9. See *The Noble Eightfold Path and its Factors Explained* (The *Maggaṅgadīpanī* of the Venerable Ledi Sayādaw), Wheel No. 245-247 from B.P.S. Kandy, and Francis Story, *The Four Noble Truths* (Wheel 34/35) B.P.S. Kandy.

where he analyzes the conditions for non-conflict. And he does not only condemn broad generalities but in the following paragraphs shows how true statements should be phrased so as to avoid over-rating, under-rating and not speaking Dhamma.

The examples given here are interesting since sweeping condemnations and commendations involving masses of people are put aside by the Buddha in favour of pinpointing precisely what is right or wrong—the Dhamma (or mental factor) "not being engaged" or "being engaged." It is not "all those people" who are wrong or right, but certain very exact mental attitudes; "being engaged" here is another way of saying "attachment"—and attachment (*upādāna*) always brings *dukkha*. "Not being engaged" on the other hand, is the same as "detachment," a mental state which will enhance non-conflict. In the case of the last pair, in both paragraphs seven and eight, which concern "the fetter of being", in the first case one has again an inaccurate formulation: "All those ..." but in the second the formulation is precise and cannot be misunderstood:

"As long as the fetter of being is 'unabandoned,' being is 'unabandoned'" and "When the fetter of being has been abandoned, being is abandoned." What lucid and wonderful depths of Dhamma these few precise words hold!

When one speaks in this way then one speaks according to Dhamma without distortion: Undistorted Dhamma is a great aid to non-conflict.

And with non-conflict we come back to the basic problem of happiness or "pleasure" (*sukha*) as Venerable Ñāṇamoli renders it. "Knowing how to define pleasure" means being clear in one's mind as to what actually produces untainted satisfaction, unregretted happiness. First, the Buddha runs through the formula defining the "five *cords* (note the bondage inherent in this word) of sensual desire," "that are wished for, desired and provocative of lust." We have already outlined some thoughts upon these in connection with the first subject dealt with in the *Sutta*. But the Buddha adds some words describing these desires and pleasures which give us a pause: "pleasure in filth, coarse pleasure, ignoble pleasure." This may seem too strong for many people, especially when it applies to some "innocent" and aesthetic diversion such as listening to inspiring music. How can this be called "filth" and so on? Of course, it depends on one's scale of values. The higher aesthetic pleasures seem to be the peak of subtle enjoyment, until one has meditated, until one has gained *jhāna.*

The four jhānas, which are described in outline, completely transcend the limitations of sensual aesthetics. They do not require an exterior object for stimulating the senses, nor do they require the senses to be active. Thus they surpass sensual experience, even the finest, since they cannot cease because of the cessation of a sensual object but only because one withdraws from meditation, and since the senses not being active, the mind becomes brilliantly and forcefully one-pointed. The objects of *jhāna* are internal and thus much more easily controlled than those of sense-stimulation. From the viewpoint of a *jhāna*-gainer (*jhānalābhi*) the sense-pleasures, however subtle, appear like wavering shadows so easily displaced. And the fact that sensual desires are "provocative of lust" and therefore involve the activities of the three roots of unwholesomeness—greed, aversion and delusion—is sufficient reason for labelling them "pleasure in filth." It is in points like this that one sees clearly the need to distinguish who the Buddha was speaking to. And on this occasion it was to Bhikkhus, those who have left behind the household life and its associated sensual pleasures. They can appreciate the use of such labels while it may be more difficult for lay people to do so.

While the happiness (or pleasure) derived from the senses should not be cultivated, that which arises in *jhāna* should be. The first is to be feared but the second is not. What does this mean? Fear arises dependent upon the unstable nature of the sense-objects and from the desire to possess, to make mine, to support my sense of self. This is all an elaborate fabrication of the mind. What I call "myself" is a collection of changing physical and mental processes in which no abiding "self or soul" can be found. All other existent objects are also changing processes, some with sentience—other beings, some without it. They cannot be really made "mine." So fear lurks behind this complicated facade, for just as the ordinary liar fears that his inventions may be seen through, so the ego or self fears that the truth might be seen—and thereby dissolve it away. Then fear arises too from that very nature that things have—impermanence, that they may age, break, disappear, get lost or stolen. In this way fear lurks inseparable from sensual desires and their objects.

From knowing how to define pleasure and its true pursuit, we pass to speech that conduces to non-conflict. "Covert" speech includes words having a meaning different from what they seem to convey, a concealed or secret meaning. Now it is noticeable that the Buddha refrained from concealed and secret methods of teaching (although there are some who teach in his name, "esoteric Buddhism') and condemned religious secrecy.[10] His words and methods are straight-forward and there is nothing "hidden" for favoured disciples to discover. In this he differs from many Indian teachers who have passed on their esoteric secrets to their favourite disciples. Religious secrecy, he perceived, easily became the shelter for the fraud, for the credulous and for all manner of priest craft which he as one intent on laying bare the truth, avoided, and required his disciples to avoid.

Covert speech has been classified by the Buddha into three:

1. Untrue and harmful: utter on no account;
2. True and harmful: try not to utter it;
3. True and beneficial: utter it knowing the right time.

The first is lies and slander breaking the fourth Precept, the second is matters which, though true, lead to harm, while with the third, one should have wisdom to know when it should and should not be said. For instance, true and beneficial matters can, if spoken at the wrong time, be embarrassing to some people.

So the Buddha has allowed covert speech which is true and beneficial, as when perhaps only a hint is needed to correct someone. Similarly, the Buddha allowed overt, sharp speech which is both true and beneficial. This can be illustrated by a severe reprimand which can turn some person away from evil and back to practising Dhamma. But overt, sharp speech which is untrue and harmful, as spoken by an angry man trying to lay the blame on someone else, or that which is true and harmful—as a reprimand might be if spoken at the wrong time or in the wrong company, neither of these should be employed.

Other kinds of speech too help or hinder peacefulness. Consider the impetuous person who rushes into saying things but when only halfway through changes his mind so that his

10. See *Aṅguttara, Threes,* No. 129.

speech rushes off elsewhere. People who speak hurriedly tire themselves out and are tiresome to others, besides showing a great deal of their confused mental state in their way of talking. The Buddhist ideal in speaking is shown in this Sutta—speaking unhurriedly in a well-considered and mindful way. The Buddha gives six advantages of this and even then does not exhaust the range of benefits. Steady, mindful speech is related to a "mindful mind" and when one cultivates this type of speaking it conduces to more mindfulness.

With "local language" and "normal usage" the Buddha touches upon some other important points favouring non-conflict. In northern India then, as now, there were many dialects and sub-languages. If someone insists on using special dialect forms their rigidity is a kind of dogmatism founded on pride: "Only this is true; anything else is wrong." Conforming to normal usage straightens out a number of difficulties for a speaker. The Buddha always recommended the use of language which everyone could understand. Thus Pāli bears the marks of being a spoken and popular tongue, which has never been true of Sanskrit. The Buddha wished all to understand his words and so used popular and normal forms of speech.

The Discourse on Non-conflict closes with a long passage showing why some factors lead to conflict and others to non-conflict. All that remains for us is to select carefully those factors which will promote non-conflict in our own lives, until the very highest aspect of non-conflict is won in our own hearts, as was the case with the Venerable Subhūti Thera who was an Arahant.

Three Symbolic Ways of Life

by

Carlo Gragnani

WHEEL PUBLICATION NO. 270

Three Symbolic Ways of Life

Let us start with an example and, to be fashionable, let us take anxiety (although any other example would do). The question I will try to answer is the following:

"In what fundamental way can I be connected with anxiety?"

Well, one way is what I am doing this very moment: *writing* about anxiety. I might talk or think about it. In all these cases I would use words. Whenever I operate in that way, I am in an area which might be called: "verbal plane."

What are its characteristics?

Obviously, I have to arrange words, to combine them in a certain order; my sentences must abide by certain principles and rules or else I would talk nonsense.

Words are signs which stand for something else. If I say: "bla-bla-bla," I simply utter sounds without any meaning. If I say: "table simultaneously procrastination," although each of these words taken separately has a meaning, the whole phrase has not. Grammar and syntactic rules have not been observed and, again, my sentence is not intelligible. Besides, verbal expressions must fit into one of the various logical systems. "A table is a table" is not a very exciting but a correct statement according to Aristotelian logic. Not so this one: "A table is and is not a table," although it is correct from the point of view of Hegel and perhaps of Nāgārjuna.

Now, what I want to stress is that the observance of these principles and rules (which are flexible in time and/or space, but within limits) confers stability, fixity, to what is expressed in words. Through language, the world appears solid, lasting, orderly, rational; things may be temporarily not present to our consciousness, but we consider them still as existing, although absent, and we recognize them when they appear again.

All this allows us to classify, to categorize, to establish correlations, laws. A trivial example taken from abstract thinking: $2 + 2 = 4$ is an eternal truth, of which I can make use for actual calculations, or not; however, it does not cease to exist and to be true even when nobody resorts to it.

To live on the logical level, therefore, is to live in an orderly, rational, stable, durable, recognizable world, where there are truths, certitudes, to stand on, a world where "I am I" and "you are you", where we can understand each other, so that if I ask the waiter for a steak, there is little risk that he will bring me a box of matches.

The verbal level is very reassuring, it gives the sensation of being on solid ground, of being sane, so much so that to see the world in a radically different way would be interpreted as a sign of mental disorder.

Another fundamental way to be related with anxiety—to pursue our example—is to *experience* it. Faced with this sensation, I may try to repress it by applying myself to some engaging task, I may take a tranquillizer, or I may just live with my anxiety.

More generally, this second fundamental way of relating myself consists of action with the aim of abolishing a sensation or modifying or creating one. In so acting, I am in direct contact with things, I use them (instead of talking about them as I do on the verbal plane).

So, on the one side we have *words*, on the other, *action*. Through words we understand intellectually; through action we try to reach our aims. In the first case, it is the mind that is mainly involved; in the second, it is the body—with its five senses.

But these distinctions do not represent reality faithfully: they are too sharp, too clear-cut. In fact, the relationships, the interconnections between the verbal level and what might be called the "action level" are many.

The two sectors are distinct, not separated. To continue our example, while words may start anxiety, anxiety may be assuaged by words, by talking about it. More generally, if it is true that the verbal level engages mainly the mind, it is also true that talking, writing and even thinking are not possible without the participation of the body. Conversely, acting consciously involves some mental implications which, directly or indirectly, refer to verbal activity; even the movements of the artisan (who is so familiar with his tools that he handles them automatically) are based on the recognition of things: when he needs a hammer, he takes just a hammer and not something else. This means that the world is categorized, classified, by him. And what is that, if not language at a deep level or, if you like, the necessary basis out of which language emerges?

That having been said, the fact still remains that words and action are different and, in a way, even alternatives: the taste of tea is not a good description of it; a dinner is not its menu card; the word "tiredness" is not tiredness itself.

* * *

The verbal level may be geometrically symbolized by the straight line. Verbal expression is linear, analytical; words come one after the other in succession; meaning has no form, no dimension. Like the straight line, reasoning is unidimensional and potentially infinite; it never reaches either definite conclusions or its origins; thoughts engender other thoughts ...

Action, on the contrary, radiates in many directions at the same time; it is multidimensional; it evokes form. Even the (mental) planning which prepares and accompanies action proper is synthetic: the chess player looking at the board before making a move gets a panoramic view of the situation as a whole. Therefore, action, doing, can be symbolized by space: in geometrical terminology, by the plane.

* * *

At one moment we live and are engaged chiefly on the verbal level, at the next on the action level—the two covering the whole range of human activity. Sometimes we can distinguish an experience from its verbal expression; sometimes we mistake one for the other, as when we believe ourselves to be compassionate but are in fact simply in love with beautiful compassionate words.

In any event, however, the two levels have in common the characteristic of being goal-oriented. We constantly try to reach our aims, however big or small they may be. Even the simple act of going to the office is evidently goal-oriented and therefore needs some planning.

Now, to be goal-oriented may mean two things, depending on whether the accent is put on the first or on the second word; one may be oriented in order to reach a goal or one may have a goal in order to be oriented.

The first attitude seems to be the only rational one:

I want something; therefore, I pave the way to obtain it. However, man is inclined to follow also the second path, irrational as it may appear. Goals are very often an excuse to justify our action to reach them.

Is it not true that we very frequently work—and sometimes very hard—only to neglect the result of our effort? Why is this? Why, as soon as one goal is attained, do we immediately pursue another one, without enjoying the first? When eating a slice of apple pie, why, instead of tasting it, do we think about how to get an additional portion? Or, when there is no apple pie left, why is it that disappointment prevents us from relishing what we are eating? And this happens in every field: one strives for years and years to become an Ambassador only, after becoming one, to feel frustrated because the time for retirement is approaching.

There are also more subtle ways in which the same development occurs. Take the case of a camera fan. At the very beginning, his interest in photos is no doubt prompted by his desire to recapture, at home by the fireside, to his own contentment and to the ill-concealed boredom of his guests, the beautiful views he has admired, let us say, during a trip. But as time goes by, be becomes increasingly interested in panoramas and monuments not for themselves but as occasions for taking a few shots. Then, the interest shifts to cameras; our friend starts talking at length about lenses and other components. Soon, the camera industry comes into the picture: different types of productions technical details ... At this point, photos are almost forgotten: the recipe has supplanted the meal.

So, in one way or another, man does not dwell long enough on his experiences for getting the full "taste" of them; he passes through everything hastily, anxiously ... to get *more* things that will probably be used *more* hastily, *more* anxiously ... So he finds himself void of the "fullness," the fulfilment that he looked for.

How is it that to stay happily with the coveted object is so difficult? The usual answer, that it is due to our restlessness, amounts to nothing more than a mere name for the phenomenon without an explanation of it: therefore, it is not satisfactory. We have to find out the basic cause for this state of affairs, however much social or other conditions may contribute to strengthen this cause.

Well, the core of the matter lies in the dichotomy between the world as it is normally conceived and the world as it is experienced.

As said above, we conceive the world as solid, stable, lasting. If it were not for language, we could not see the world that way. But it must be added that, if it were not for our likes, dislikes, interests and desires, we would not accept this conception of the world so uncritically. Passions induce convictions; so much so that right at the beginning our perceptions are often coloured by our feelings and emotions. If I am afraid of ghosts, I shall see them; if I am thirsty in a desert, I shall soon see mirages. Everybody would agree that imaginary things are perceived in such extreme circumstances. *But in fact, we see imaginary things all the time.*

What we see in things is lasting pleasure or displeasure or indifference. Since indifference is boring, we more often see things that seem worthwhile having (because of the pleasure that we hope to derive from their possession), or things that are worthwhile rejecting (because of the displeasure we fear we shall feel in having them).

The extent to which imagination influences our perception can be found out through our experience, which regularly belies our expectations. Things and—what is more important—feelings do not stay put; they "wobble," to say the least. What appeared to be lasting, and therefore worthwhile having or rejecting, reveals itself to be of a quite different, even opposite, nature.

Because we assume that things and feelings are persistent, durable, we think how beautiful it would be to listen to music for hours on end or to live on a remote small island for months. But we would indeed be in a predicament if those wishes were fulfilled. Sometimes I imagine what it would be like if there were some malevolent deity who instantly fulfilled the desires of human beings the moment they entered the mind: if someone wished he could travel his whole life long, lo and behold! he would immediately start travelling for the rest of his days! Man does not always realize how lucky he is that he is not always able to do what he would like to do. If he realized that, he would be more attentive to "what is" and less to "what he would like to be, or to have."

So, we suffer from an unresolved dichotomy. We do not learn the lessons of our experience; instead, we again and again try to obtain the impossible, justifying the preceding failure with all sorts of rationalizations.

In fact, we cannot learn our lesson because a lesson learned intellectually or even through experience is not enough when strong feelings are involved. If this were not so, the neurotic, conscious of his state, as many of them are, would be cured immediately.

And our experiences indeed involve strong feelings. One of the most powerful and prominent of them is the feeling of security, directed at preserving and promoting the most important of the durable, solid entities that we conceive on the verbal level: our ego, which, like other components of the world, we imagine as an entity with a core, that remains unaltered and unalterable despite changes that occur here and there; some sort of identity in continuity, or "invariant under transformation," to use the language of modern physics.

Not only do we try to defend our ego, to promote it and to make it last longer and longer, but we also try to protect our conviction that we are such an entity—a conviction which is constantly contradicted by fact and experience.

The fact is that our view of the world as solid and durable and our similar view of the ego mutually support each other: the ego could not live its own life in an ephemeral world; conversely, from an ego-less point of view, the world could not be conceived as it appears to us. And this tragicomedy goes on and on, with a Sisyphus-like character on the stage, trying unsuccessfully to grasp at perceptions, feelings, and what not, which are continuously slipping through his fingers.

In order to end this ordeal, to stop "looking for something which does not exist" and to start "looking at things as they are" instead, one must be really fed up with all of this; but the great majority of people are not. Like flies in a bottle, they do not see or do not want to see the way out through the neck of the bottle and endlessly repeat the same unsuccessful attempt to reach salvation, freedom.

* * *

Now, for those who are fed up, how to get out of this tangle?

As long as the world is looked at with the attention directed to the ego, that is, an attention "wanting" to see things in conformity with the ego requirements, as long as the world is experienced with the intent of looking for lasting pleasure, in the framework of a verbal structure supporting this notion—the vicious circle of desire and dissatisfaction will be doomed to repeat itself.

It would be preposterous to suggest the renunciation of passions and feelings as a means of breaking this circle. In any case, it would be practically impossible to achieve this through deliberate effort alone, as the passions and feelings would only be repressed, not eliminated.

The only line of attack would seem to be rather a new way of looking, perceiving, and being attentive.

It may seem strange to reduce such a vital point to a question of attention; but the fact is that attention is the point at which things may go right or wrong. Much depends on its quality and intensity. Attention is a key: the key to Paradise is not the same as the one to Hell and the difference between them may be a question of millimetres. But a small differentiation at the source very often leads into opposite directions.

We are not accustomed to consider how to cultivate this faculty of attention. We do not learn how to be attentive any more than we learn how to walk or to stand up. But, as many of us walk and stand up badly (to the point that malfunctioning of the body ensues), so many of us direct our attention wrongly, which also has ill effects. Let us see how.

We are goal-oriented. This means that our interest is focused on certain things; and since interest stimulates attention, the latter cannot but be partial and discriminatory. In fact, attention is mostly directed from a preconceived view point or desire; it lights up what interests us and leaves the rest in the dark. (Odd situations arise from this. He, who tries to demonstrate the virtue of tolerance in a discussion, does not realize how intolerant he himself sometimes is with his interlocutors. Similarly, he who fights vehemently for the cause of love and peace is not aware how full of hate he is for his opponents.)

Now, discriminatory attention contributes to the general dichotomy: subject/object or, if you like, ego/world, where the factors left in the dark accumulate around attention and restrict it. Thus, we are attentive with an admixture of impatience or desire or worry, etc. This aggregation forms an obscure, but very much real, conglomerate which is individualized as the ego.

(And that, incidentally, is an additional reason why the existence of the ego is not generally disputed, although extreme vagueness surrounds any definition of it.)

The existence of the ego is affirmed as a certainty because the conglomerate constituted by attention and its associated elements is felt either as a unit or as something needing a support; but, since attention does not clarify these uninteresting objects—sometimes neglected because they are unpleasant to look at!—the definition of this fabricated whole, the ego, cannot but be vague. In other words, the ego, like a ghost, is felt to be a certainty as long as it is not analysed.

Normal attention, besides being partial and discriminatory, is also generally not sharp enough, being not well focused: it is like a badly adjusted telescope. This is because there is no proper balance between attention and mental absorption (or full concentration).

What does that mean and what are the implications?

Let us see. To be attentive is very different from being totally absorbed. Attention requires space, distance from the object one is attentive to. Absorption, on the other hand, if it is total, eliminates all distance; it is union, identification, "disappearance through incorporation in something," as the Concise Oxford Dictionary defines it. When one is absorbed, locked into the object, one is incapable of seeing it, of describing it; besides, the natural flow of events or the "stream of consciousness" is interrupted.

However, a good measure of absorption is nevertheless necessary for attention to be operative. Attention that is too distant (in the real and the figurative sense) runs the risk of being so little involved as to miss the object; a risk that is always run by those who are afraid of being over "subjective." An extreme example of this is the case of the art critic who, jokingly, refused to see the painting he had to judge, so as not to be influenced by it, to be "objective" in his judgement!

The problem is now to find a good equilibrium between being *in* and being *out*. This balance is rarely kept, or even aimed at. Thus, either we do not know what we are doing because we are what we are doing, or we do not know what we are doing because we are too far removed from what we are doing. The result is the same in both cases.

The two main characteristics of our everyday attention (discriminative and out of focus) contribute greatly to our normal vision of the world, distorted by passion and egotistic interests.

Instead of being a sovereign master who tries to exercise his power in the best possible way, attention lets itself be degraded and allows its sphere of authority to be infiltrated by intruding elements (interests, passions ...), to which it becomes subservient.

It is no wonder, therefore, that the resulting conception of the world (including that of the ego) reflects those interests and passions. It may be said that interests and passions engage in narcissistic contemplation of themselves, creating the deceptive image of a solid, lasting world.

We can now easily come to the conclusion that a "non-deceptive" type of attention should have the opposite characteristics to those mentioned above: it should be non-discriminatory and well focused, in the sense implied earlier. To be non-discriminatory, it must be directed to anything that is present to our consciousness, regardless of inclinations, preferences and the like. (Should the latter make themselves felt, they, like anything else, would become the object of attention.) To be well focused, it must be well balanced with absorption, achieving a combination of maximum identification and maximum detachment.

Such pure, detached attention cannot function from a preconceived view point: it must maintain contact with whatever is happening at the moment, with what our senses bring to the fore of our consciousness, with what is present here and now, which is always one thing at a time, just as only one point of a turning wheel is in contact with the ground at a time.

All this is easily said; many things are easy on the logical level (where we now are). It is not so easy, however, to put them into practice, so that the very nature of reality may be experienced in such a poignant, matter-of-fact way that our behaviour is instinctively attuned to such experiences and in harmony with them. Training methods have been devised to facilitate the process, with the main emphasis on learning to determine the obstacles that prevent pure attention from emerging; but the subject is too large for discussing it here.

The new way of perception goes against long-standing habits. It is not easy just to *look* at inclinations and likings, instead of trying to satisfy them; the temptation to fall back into the old habit is always present and often succumbed to.

But insofar as the new system works properly, attention stands unencumbered and alone: it is no longer associated with unnoticed but actively present elements, because, in this way of practice, there is nothing actively present that is not observed. There is no longer any "looking with ..." but always and only "looking at ...." This means that the dividing line between subject and object has moved, so that everything is now on the side of the object. To put it differently, the dichotomy subject/object has changed into attention/object. The "I" has become an eye. The ego has dissolved into the ephemeral state of consciousness; its apparent compactness has lost its glue. It is as if everything happens impersonally, is watched anonymously, impartially.

The difference between the new kind of attention and total absorption is now quite evident. In total absorption, the ego is neither dissected nor examined in its separate components but simply put into abeyance, forgotten for a while—for as long as the absorption lasts. Total absorption (no matter whether the identification is made with God or with a rose) is a mystical state: only one thing lives from "within," the rest is blotted out. And what happens to the compactness of the ego when pure attention is applied happens also to the rest of the world. Reality no longer appears as solid and lasting but as small, short-lived, almost evanescent, interdependent units. In terms of the logical class theory, we have passed from a class to its components or, better still, from the characteristics of the first to those of the latter. Or, to use musical terminology, what was read before as "legato" is now read as "staccato." The *ringing of the alarm clock* in the morning and the consequent *getting up* are now seen as labels covering a variety of experiences: the sound in all its modulations; its meaning (getting up); the unpleasant feelings connected with having to do that; the movements of the body; the thoughts about the first appointment at the office ... and so forth; all these elements of units being taken not in a preconstituted order, but as they present themselves to the attention; felt separately, distinctly, in their own taste, in their own appearance, duration, disappearance, and, finally, in their interconnections.

In pure attention, any event which comes to the consciousness bears the mark of its place in time. And that place in time can only be the present, since consciousness can be aware only "now." Thus, fear of death is a "now fear" of something that is not present; the presence concerns the fear, not the death; a souvenir of something that happened two years ago is a now souvenir of something no longer present.

To realize this eternal, inevitable present, this inescapable time to which waking life is linked, is to avoid being lost or alienated in the past or in the future, as is frequently the case in everyday modes of life. It also means being constantly vigilant. The stage is lighted; when the light is on, confusion either disappears or becomes ineffective.

Only he who is dead to the past lives in the present. The death of the past does not mean that it has been forgotten; it means that the emotions connected with it have spent themselves. What remains is a mere recollection of it (greatly enhanced, by the way, by constant awareness of the present).

Only he who is dead to fears and hopes about the future lives in the present. To be dead to fears and hopes about the future does not necessarily mean that they have been eradicated (although so much the better if so); it means that they are lived as present happenings, belonging to and unavoidably connected with the moment at which they occur.

When only the present is alive, newness is alive. Each and every event is experienced as individual and unmistakably itself, yet related to others. Because pure attention includes absorption, every *form* is vividly detached from its *background*, is unique and unrepeatable. Because pure attention implies distance, detachment and perspective, every *form* belongs to its family or class.

Nietzsche has written "He who cannot stand on a point without dizziness and fear, like a deity of victory, will never know what happiness is and will not be able to do anything to help others to be happy" (*Vom Nutzen und Nachteil der Historie für das Leben*).

But we do not usually know how "to stand on a point," how to live in the present. So we cannot have the sense of newness; we cannot be happy. Everything carries with it an oppressive past. We write books about books; ideas follow ideas. What we hear we have already heard; what we see we have already seen. Any message is dissolved in reminiscent echoes. Anything new has an old flavour. On the other hand, we are also bent towards the other slope; we are always projecting something or ourselves into the future. Martin Buber relates the answer given by Rabbi Jizchak to the question: "What was the real sin of Adam"—"He worried about the following day."

* * *

If the straight line represents the verbal level, and the plane the realm of action, the curve is perhaps the geometrical figure best suited to symbolize the "pure attention level."

Pure attention, being focused on one object after another, has a linear development but, in contradistinction to the verbal level, in pure attention everything changes from moment to moment; everything is and is not itself. In order to indicate these changes, the line is curved and not straight.

To go into more detail, normal attention (which is discriminative) may be represented by the straight line, since both are exclusive. As the former excludes objects that are not the chosen ones, so the latter excludes directions that are not its own.

On the contrary, pure attention (which is not discriminative), directs itself to anything present to the consciousness; thus, as soon as one direction is taken, it is abandoned for another one. There is no "follow up." The geometrical representation of this state of affairs is the curve, since it is the place where all these incipient stages of events are linked; each point of the curve may be considered as the departure of a straight line which was never traced, because attention, instead of following the verbal pattern, immediately turned to the next event that emerged on the stage of consciousness.

Let us see what may happen at this very moment, as I am writing on pure attention and its geometrical representation. There are two possibilities: either the subject matter is dealt with on a verbal level, as is usually the case; or pure attention not only focuses itself on what is or had to be written, but also directs itself to whatever makes itself felt as a presence: intruding thoughts, imaginations, body sensations, and so on. In the second case, what is written now would emerge from a living curve, from pure attention in operation.

* * *

Pure attention has no support; it is self-supporting, so to speak: a watching from no-man's land or—which amounts to the same thing—from a dimensionless point, from nowhere.

Living on the curve—it is clear now—does not mean refraining from thinking and acting (which, incidentally, would be impossible). But the thoughts and actions—or life in general—are watched from that vantage point which is nowhere. Leaving the talk to the talking, the walk to the walking, and so on, means liberating energies that were previously invested unnecessarily in those activities and thus enabling them to be invested in pure, vigilant attention. It might be worth stressing that the functioning of the latter is not tantamount to "considering" or "pondering" and the like. If it were, it would be an extra dose of thinking, another straight line added to the others! But it is not, although this is a trap the beginner is bound to fall into innumerable times! The function of pure attention is more akin to "tasting," "feeling," like tasting food or touching a piece of cloth. This sort of knowledge, which can be called "tasting" or "feeling" only metaphorically, can be applied to the activity of our six senses (the five traditional senses plus the mind). And each sense has a flavour of its own. Seeing "tastes" different from hearing, smelling, touching, tasting (proper), and thinking and, of course, each one of these "tastes" different from the rest. Even "thinking," the least corporeal of the senses, has a "taste" (a pretty dull one, I am afraid!).

Pure attention perceives, recognizes and acknowledges all this and makes a mental note of it: a rather unusual activity which, if judged by its description, may appear boring and purposeless. But it would indeed be purposeless to argue the point, for any practice is for practising and this case is no exception.

Only he who is aware of his perceptions, feelings and mental states in the manner outlined above, that is, through intimate contact with their texture, caught in the process of its making, can really know what seeing or being angry or being worried or what not, are like.

The proof of the pudding is in the eating.

* * *

But, let us face it: the chances are that not only the cooking of the pudding goes against the grain, but that even the result (especially if the recipe has been scrupulously followed) tastes rather disgusting! Leaving aside the metaphor, not only does the practice of pure attention counter old habits and long-time inclinations, but also the reality revealed by that practice manifests itself as rather disagreeable.

In fact, what is experienced through pure attention is a high degree of impermanence: our "*bête noire*" a "black monster." We do not want to admit that everything that is born must die and that what must die, is in a sense, already dead. We discard this view too easily as being pessimistic, whereas it is neither pessimistic nor optimistic but reflects only what is. We angrily flog dead horses but this does not even make us a taxidermist; it makes us only more and more similar to that neurotic who knew that 2 + 2 = 4, but who got angry about it.

The glaring realization that reality is utterly impermanent makes reality itself even more unsatisfactory, because desires, fears and hopes—still at work—have no firm hook to hang from. And, what is worse, we can do nothing about it, because our ego is revealed by pure attention as a "pathological phenomenon," as an illness that consists of the ego's claim to exist and its self-promotion or consists in its being ego-less, to put it in one word. Such an ego, or rather non-ego, cannot modify this state of affairs. Our supposed all-of-a-piece self is not the master of impermanence, because it is impermanent itself.

But, sooner or later, this situation draws to a climax, which is also a turning point. Sooner or later, a "giving up," a "letting go," manifests itself: reality is accepted as it is; any dichotomy between what is and what should be disappears; life and reality become one, not in the sense of a mystical union, but in that of being attuned to one another. And that is peace, harmony, not because everything is going smoothly but because everything is inescapably the way it is and therefore cannot be otherwise. The deep recognition of this fact does not leave any leeway for vain speculation.

This is not fatalism. The chances of missing the bus are reduced by running for it; but once the bus has been caught or missed—to one's contentment or disappointment—this result (including the contentment or disappointment) is the unchangeable effect of what has gone before. Apart from that, the new practice also teaches us that we often run unnecessarily; we interfere unduly. Things have a way of doing themselves by themselves. "I hope to find what I am going to say interesting" was the witty remark I heard from an excellent speaker, one minute before he delivered his speech.

* * *

The "way out" need not have a dramatic turning point; its development may be smoother, marked by many insights along the road. It seems advisable not to make too much fuss about them. Are they genuine? Or not? Too much doubting is itself a clear sign that the ego is not very far off. In any case, the best mark of the true value of these insights resides in one's ability to receive them, spontaneously and in a spirit of humility. Obviously, one cannot *want* to be spontaneous, although this double constraint plagues many unprepared beginners. On the contrary, boasting about flashes of insight, playing the role of the noisy convert, is a symptom of inauthenticity. Sometimes these manifestations are allowed to pass under the complacent cover of helping others to follow suit. But this end is better served by examples than by words: the most effective help comes especially when it is unintentional and in the form of a by-result of what one is.

* * *

Nobody can help you to an insight, *nobody* can even put you on the curve; least of all *yourself.* Effort and discipline may be required but not *your* effort or *your* discipline; in other words, they should not be the issue of an ego. And yet the starting point cannot be other than where one is, that is to say, it is most likely in a full-fledged ego that wants to become ego-less and is therefore striving to reach this goal. Now, an ego-less situation cannot be the product of an ego's desire and planning. All the same, and paradoxically, this almost inevitable false start may eventually have happy turnings. Ambroise Parè, a famous French surgeon of the XVIth century, used to say of every patient he could keep alive: "*Je le pansay, Dieu le guarist*" ("I have bandaged him, God has cured him"). In non-theological terms, any result is at least in part the effect of uncontrollable circumstances.

In the same spirit, we can say that the passage from self to no-self must be prepared, although it cannot be determined. It comes with a leap that takes no time and covers no space. It is an arrival without previous departure. More than an event, it is an advent. Being beyond time, it cannot be explained or described. What can be explained and described must have a temporal nature; hence, endless references in both directions: the past and the future. Insight, however, is a vertical break in the horizontal, temporal line. It bears no "before that," no "after that."

Insight is THAT.

* * *

A few words of acknowledgement.

In the preceding pages, the Buddhist reader will have recognized, as a sort of watermarks, some of the vital points of the *Dhamma*, Suttas have not been quoted, nor have Pāli words been cited. The intention was to deal—in today's language—with problems that are as important for man at present as they have been at all times in the past. As Buddhism is independent of "source references," the attempt seems to be legitimate. But it may, of course, be off the mark; which would not be so strange: *paṭiccasamuppāda* was at work while it was written.

Bag of Bones

A Miscellany on the Body

by

Bhikkhu Khantipālo

WHEEL PUBLICATION NO. 271/272

"Bhikkhus, they do not savour the deathless
who do not savour mindfulness of the body;
they savour the deathless who savour
mindfulness of the body." (A I 45)

"A skeleton wrapped up in skin ..." (MN 82)

Introduction

The body is thought to be most obviously "me," what I regard as the most tangible part of myself. Around it therefore are constructed many views, all of them distorted to some extent, which prevent insight arising into *the body as it really is*. This book is a small anthology relating to the body in various ways, and presents material, which, if contemplated by the earnest and sincere student of Dhamma, will eventually provide fruitful insight and, thereby, freedom from the many desires and fears centred on the body.

Such desires for pleasures in which the body is the instrument (though it is in the heart-mind where they dwell), awaken and intensify greed of all kinds, for food or sex for instance. Greed which is often accompanied by pleasurable sensations—and therefore desired—needs a rather bitter medicine to combat it: hence the number of pieces here on the unattractiveness of the body, its decay and death—all unpleasant matters. Some of the material, concerned with bodily unattractiveness, is like a medicine which need only be taken while the disease of greed-lust is active, and afterwards may be discontinued. It is important to understand this, and not to form the mistaken impression that the Buddha advocated viewing all beauty as loathsome. It is only that there is a hook in beauty which tangles with the greed in one's own heart and leads to more and more complications and difficulties.

Fears centre around ageing-decay, disease and death. They are not overcome by pretending they do not exist, as the ostrich is said to bury its head in the sand at the approach of enemies. Only resolutely facing these inevitable features of life can bring insight and relief from fear.

The Buddha's instructions on the contemplation of the body are addressed to those who are able, through their lifestyle, to practice them. This means in effect monks and nuns, together with dedicated lay people. The former group have this contemplation given to them by their Teachers at the time of Going-forth from home to homelessness, and they need such a medicine to combat lust, which is destructive to the celibate Holy Life. Lay people keeping the Five Precepts have contentment with their partners as an important part of their practice. Sex is a natural part of their life but should still be restrained and kept within the bounds of the Third Precept. If not, how much trouble follows! But some of them may wish to live without sexual attachment, and this cannot be done in the way of Dhamma by ignoring the power of the sexual drive, or by suppressing it. Only when it is treated with mindfulness can it be transcended. The aspect of mindfulness which is needed for this is the subject, or rather the interrelated subjects, of this book.

In the world today people are subjected to a bombardment of sensuality by way of the mass media. Sex especially is used as a bait to sell things, and as a titillation of sensory experience. When this subjection is continued, the defilements of the mind, notably lust, greed, and attachment, are sure to be strengthened. Then when this has happened, the result is not more happiness, only an increase of dukkha, suffering, trouble, and difficulties. The medicine for such over-indulgence and over-stimulation is given in this book.

It is said that this subject of meditation is unique to the Buddha's Teachings and that elsewhere it is not clearly taught. This is not surprising as we find that desire is sometimes accepted as being "natural." Wherever desires are viewed as "natural," that is, inherent in one's nature or self, nothing much can be done about them. But the Buddha analyzed desires into those which are wholesome—to practice Dhamma, for instance—and the unwholesome ones, among which are greed and lust. They may not be gross either, as in the case of the meditator who is greedy for bliss, or visions, and attached to such things. The Buddha has provided the medicine for all unwholesome desires, and according to our various ways of life we can use it to effect partial or complete cures.

When the emphasis is so much on sensuality, youth, and beauty as we find now, the darker sides of life get pushed away and attempts are made, always unsuccessful, to sweep them under the carpet. Those who try to do so will not be pleased with the exercises contained in the Buddha's contemplation of the body. Such things will appear to them as morbid and unnatural. Yet they are also a part of this life and should not be ignored. And if the effort is made to ignore what is unpleasant about the body, sooner or later one will be jolted into the recognition of these things. Such jolts are not pleasant. Rather than leave it until one is forced to know the body's unpleasant sides it is better to acquaint one's emotions with this knowledge gradually.

In this spirit, *Bag of Bones* is being published. Unfortunately, being only a book it cannot give person-to-person advice on special problems. It can only offer some general guidelines to people who are interested in reducing their greed and lust.

A word of warning: meditation on the unattractiveness of the body can be very potent and should only be practiced with moderation and care, especially if one has no personal contact with a Teacher of Buddhist meditation. If fear and anxiety, or other extreme unwholesome emotional states arise after practice of it, then it will be better to lay it down and take up Loving-kindness (*mettā*) or Recollection of the Buddha (*Buddhānussati*) as one's meditation instead.

This book, therefore, is not so much for beginners in Buddhism but rather for those who have already practiced for some time. May it inspire many people to practice the Dhamma more intently!

Translations which have no one's name after them are by the compiler. And all other reflections, dialogues, and poems too are his work, and have been jotted down as they occurred to him, mostly in the peaceful Forest Hermitage of Ven. Nyanaponika Mahāthera outside Kandy. [Editor: *Note that no quotation marks are added around these translations, reflections, dialogues, and poems by Bhikkhu Khantipālo.*] May I also here acknowledge the Venerable Mahāthera's kind advice and help in bringing this collection to print.

Bhikkhu Khantipālo
Wat Buddha-Dhamma
Forest Meditation Centre
Ten Mile Hollow
Wiseman's Ferry, N.S.W. 2255
Australia

Bag of Bones

1.

"Bhikkhus, when *one dhamma* is developed and cultivated it leads to a great sense of urgency, to great benefit, to great safety from bondage, to great mindfulness and full awareness, to obtainment of knowledge and insight, to a pleasant abiding here and now, to realization of the fruit of true knowledge and deliverance. What is that *one dhamma*? It is mindfulness occupied with the body."

AN 1:21, trans. Ven. Ñāṇamoli

2. The Advantages of Mindfulness of the Body

1. One conquers aversion and delight,
2. And fear and dread as well.
3. Besides, one can stand cold and heat, hunger and thirst, troublesome things in the world, harsh words and painful feelings.
4. One obtains all four *jhānas*,
5. And supernormal faculties,
6. The heavenly ear element (clairaudience),
7. Knowledge of others' minds,
8. And of all one's past lives,
9. And sees besides, how beings appear and pass away according to their dukkha.
10. Finally one enters upon the two deliverances (of the heart and by wisdom), and all taints (*āsava*) are abolished.

MN 119, Mindfulness of the Body

3.

"When anyone has developed and repeatedly practiced mindfulness of the body, he has included whatever wholesome *dhammas* (mental states) there are that partake of true knowledge (*vijjā*).

"Just as anyone who extends his mind over the great ocean has included whatever streams there are that flow into the ocean, so too, when anyone has developed and repeatedly practiced mindfulness of the body, he has included whatever wholesome *dhammas* there are that partake of true knowledge."

MN 119, trans. Ven. Ñāṇamoli (revised)

4. Insight Knowledge

"This my body consists of the four great elements, procreated by a mother and father, is built up out of boiled rice and bread, is of the nature of impermanence, of being worn and rubbed away, of dissolution and disintegration, and this my consciousness has that for its support and is bound up with it."

MN 77, trans. Ven. Ñāṇamoli

5.

"Now, this body that has material form consists of the four great elements, it is procreated by a mother and father, and built up out of boiled rice and bread, it has the nature of impermanence, of being worn and rubbed away, of dissolution and disintegration. It must be regarded—

as impermanent—as (liable to) suffering,
as a disease—as a cancer,
as a dart—as a calamity,
as an affliction—as alien,
as a falling to pieces—as void,
as without a self.

"When a man regards it thus, he abandons his desire for the body, affection for the body, and his habit of treating the body as a basis for his inferences."[1]

MN 74, trans. Ven. Ñāṇamoli

6.

You live by *"following the body?"* Eating when it's hungry, resting when it's tired, dressing when necessary, urinating, defecating,

1. Or "habit of following the body, being dependent on the body."

going to work to get money—all for what? For this body? Then what about the time when its end comes? What was it all for?

7.

How much time do you spend on your body—
to feed it—to clothe it,
to cleanse it—to wash it,
to beautify it—to relax it,
to rest it?
How much time do you spend on your mind?

8.

Three things we never forget to do for the *body*:
wash it,
feed it,
medicate it.
Three things we usually forget to do with the *mind*:
wash it (with the purity of calm meditation),
feed it (with good *Dhamma*),
medicate it (mindfully ridding ourselves of the diseases of greed, aversion and delusion, with the supreme medicine of *Dhamma*).

The mind gets dirty and needs washing, it becomes hungry and needs nutriment, and it is most of the time diseased and needs curing.

Why are we so forgetful of our own good?

9. Gratification and Danger in Form (Body)

"And what is gratification in the case of form (body)?

"Suppose there were a girl of warrior-noble caste or brahmin caste or householder stock, in her fifteenth or sixteenth year, neither too tall nor too short, neither too thin nor too fat, neither too dark nor too fair: is her beauty and loveliness then at its height?"

"Yes, venerable sir."

"Now, the pleasure and joy that arise in dependence on that beauty and loveliness are the gratification in the case of form.

"And what is danger in the case of form?

"Later on one might see that same woman here at eighty, ninety or a hundred years, aged, as crooked as a roof, doubled up, tottering with the aid of sticks, frail, her youth gone, her teeth broken, grey haired, scanty-haired, bald, wrinkled, with limbs all blotchy: how do you conceive this, bhikkhus, has her former beauty and loveliness vanished and the danger become evident?"

"Yes, venerable sir."

"Bhikkhus, this is the danger in the case of form."

MN 13, "The Mass of Suffering,"
trans. Ven. Ñāṇamoli

N.B. Women reading this should change the sex of the person in the above.

10. Reflections on her body by the former beautiful courtesan, later the *arahat* nun Ambapāli

Black was my hair, the colour of bees, curled at the ends;
with ageing it's likened to fibres of hemp—
not other than this are the Truth-speaker's [2] words.

Fragrant was my hair, full of flowers like a perfume box;
with ageing it possesses the smell of dog's fur—
not other than this are the Truth-speaker's words.

Thick as a well-planted grove and comely with comb, pin and parting;
with ageing it's thin here and there—
not other than this are the Truth-speaker's words.

Braided well, adorned, black masses beautified by gold;
with ageing has the head become quite bald—
not other than this are the Truth-speaker's words.

My eyebrows then as though by artists were well-drawn;
with ageing they are wrinkled, hanging down—
not other than this are the Truth-speaker's words.

2. The Truth-speaker (who speaks the truth of impermanence) is the Buddha.

Flashing and brilliant as jewels, black and long were my eyes;
by ageing overwhelmed no longer beautiful—
not other than this are the Truth-speaker's words.

Long, beautiful and delicate my nose in the bloom of my youth;
with ageing has become quite pendulous—
not other than this are the Truth-speaker's words.

Fair my earlobes, formerly as bracelets well and truly crafted;
with ageing they are wrinkled, hanging down—
not other than this are the Truth-speaker's words.

Then were my teeth beautiful, the hue of plantain buds;
with ageing they have broken and yellowed—
not other than this are the Truth-speaker's words.

Sweet was my singing voice as cuckoo in the forest grove;
with ageing it is broken now and then—
not other than this are the Truth-speaker's words.

Formerly my throat was beautiful, polished like a conch;
with ageing decayed it is and twisted—
not other than this are the Truth-speaker's words.

Round as door-bars then were my arms beautiful;
with ageing they are weak as the trumpet-creeper—
not other than this are the Truth-speaker's words.

Adorned with gold and delicate signet rings my hands were beautiful;
with ageing just like knotted and twisted roots—
not other than this are the Truth-speaker's words.

Full and round were my breasts, close together, lovely and lofty;
pendulous they hang now as water-skins without water—
not other than this are the Truth-speaker's words.

Fair was my body then as a well-burnished tablet of gold;
now it is covered all over with very fine wrinkles—
not other than this are the Truth-speaker's words.

Lovely both my thighs as the trunks of elephants;
with ageing they are as a bamboo's stems—
not other than this are the Truth-speaker's words.

Fair were my legs adorned with fine golden anklets;
with ageing stick-like as the sesame—
not other than this are the Truth-speaker's words.

As though filled out with down my feet so lovely;
with ageing they are cracked and wrinkled—
not other than this are the Truth-speaker's words.

So was this congeries; decrepit now, abode of dukkha;
old house with its plaster falling off—
not other than this are the Truth-speaker's words.

Theragāthā, Verses of the Elder Bhikkhunīs,
verses 252–270

11.

"Come, bhikkhus, abide contemplating ugliness in the body, perceiving repulsiveness in nutriment, perceiving disenchantment with all the world, contemplating impermanence in all formations."

MN 50, trans. Ven. Ñāṇamoli

Directly counter goes this to the world's way which is: to see beauty in the body or at any rate disguise the ugliness, to delight in food both physical and mental, to be enchanted with (the beauty of) the world (and forget the other side), and to regard mental formations as a basis for a permanent self or soul.

12.

Rohitassa, a deva: "Lord, the world's end where one is neither born nor ages nor dies, nor passes away nor reappears: is it possible to know or see or reach that by travelling there?"

The Buddha: "Friend, that there is a world's end where one is neither born nor ages nor dies, nor passes away nor reappears, which is to be known or seen or reached by travelling there—that I do not say. Yet I do not say that there is ending of suffering without reaching the world's end. Rather it is in this fathom-long carcass with its perceptions and its mind that I describe the world, the origin of the world, the cessation of the world, and the way leading to the cessation of the world."

SN 2:26, AN 4:46, trans, Ven. Ñāṇamoli

13.

The current rash of so much porn has the effects we see, increased and open expression of greed and lust. The meditation techniques which can cure these diseases are all the different aspects of mindfulness concerned with the body—for they cut the body down to size, without harming it, while emphasizing the importance of the mind.

14.

Contemplation of the body's unattractiveness is not a popular meditation. People are happy to try to rid themselves of anger and hatred because they are painful. This can be done by the well-known meditations developing loving-kindness (*mettā*). But meditating upon the nature of this body dulls the appetites rooted in greed—and greed is often associated with pleasure. And isn't pleasure what this life's all about?

Safely bagged by Māra—Death and Lord of the sensual realm!

15.

When the body is not washed it attracts flies and vermin which feed on it. When the mind is not purified but is full of lust, hate and delusion what does it attract ...?

16.

The body is so near, yet like an unexplored continent. Large areas in it are a blank. While this is so, greed, lust and craving dwell safely in the jungles of ignorance.

17.

People's attitudes to the body are liable to swing from the extreme of indulging the desires connected with the body, to the other extreme of mortifying it.

The Middle Way of mindfulness regarding the body is unknown to them.

18.

When desires connected with bodily pleasures can be indulged, which means that *greed* rules the mind, *aversion* only arises if one's aims are thwarted; but when a person has undertaken some method of self-discipline not guided by wisdom (*paññā*), then suppressed desires find their outlet not only by aversion but also by bodily mortification. As though the body was responsible! So, having no wisdom, people subject their bodies to "disciplines" and rigors of various kinds in order, they think, *to control strong desires.* Then *aversion,* that is self-hatred in a more or less subtle form, reigns supreme and sufferings are increased. Desires can never be understood in this way, only suppressed. The only way to understand desires is through mindfulness, and the various exercises on mindfulness of the body are for this purpose.

19.

There are very few beings who do not suffer from lust, in this world of sensuality at any rate. It is a great sickness of the mind, an epidemic with no beginning, and no end in sight for most beings. Wise men want to be cured of this disease and the Buddha offers for this the medicine of contemplating the unattractive in one's own body. One should not try to see the ugly or foul in others. This could turn to hatred—even if not, it could result in a "sour grapes" attitude to them. Towards others maintain one of the Divine Abidings: loving-kindness, compassion, joy-with-others, or equanimity, but towards one's own selfish desires for pleasure develop the seeing of unattractiveness.

20.

True love, which is cool, unattached *mettā*, and compassion for others' sorrows, do not grow when people are bound up with greed and sensuality.

21.

When lust arises in the mind, which leads to more defilements, more burning desires in future, just take a look at this butcher's shop of a body. Anything attractive about red meat? Are white bones especially lovable? Or coiled "innards" desirable? Lust soon disappears when the body is regarded in this way. Repeating this practice, lust becomes weaker and arises less often.

22.

"... no one who searches earnestly throughout the whole of this fathom-long carcass, starting from the soles of the feet upwards, starting from the top of the hair downwards, and starting from the skin all round, ever sees even the minutest atom of pureness in it such as a pearl or a crystal or a beryl or aloes or sandalwood or saffron or camphor or talcum powder, etc; on the contrary, he sees nothing but various very malodorous offensive drab-looking sorts of impurity consisting of head-hair, body-hairs, and the rest."

Minor Readings (and Illustrator), III 4, transl. of Khuddakapāṭha by Ven. Ñāṇamoli.

23. The Thirty-two Parts of the Body

The practice of this mindfulness attending to the body can begin by reciting this passage:

"In this very body, from the soles of the feet up, from the crown of the head down, surrounded by skin, full of these various mean impurities, he reviews thus:

"There are in this body:

Kesā—head-hair
Lomā—body-hair
Nakhā—nails
Dantā—teeth
Taco—skin
Maṃsaṃ—flesh
Nahāru—sinews
Aṭṭhi—bones
Aṭṭhimiñjaṃ—bone-marrow
Vakkaṃ—kidneys
Hadayaṃ—heart
Yakanaṃ—liver
Kilomakaṃ—membranes
Pihakaṃ—spleen

Papphāsaṃ—lungs
Antaṃ—large gut
Antaguṇaṃ—small gut
Udariyaṃ—gorge
Karīsaṃ—dung
Pittaṃ—bile
Semhaṃ—phlegm
Pubbo—pus
Lohitaṃ—blood
Sedo—sweat
Medo—fat
Assu—tears
Vasā—grease
Khelo—spit
Siṅghānikā—snot
Lasikā—oil of the joints
Muttaṃ—urine
(to which is added "brain in the skull" to make up 32 parts).

"In this very body, from the soles of the feet up, from the crown of the head down, surrounded by skin, full of these various mean impurities, he reviews thus."

MN 10, Satipaṭṭhāna Sutta, trans. Ven. Ñāṇamoli

24.

There is no unhealthy self-disgust or aversion here, just seeing what is unattractive as it really is. But in later times some teachers (such as Śāntideva in his *Bodhicāryāvatāra*)[3] went to extremes in this matter. One must suspect in such a case not the proper dispassion with the body but rather perverted passion. Lust can switch to aversion and hatred quickly.

25.

It is a remarkable thing that the first five parts on this list—the "person" we see—are all dead! Hair of the head and body lives only at its roots, we see dead hair. Nails that we see are dead nails, the quick is painful and hidden. The teeth, all

3. Many verses in Chapter 8 of that work are certainly "sick."

that is visible, are dead, and their tender living roots we only experience painfully from time to time. Outer skin is dead—horrible if it was not, for it is sensitive enough already. The living skin below is more painful.

So when we get excited about a visual form—someone else's body—we are stimulated by impressions of what has died already. Strange to be excited by what is dead on the outside and dying within! However, the real lure is in our own minds: the thoughts of lust that arise there and embellish the corpse before us.

Apart from this, live bodies and dead ones differ only in degree. Lust fastens only on the body. But loving-kindness and compassion are concerned with the well-being of peoples' minds and bodies.

26.

When we see a "person," we see just the first five of the 32 parts: head-hair, body-hair, nail, teeth and skin. When *head-hair* is of certain colours and forms, *body-hair* present or absent according to sex and race, *nails* cut and cleaned, *teeth* white, polished and with none missing, and *skin,* well washed and unblemished by scars or wrinkles and covering flesh of certain shapes—then with all these conditions fulfilled, desire arises!

What about grey or white hair on the head or body—thin and straggly, nails cracked, dirty and broken, teeth yellow or mostly missing and skin wrinkled and blotchy? Who gets excited?

27.

Staring at corpses as recommended by commentary-writer Buddhaghosa in his *Path of Purification* is not really to the point. One has *inwardly* to stare at *this* corpse to accomplish anything.

And he gets much too complicated in his descriptions of how to do the actual practice, which does not require a lot of categories and analysis, or things to be learnt by heart. This applies to both the meditation on corpses and to the 32 parts of the body.

In the latter case, just a few parts are needed for repetition and inspection, and even one will be sufficient if one's mind wanders. Simplicity and directness cut out the clutter of thoughts—and clearing those out is the way to get into meditation.

28. Meditation on Bones

"Bones in a pattern ordered
Standing end to end
With many joints, whose shaping
On no one does depend;
By sinews held together,
Menaced by ageing's threat,
Incognizant, resembling
A wooden marionette."

M R. III 22

29. Contemplation of the Body: Charnel Ground Meditations

"Again, a bhikkhu judges this same body as though he were looking at bodily remains thrown on a charnel ground, bones without sinews scattered in all directions: here a hand bone, there a foot bone, there a shin bone, there a thigh bone, there a hip bone, there a back bone, there a rib bone, there a breast bone, there an arm bone, there a shoulder bone, there a neck bone, there a jaw bone, there a tooth bone, there the skull.

"This body too is of such a nature, it will be like that, it is not exempt from that!

"In this way he abides contemplating the body as a body in himself, or he abides contemplating the body as a body externally, or he abides contemplating the body as a body in himself and externally. Or else he abides contemplating in the body its arising factors, or he abides contemplating in the body its vanishing factors, or he abides contemplating in the body its arising and vanishing factors.

"Or else, mindfulness that 'There is a body' is simply established in him to the extent of bare knowledge and remembrance (of it), while he abides independent, not clinging to anything in the world."

from MN 10, trans. Ven. Ñāṇamoli

30.

When the mind is calm, look into this bony frame to see its emptiness, how the wind blows through it. Who owns these bones?

31.

It seems that as the Elder (Mahā-tissa) was on his way from Cetiyapabbata to Anurādhapura for alms, a certain daughter-in-law of a clan, who had quarrelled with her husband and had set out early from Anurādhapura all dressed up and tricked out like a celestial nymph to go to her relatives' home, saw him on the road, and being low-minded, she laughed a loud laugh. (Wondering) "What is that?", the Elder looked up and finding in the bones of her teeth the perception of foulness, he attained arahatship. But her husband who was going after her saw the Elder and asked "Venerable sir, did you by any chance see a woman?" The Elder told him:

> "Whether it was a man or a woman
> That went by I noticed not;
> But only that on this high road
> There goes a group of bones."

The Path of Purification, I.55

32.

A mound of about five feet high of bones, skulls, long bones and vertebrae all mixed up. No knowing where one person's bones ended and another's began. Over them all the hot sun beat down and bleached them, the rains lashed down and washed them; these remains of unknown poor people waiting to be cremated in a Chinese graveyard in Bangkok. A rare and stirring sight in these days of "window-dressing."

33.

Suppose, that during meditation, this bony frame appeared to one's mind's eye but when one opened the eyes at the meditation's end, the bones of the hand, or other parts, were still visible without their covering of "decent" flesh—how upsetting for oneself—and others if they too could see it. How very odd to be so fearful of a part of one's "own" body!

34. Story

Once there was a man who had charge of a hothouse in which a great variety of tropical water-lilies and gourds were growing. On this particular afternoon it was cold and raining outside, so that a continuous stream of visitors entered to warm themselves and admire the exotic plants. Having sprayed the plants over with water from a hose the man bent down to turn off the tap. When he raised his eyes he saw, not people, but a procession of skeletons. The vision lasted a moment and was gone. An indication of what sort of meditation he should practice, perhaps?

35.

"Bhikkhus, the bones of a single person journeying on, wandering on for an eon, would make a cairn, a pile, a mound as great as Mount Vepulla, were there a collector of those bones and if the collection were not destroyed."

Itivuttaka 1

36.

"Just as when a space is enclosed by timber and creepers, grass and clay, there comes to be the term 'house,' so too, when a space is enclosed by bones and sinews, flesh and skin, there comes to be the term 'form.'"

MN 28.36, trans. Ven. Ñāṇamoli

37.

Or again, the Ancient Teachers said:
"Nine hundred sinews all round
In this fathom-long carcass found
Whereby its bony frame is bound
As creepers serve a building to compound."

M.R. again

38.

Or how about this for the body?
"A tumour where nine holes abide [4]
Wrapped in a coat of clammy hide
And trickling filth on every side,
Polluting the air with stenches far and wide."

M.R., quoting *Questions of Milinda,* p. 74

39. An Ulcer

Monks, it is just like an ulcer that had been growing for many years, having nine gaping wounds, nine lesions, and whatever discharged and oozed out of it would be foul and stinking, it would be loathsome.

"Ulcer," monks, is a name for this body consisting of the four great elements, procreated by mother and father, and built up out of rice and bread. It is subject to impermanence, to breaking up and wearing away, to dissolution and to disintegration, having nine gaping wounds, nine lesions. Whatever discharges and oozes out of it is foul and stinks, it is loathsome.

Therefore, monks, turn away from[5] this body.

AN 9:15

40.

"A man's body is structurally simply a hollow ring. A hollow ring elongated into a hollow cylinder, with the inner portion further lengthened and coiled; and above the upper orifice there bulges a head and between the upper and lower orifices the limbs stick out.

---

4. (Two) eyes, (two) ears, (two) nostrils, mouth, urinary duct, and anus.

5. Pali: *nibbindatha.* This can also be rendered "be weary of" or "be averse to" or "be disgusted with." But none of these renderings conveys the flavour of very subtle *Dhamma*-practice; they are too gross and convey negative or defiled states of mind. We should note that the Buddha is speaking to monks—that is, to those who practice *Dhamma* full-time, and if we knew the circumstances in which these words were spoken, we should probably find that the monks addressed needed such a "severe" exhortation in order to overcome greed or attachment.

The world passes in small portions through the ring, helped in by spoon and gulping, and out by pressure and paper."

A Thinker's Notebook by Ven. Ñāṇamoli § 240,
March '56

41. Tale:

A woman, infatuated, came to a bhikkhu and stripped off her clothes. The bhikkhu, without batting an eyelid, said—"Now take off your skin."

42.

"Beauty is skin-deep"—how true this saying is! Who wants a beautiful body without skin? How fragile is skin, but how strong is lust!

43.

Another view of the body:
"A carcass daubed with bits of meat
Nine times a hundred when complete,
Where swarming clans of worms[6] compete
To share the rotting midden for their seat."

44.

On this subject we have also:

"*As to sharing the body with many:* This body is shared by many. Firstly, it is shared by the eighty families of worms (parasites). There too, creatures live in dependence on the outer skin, on the inner skin, on the flesh, on the sinews, on the bones, on the marrow, feeding on these things. And there they are born, grow old and die, evacuate and make water; and the body is their maternity home, their hospital, their charnel ground, their privy and their urinal. The body can also be brought to death with the upsetting of these worms. And just as it is shared with the eighty families of worms, so too it is shared by the several hundred

6. "Worms" means not only the parasitic worms, but all the other parasites, visible or of microscopic size, which make this body their home.

internal diseases, as well as by such external causes of death as snakes, scorpions and what not."

The Path of Purification, VII.25

45. The Discourse on Victory

(The Buddha:)

Walking or standing, sitting, lying down,
He bends it in or stretches it: this is the body's movement.
This body by bones and sinews bound, bedaubed with membrane, flesh,
And covered up with skin—is not seen as it really is.
Filled with guts, with belly filled with liver-lump and bladder,
With heart, with lungs as well, with kidneys and with spleen,
With snot and spittle, and with fat and sweat,
With blood, and oil for the joints, with bile, and grease of the skin;
Then by nine streams the unclean flows forever from it:
Eye-dirt from the eyes, ear-dirt from the ears,
Snot from the nose, now from the mouth bile is spewed,
Now is spewed out phlegm, and from the body sweat and dirt.
And then its hollow head is stuffed with brains;
The fool thinks (all is) beautiful—led on by ignorance.
But when it's lying dead, bloated up and livid blue,
Cast away in the charnel ground, even kin do not care for it.
Dogs eat it and jackals, and wolves and worms,
Crows and vultures eat it, and whatever other creatures are.
Wise the bhikkhu in this world who having heard the Buddha-word,
The body he knows surely and thoroughly, he sees it as it really is,
(Thinking): As this (living body) so that (corpse was once),
As that (corpse is now) so this (body will surely be)—
So for the body, within and without, discard desire.
Such a bhikkhu, wise, discarding desire and lust in this world,

Attains to deathlessness, to peace, Nibbāna the unchanging state.
Pampered is this foul, two-footed, fetid thing,
Though filled with various sorts of stench and oozing here and there:
He who with such a body thinks to exalt himself,
Or should despise another—what else is this but blindness?

Sutta-Nipāta, Vijaya Sutta, Verses 193–206

46. Dhammapada Verses on the Body

41.

Not long alas—and it will lie
this body here, upon the earth!
Rejected, void of consciousness
and useless as a rotten log.

46.

Having known this body likened unto foam
and understanding thoroughly its nature mirage-like,
cutting down the shafts of Māra, flower-tipped,
unseen one can go beyond the king of death.

147.

See this body beautiful,
a mass of sores, a congeries,
much considered but miserable
where nothing is stable, nothing persists.

148.

All decrepit is this body,
diseases' nest and frail;
this foul mass is broken up—
indeed life ends in death.

149.

These dove-hued bones
scattered in fall
like long white gourds,
what joy in seeing them?

150.

This city is made of bones
plastered with flesh and blood;
in it are stored decay and death
as well as pride, detraction.

151.

Even rich royal chariots decay;
this body also reaches to decay;
but the Dhamma of the good does not decay;
so the good make it known to the calm.

293.

But those who always practice well
bodily mindfulness,
do never what should not be done
and ever do what should be done;
mindful, clearly comprehending,
their pollutions out of existence go.

299.

Well awake and watchful
ever are Gotama's *sāvakā*,[7]
who constantly by day and night
are mindful of the body.

7. Disciples, literally "listeners."

47

Two Pairs of Verses on the Contemplation of Beauty and Unattractiveness

7.

One who lives contemplating beauty,
with faculties of sense unrestrained,
who knows not moderation in his food,
and who is indolent, of little effort;
him indeed does Māra overthrow
as wind a tree of little strength.

8.

One who lives contemplating foulness,
with faculties of sense well-restrained,
who does know moderation in his food,
and who has faith, of roused-up effort;
him indeed does Māra never overthrow
as wind does not the rocky mount.

349.

One who contemplates the beautiful,
of agitating thoughts and active lust,
craving in this person constantly increases;
that one indeed makes strong his bonds.

350.

But who delights in calming thoughts,
he develops foulness ever mindfully,
he indeed will make an end;
that one will sever Māra's bonds.

48. Verses of the Arahat Kappa Thera

Full of many kinds of filth,
producer of much excrement,
as ripe as a midden-pool,

a tumour, a great wound
filled up with pus and blood,
as though sunk in a cesspit
the body oozes water
and ever filth outflows.
Tied together by sixty tendons
and plastered with plaster of flesh,
tightly jacketed with skin—
with no value, this body of filth.
A connected skeleton of bones
bound together with sinew cords
producing various postures
by conditioned things combined.
Set out with certainty of death
and near to King Mortality
but having rejected it[8] just here
a man goes as he likes.
Covered over with ignorance
and tied with the fourfold tie,
enmeshed in the net of tendencies
this body sinks in the flood.
Hitched to the five hindrances
and so, affected by thoughts,
accompanied by craving's root
and wrapped by delusion's wrappings—
this body continues on,
made to go by kamma's means,
its existence in the end destroyed,
all sorts of beings perish.
Those ordinary people, blinded fools,
thinking their bodies belong to them
fill up the fearful cemeteries
and seize repeated birth.
Those who abandon[9] this body
as one would a dung-smeared snake,

8. As "me" or "mine."
9. Abandon attachment to it.

having vomited being's root,
will, taintless, Nibbāna attain.

Theragāthā, Verses of the Elder Bhikkhus,
verses 567–576

49. Verses of the Arahat Nandaka Thera

Shame on it then, full of stinks
and oozing, Māra's partisan, [10]
in your body nine streams are
leaking out continually.
Do not conceive of these filled-up things,
they are not praised by Tathāgatas
who desire not even the heavens,
not to speak of the human world.
But those who are foolish, stupid,
ill-counselled, dullness-shrouded,
such do indeed desire it
thrown down by Māra's snare.
Those in whom desire and hate
and ignorance are discarded—
such do not desire it,
severed their ropes—unbound!

Theragāthā, Verses of the Elder Bhikkhus,
verses 279–282

50. Verses of the Arahat Sabbakāma Thera

This foul two-footed thing,
full of many kinds of filth
flowing out from here and there,
ill-smelling—dearly loved it is.
As by a trap the wary deer,

---

10. Why is the body called "Māra's partisan" (lit: on the side of Māra)? Because the body is subject to all sorts of pain, dismemberment, death, as well as unwholesome desires connected with the body—such as to overeat or for sex, which are obstacles to purity of mind, riddance of defilements, and enlightenment.

as by the hook the fish,
just as the monkey's caught with pitch,
so ordinary men are trapped.
Forms, sounds, smells and tastes
and tangibles, delighting the mind,
these are the five cords of desire
seen in a woman's form.[11]
Those who pursue them–
ordinary men with minds enflamed–
fill up the fearful cemeteries
and heap up further birth.
But one who does avoid it
as the feet a serpent's head,
mindful, such a one transcends
clinging to this world.
Seeing the danger of sensual desires,
renunciation seeing secure,
escaped from all desires [12]
to exhaustion of taints attained.

Theragāthā, Verses of the Elder Bhikkhus,
verses 453–458

51. Verses of the Arahat Raṭṭhapāla

His family tried to snare him, with the bait of his former wives and good food, into returning to the household life, at which he said:

"Behold a puppet here pranked out,
A body built up out of sores,
Sick, and much object for concern,
Where no stability abides.
Behold a figure here pranked out
With jewellery and earrings too,
A skeleton wrapped up in skin,
Made creditable by its clothes.
Its feet adorned with henna dye
And powder smeared upon its face,

11. Women reading this must substitute "a man's form."
12. This thera's name means "all desires."

It may beguile a fool, but not
A seeker of the Further Shore.
Its hair is dressed in eightfold plaits
And unguent smeared upon its eyes.
It may beguile a fool, but not
A seeker of the Further Shore.
A filthy body decked without
Like a new-painted unguent pot,
It may beguile a fool, but not
A seeker of the Further Shore.
The deer-hunter sets well the snare
But the deer springs not the trap;
We eat the bait, and we depart,
Leaving the hunters to lament."

MN 82, trans. Ven. Ñāṇamoli

52.

The vast array of "beauty products," for both male and female, should make people think. If it is so necessary to beautify the body what is it really like?

53.

This impure body
like a wave that rises suddenly,
breaks and disperses.
This impure body
like a speck of dust
in a desert land
where mirages are seen.

Wijayasiri Amaratunga

54.

The body is like a leaky barrel, oozing all the time. But a barrel can be bunged up, while the body must continue oozing its whole life.

55.

A drum has four characteristics—it is round in section, covered by hide, is beaten frequently, and emits sound. In the same way the body has four characteristics: it is round in section or fairly much so, it also is covered by hide, it is beaten by the many sorts of physical and mental dukkha, and emits sound—that is, the sounds indicating pleasure which is unreliable and impermanent, and those which accompany sufferings such as weeping and lamentation. And who is the beater? His name is *Craving*.

56.

The Buddha said:

"Birth is dukkha,[13] disease is dukkha, decay is dukkha, death is dukkha"—all this is dukkha related to this body. It is interesting that each sort of dukkha has special institutions in Western society to screen it off from the generality of people, who are "in between" these events so to speak. Birth takes place in maternity wards and nursing homes. Other parts of the same hospital take care of "disease." For "decay" we have old peoples' homes and the geriatric wards, while "death" may occur in all such places, the corpse then going on to the undertakers' chapels, and to religious rites. Things hidden away are unhealthy. Look at the dukkha! Look at it!

57.

When one considers how many things afflict this body, it is a wonder that it keeps going so well and for so long!

Many, many kinds of dukkha!

58.

There is so much dukkha connected with this body, which people never notice due to shifting around from one position to another. When tired of walking or standing, they sit down; when tired of sitting, they stand or lie down; when they have enough of lying down, they get up. Walking an unexpectedly long distance is dukkha. Standing long in queue is dukkha. Sitting in even a

13. Suffering of all kinds, physical and mental, and suffering due to the impermanence of everything.

comfortable chair for hours is dukkha. Lying in a hospital bed for days or weeks is dukkha. By changing position we evade the dukkha, or make it less obvious. But when someone starts to meditate, spending hours on walking meditation, hours on sitting meditation—then this bodily dukkha can be felt and investigated.

59. Pain and the Body

"The uninstructed ordinary person, bhikkhu, has a saying: 'There is a bottomless abyss in the great ocean.' But the uninstructed ordinary person speaks of what does not exist, of what cannot be found, that is that there is a 'bottomless abyss in the great ocean.' A designation for painful bodily feeling, bhikkhus, is this term 'bottomless abyss.' When an uninstructed ordinary person experiences painful bodily feeling, he grieves, is afflicted laments, beats his breast, cries out loud, and becomes distraught. So it is said, bhikkhus, the uninstructed ordinary person has not emerged from the bottomless abyss, has not obtained a firm foothold.

"But, bhikkhus, when an instructed Noble Disciple experiences painful bodily feeling he does not grieve, is not afflicted, does not lament, nor beat his breast, nor cry out loud, nor become distraught. So it is said, bhikkhus, the instructed Noble Disciple has emerged from the bottomless abyss and has obtained a firm foothold."

SN 36:4, trans. Ven. Nyanaponika

60. This "form" (=body)

"Why does one say 'form' (*rūpa*)? It is deformed (*ruppati*), that is why it is called 'form.' Deformed by what? By cold and heat and hunger and thirst, by contact with mosquitoes, flies, wind, sunburn, and creeping things."

SN 12:79, trans. Ven. Ñāṇamoli

61.

One could play similar word games in English: Why is it called a *body*? Because it is one's *abode,* therefore it is a *body*; or again because it *bodes no good,* therefore it is a *body* —though this is rather pessimistic perhaps. To balance up one could etymologize thus: It is called a *body* since depending on it *bodhi* is discovered.

62. The Body's Needs as the Buddha Summarized Them

Clothing to cover it,
food to sustain it,
shelter to keep it from harm,
and medicine to cure it.
Buddhist monks recollect these four "supports" every day.
A way of cutting down greed:
Few and simple clothes cover it
enough wholesome food sustains it,
a small shelter keeps it from harm,
and appropriate medicine cures it.
How many sets of clothes can you wear at once?
How many different dishes do you need to eat?
How much room does this body fill?
How may pills and powders to keep in health?

63. Greed and the Body

Look at it like this:

There's a wardrobe with lots of clothes to cover your body. Are they all needed? (There are some clothes-less poor in this world.)

There is a pantry (a refrigerator and a freezer?), stacked with food. Is all that variety and quantity needed? (There are people starving in this world.)

There's the house one lives in with its furnishings. Is it too large or too luxurious? (There are house-less people in this world.)

There's that medicine chest of pills and creams and whatnot. Can you use them all? Are they all needed? (How many people have no medicine in this world?)

64. Overeating? Gluttony?

Then read these verses:

The food and drink so greatly prized—
The crisp to chew, the soft to suck—
Go in all by a single door,
But by nine doors [14] come oozing out.

---

14. Go in by the mouth but can come out from the eyes (2), ears (2), nostrils (2), mouth, urinary duct, and anus, as various sorts of "dirt."

The food and drink so greatly prized—
The crisp to chew, the soft to suck—
Men like to eat in company,
But to excrete in secrecy.
The food and drink so greatly prized
The crisp to chew, the soft to suck—
These a man eats with high delight,
And then excretes in dumb disgust.
The food and drink so greatly prized—
The crisp to chew, the soft to suck—
A single night will be enough
To bring them to putridity.

The Path of Purification, Ch. XI para. 23
(Remember while eating!)

65. Reflections on a Loo

Earth and water elements inside
press to get out,
all that solid food, and drink
ingested, must be in time extruded.
No polished "sanitary ware"
adorns my forest loo
all natural
a wooden platform raised upon a pit.
Where I walk up and down
pacing steadily to still the mad mind,
at the end surrounded by trees—
my lovely loo.
Trees with asbestos sheeting broken up
nailed to the trunks—for privacy,
where only trees can watch
bored—but nourished—by this necessity.
To climb up to my toilet
six feet up swaying with the trunks
of trees, two logs are driven in the ground
as steps up to the throne.
A platform with a hole
through which one can look down

ten feet to the papered pit below
and watch the great black dung-
beetles at work burying the mess,
hygienic from our point of view
but what a birth to get,
perhaps for perverters and pornographers?
Anyway, I squat lordly far above
while water and earth elements within
join water and earth elements without.
when within I call them "mine";
when in the pit they're not me—
where does the change take place?
Strange mind which loves this stinking form
But loathes the stink down there.
Rejoicing in fine flavours,
Detesting stench and excrement:
"I" am made up of all this
rejoicing and detesting.

Vassa, the Rains, 2515/1972

66.

Food arranged nicely on plates is attractive to the eyes and nose. "It looks good!"—"It smells good!"—people say. When it reaches the mouth it is attractive to the tongue and touch. They say "How good it tastes!" or "Real crunchy!" (crackly, creamy, or whatever). But just spit it out—attractive to the eyes now or not? Greed can only arise if conditions are right for it. And how attractive is the same food spewed up after a few hours in the belly? It becomes even less desirable when after a day or two its remains are expelled. Three stages for contemplation!

67.

As the meditator finds out, without food the body becomes weak, with much food it is heavy and disturbed: two kinds of dukkha. The only way is to know moderation in food, neither altogether abstaining, which can easily become the extreme of self-mortification; nor overeating, which is just the other extreme of sensual pleasure

68. Remind Yourself:

"This requisite that accrued to me—
it's just mere various elements,
that is, these clothes
and the person using them—
just elements,
not a person,
not a being,
just void.
"This requisite that accrued to me—
it's just mere various elements,
that is, this shelter
and the person using it—
just elements,
not a person,
not a being,
just void.
"This requisite that accrued to me—
it's just mere various elements,
that is, this food
and the person using it—
just elements,
not a person,
not a being,
just void.
"This requisite that accrued to me—
it's just mere various elements,
that is, this medicine
and the person using it—
just elements,
not a person,
not a being,
just void."

Translated from a traditional Pāli recollection,
"*Yathā paccayaṃ* ..."

69. A Fleck of Foam

At one time the Lord was staying at Ayojjha on the bank of the river Ganges. There the Lord addressed the bhikkhus as follows: "Suppose, bhikkhus, a large fleck of foam were floating on this river Ganges and a clear-sighted man were to see it, observe it and properly examine it. Having done this it would appear to him to be empty, insubstantial, without essence—for what essence could there be in a fleck of foam?

"In the same way, bhikkhus, whatever body, past, future, or present, in oneself or external, gross or subtle, inferior or superior, far or near, that a bhikkhu sees, observes and properly examines ... it would appear to him to be empty, insubstantial, without essence—for what essence could there be in a body? ..."

> The Kinsman of the Sun made clear:
> Form compared to a fleck of foam,
> Feeling to a bubble compared,[15]
> And perception to a mirage,
> Thoughts compared to a plantain-tree [16]
> And consciousness to a magical trick. (SN 22:95)

70.

> "My" body, but mosquitoes like to suck its blood.
> "My" body, but fleas and bugs find on it a feeding place.
> "My" body, nits and lice enjoy it too.
> "My" body, which makes a cattle-tick a meal.
> "My" body, where worms live happily.
> "My" body, attacked by microscopic foes.
> "My" body, sure it gets sick without permission.
> "My" body, which is not well though I want it so.
> "My" body, getting old from day to day.
> "My" body, though I want youth, ever ages.
> "My" body, goes and dies against my cries.
> "My" body, buried or burned to elements turned.

---

15. *Bubbulūpamā* is translated in Thai as "a wave compared," a wave being a very suitable simile for feeling.

16. A banana-plant.

"My" body—how come?
"My"? Who's the owner here?

71. A Rationalist and a Buddhist

B. Whose is that body?

R. It's mine, of course!

B. Better be careful with that "of course." Anyway, how do you know it's your body?

R. Well, I see it—every day for years.

B. So it's yours because you see it?

R. Yes. Besides, I feel it's mine.

B. O.K. So that's another reason why it belongs to you. You feel it—right?

R. Sure! It feels like me.

B. Any other evidence that it's yours? What about the other senses?

R. I suppose you could say that I hear it too. My guts gurgle and my feet thump the deck. Of course it smells like me too. Taste? Oh I don't think that helps identify it very much. So that's all the senses, and they tell me that it is mine.

B. You've left out the most important sense—the mind. That tells you "this is my body" all the time ...

R. Yes, if you want to call mind a sense. Yes, it identifies what is mine and what is not.

B. Well, I don't think it is so easy to tell what is one's own and what is not.

R. Oh, that's easy. I have power over what is mine—like my own bank-account. I can do what I like with it.

B. I see that you have a bandaged finger. Show me how much power you have over it by healing it instantly!

R. Can't do that, you know. It's not natural!

B. Well now, what is natural? And does power over a thing signify ownership? For instance, that bit of dead wood over there. Is it myself?

R. Oh, come on ... of course not!

B. But it's quite natural, and one can do nothing about making it live again. When it lived, that life was conditioned by many factors, now it's dead because of those factors' change. Yet you say "my body"!

T. It is mine! It has belonged to me since I was born!

B. Right Then "your" body, which you can't heal—at least you know when it is going to die?

R. No ... (faltering) I've no idea ... but ...

B. But it's your body, and you can't cure it, can't stop it getting old, can't stop it dying, you don't even know when that body's going to die. But still it's your body. How much yours?

(Silence)

B. And who is the owner anyway?

(Silence)

72. Not Yours

"This body, bhikkhus, is not yours nor is it others'. It should be seen as produced by past dukkha, volitions, and feelings. Regarding this, the learned noble disciple thoroughly and systematically attends to dependent origination: This being, that is; from the arising of this, that arises; this not being, that is not; from the cessation of this, that ceases. That is to say: Unknowing conditions dukkha-formations ..."

SN 12:37

73.

The brain proclaimed: "I'm the boss here. Get up instantly, lazy bones!"

Groans from the bones: "I'm broken! I'm smashed! Who are you ordering around anyway? Yeah, who is *he*? Darn! We boss the lot, unless we are whole the contraption can't stand!"

Outcry from the tendons: "You bones will stand up by yourselves, will you? Won't do without us! Just fall to bits, a right skeleton."

A howl from the heart: "What are you all quarrelling about? No one gets anywhere without me, Old Brain least of all!"

A grunt from the guts: "Now, don't you get superior, heart! Where you goin-a-be without us workers sending you food?"

Clamour from the kidneys: "Fine mess you'll be in without us!"

Loud laugh from the lungs: "Ere, watcha gonna do without us twin windbags? Won't get very far, will you?"

Shriek from the skin: "Shut up the lot of you! I wrap you all up so that you don't look like a butcher's shop!"

And so the debate went on but no master could be found.

74. Holes and holiness

Unfillable hole
this whole body
look at it—hollow
holes for food in
and holes for muck out
holes for air both in and out
down to hollow lungs,
below is a hole of a belly
and yards of hollow tubes
a big hole of a bladder
holes everywhere;
some senses lurk in hollows—
eye-holes, ear-holes too,
the tongue in its hollow mouth
the air-holes holding smell;
one great big hole, hollow
the whole of this body
wholly empty
wholly void
all holes
wholly insubstantial
hollow ... hollow
the way to holiness.

75.

We take a bag to go shopping, and it gets filled up with what we want, if we pay the price.

In the same way this skin bag gets filled up, according to our desires. And we pay the price: old age and death.

76. The Discourses on the Arrow

The Buddha:

> Here life's for mortals, wretched and brief, unknown its end; incalculable and 'tis to dukkha joined.
>
> That those who are born will never die no means are there indeed!
>
> Having reached decay there's death, thus is the law for beings.
>
> As for fruit that is ripe there's always fear of falling, so for mortals who are born there's always fear of death.
>
> Just as vessels made of clay by a maker of pots all end by being broken, so death is (the end) of life.
>
> The young and those who're great in age, the fools together with the wise, all go under the sway of death, for all death is the goal.
>
> Those who are overcome by death and going to another world, the father cannot protect his son, nor relatives their kin.
>
> While relatives are watching, weeping and lamenting, see mortal beings one by one led as an ox to slaughter.
>
> As the world is thus afflicted by death and by decay, therefore the wise grieve not, knowing the nature of the world.
>
> Their path you do not know by which they come, by which they go.
>
> Neither end is seen by you, useless your lament!
>
> If then by lamenting, benefits were obtained, then the wise would do so, a fool just hurts himself.
>
> Not by crying nor by grief the mind attains to peace but still more dukkha is produced, the body as well is harmed.
>
> One becomes both pale and thin—one merely hurts oneself, not thus are the dead protected, it's useless to lament!
>
> By not forsaking grief one goes to greater dukkha, bewailing those who've died, one's in the sway of grief.
>
> See other men who go along, go according to dukkha, so beings tremble here with fear come under the sway of death.

However they conceive it, it's quite other than that, just so is separation—see the nature of the world!

Though one lived for hundred years or even more, such a man is separated from his kin and here he leaves his life.

So having heard the *arahats*, give up your lamentation.

Seeing the corpse (one should think): "He'll not be met by me again."

As a burning house with water should be extinguished,[17] so one wise and steadfast, a man who's wise in wholesomeness, quickly is rid of arisen grief as wind a tuft of down.

One who desires his own happiness: let him pull out his own arrow—lamentations and longings, the grief that's in himself.

Arrow withdrawn, unattached, the mind attains to peace, passed beyond all grief, griefless and extinguished.

Salla Sutta, Suttanipāta 574–593

77. The Discourse on Old Age[18]

The Buddha:

Short indeed is this life—
within a hundred years one dies,
and if anyone lives longer
then he dies of decay.
People grieve for what is "mine":
indeed possessions are not permanent
and this is subject to destruction—
see this and homeless dwell!
In death it is abandoned
yet man thinks "it is mine."
Knowing this, the wise man devoted to me
should not stoop down to making "his own."
As a man awake sees not
the things he met in sleep,

17. "Extinguished": for the putting out of the flames of greed, aversion and delusion (= Arahatship) the same verb is used, as in the last line of the verses.

18. Or on "Ageing" or "Decay."

so too the one beloved is not seen
having departed and done his time.
People now are seen and heard
and thus are called by name,
but alone shall the name remain
for the departed to be spoken of.
The greedy in "mine"-making do not give up
sorrow, lamentation, avarice
therefore sages leaving possessions
have wandered about, Seers of the Secure.
For a bhikkhu practicing seclusion,
keeping company with the secluded mind,
all are agreed and say of him
"He should not show himself again in becoming!"
The sage is unsupported in all circumstances,
nothing he makes dear nor what is not dear,
sorrow and avarice stain him not,
just as water stays not upon a leaf.
As a water-drop upon a lotus plant,
as water does not stain a lotus flower,
even so the sage is never stained
by what has been seen, heard, and sensed by him.
Certainly the wise man does not conceive
by what has been seen, heard and sensed,
nor through another does he wish for purity
for he is not attached nor yet is he displeased.

Jarā Sutta, Suttanipāta, verses 804–813

78. Contemplation of Death

Uncertain is life:
Certain is death.
Inevitable is death for me.
My life has death at its end.
Life is indeed unsure,
But death is sure,
Death is sure.

From the Dhammapada commentary story
of the Weavers' daughter

79.

"As soon as evening comes, or when the night vanishes and day is breaking, a bhikkhu reflects in this way: 'Truly there are many possibilities for me to die—I may be bitten by a snake, or stung by scorpion or centipede—and thereby lose my life. But this would be an obstacle for me. Or I may stumble and fall down, or food eaten may not agree with me. Or bile, phlegm, and piercing bodily "winds" may upset me—and thereby I may lose my life. Then men or ghosts may attack me—and thereby I may lose my life. But this would be an obstacle for me.' Then the bhikkhu should consider thus: 'Are there still found in me unsubdued evil unwholesome factors which, if I should die this day or night, might lead me to dukkha?' Now, if he understands that this is the case, he should use his utmost resolution, energy, effort, endeavour, steadfastness, attentiveness, and clear-mindedness to overcome these evil unwholesome factors."

AN 8:74, trans. after Ven. Nyanatiloka in *Buddhist Dictionary*, p. 98

80. The Arahat Raṭṭhapāla Thera's Verses Addressed to the Aged King Koravya

I see men wealthy in the world, who yet
Give not, from ignorance, their gathered riches;
But greedily will hoard away their wealth,
Through longing for still further sensual pleasures.
A king who has by force conquered the earth
And even lords the land the ocean bounds
Is yet unsated with the sea's near shore
And hungers for its further shore as well.
Most men as well, not just a king,
Encounter death with craving unabated;
With plans still incomplete they leave the corpse;
Desires remain unsated in the world.
His relatives lament him, rend their hair,
Crying "Ah me! Alas! Our love is dead!"
Then bear away the body wrapped in shrouds
To place it on a pyre and burn it there

Clad in a single shroud, he leaves behind
His property, and prodded with stakes he burns,
And as he died, no relative or kin
Or friends could offer refuge to him here.
The while his heirs annex his wealth, this being
Must now pass on according to his kammas;
And as he dies no thing can follow him:
Nor child nor wife nor wealth nor royal estate.
Longevity is not acquired with wealth
Nor can prosperity banish old age;
Short is this life, as all the sages say,
Eternity it knows not, only change.
The rich man and the poor man both shall feel
(Death's) touch, as do the fool and sage alike;
But while the fool lies stricken by his folly,
No sage will ever tremble at the touch.
Better is understanding, then, whereby
The goal can here be gained, than any wealth;
For men through different lives in ignorance
Do evil, while they fail to reach the goal.
As one goes to the womb and the next world,
Renewing the successive round, so another
With no more understanding, trusting him,
Goes also to the womb and the next world.
Just as a robber caught in burglary
By his own kammas marked a miscreant,
So people after death, in the next world
By their own kammas marked are they as miscreants.
For sense-desires so mind-alluring, sweet.
In many a different way disturb the mind;
Seeing the danger in these sense-desires
So I went forth to homelessness, O king.

From Middle Length Discourses No. 82,
trans. Ven. Ñāṇamoli Thera

81.

"Short indeed is this life of men, limited, fleeting, full of woe and torment; it is just like a dewdrop that vanishes as soon as the sun rises; like a water-bubble; like a line drawn on water; like a torrent dragging everything along and never standing still; like cattle for slaughter that every moment look death in the face."

AN 7:70, condensed trans. after Ven. Nyanatiloka,
Buddhist Dictionary, p.99

82.

If "I" am dying when this Bag of Bones packs up, then the pain is terrible indeed; but if it's just this bag of bones packing up ... then?

83.

A. What's going to die?

B. I am going to die!

A. Nonsense!

B. What do you mean?

A. The body is going to die. It's only you dying if you identify the body as yourself.

B. That's a good thought. Then I am not going to die. I shall live forever!

A. Can do, if that's what you want! But think of the sufferings, born and dying, again and again.

B. How do I get out of it?

A. Just as you don't identify with the body, so you try not identifying with the mind.

B. Wow! How come! Impossible! *I* don't identify with *my* mind. There's only one *me*.

A. Suppose you see no *me*, suppose there is just emptiness, and no *me* perceiving it, what then?

B. Oh!

84.

Interesting that religions (all of them) concern themselves so much with the dead *bodies*. Ceremonies of various sorts are all conducted round the lifeless lumps of decaying flesh. Yet each religion is concerned really with whatever is thought of as continuing. It shows that attachment to *the body as the person* is very strong.

And in English we talk of "the dead" as opposed to "the living." But for a Buddhist there are no dead people, only decaying bodies. Paradoxically, a person, while not rid of the concept of personality, never dies.

85.

Villagers in Buddhist countries are often better schooled in the body and its end than are educated Westerners. The former have plenty of chances to go to the local temple, or to see the nearest meditation teacher. And what do they hear? Again and again they hear the sound of *anicca*, dukkha, *anattā*[19] of all parts of the human being, mind and body. By hearing frequently it sinks in, so that even if people never penetrate these Three Marks of Existence in themselves, at least they have an attitude of accepting them to some extent. It helps with decay, disease, and death. And they see friends and kin cremated, not in a posh chapel with soft music, solemn colours and concealed oven, but on top of a pile of logs in the forest. That's the body burning— there's that smell of meat ... and this body too will go the same way.

These things are good to see. They are healthy, wholesome. There is no false solemnity, things are just the way they are. Undisguised.

86.

People in Buddhist lands who have so often heard teaching about *anicca*, impermanence, are more ready to accept the common end than a great many Westerners. Old age, disease and death are better accepted by Buddhists as just as natural a part of life as birth. One does not bewail the birth of a child— though painful enough for both mother and child—so why bewail the naturally succeeding events? Buddhists who know the *Dhamma* well, talk naturally and calmly about their old age and death as they have contemplated as *anicca* everything in this (and any other) world.

---

19. Impermanence, Unsatisfactoriness, No-self.

87.

There is nothing like living in a little hut in the tropical forest to make one realize how vulnerable this body is to all sorts of attack. How very small creatures can make life difficult if not precarious for this body. A city-dweller misses most of this and may easily get a false sense of security. (All those neat little suburban houses in regular rows ...)

Another thing which life in the wilds makes really necessary is mindfulness. Mindfulness where one puts one's feet, specially in the dark. And then one cannot get on without loving-kindness too, since all sorts of other beings are so near to oneself, near to this body which one fears for. Loving-kindness rids one of such fears and hatreds.

88.

We have so many fears—all things out there—ghosts, darkness, unknown people, loneliness, and so on. The really fearful things, this mind-and-body's precarious state, we never see.

89.

The body has a side which most of us don't want to see and know. We wish to hush up its dirt, stinks, belches, and farts, to disregard and overlook them. Yet finally when laid low and near to death, these stenches and filths can be disguised no longer.

90.

It is a salutary lesson, if one gets the chance, to go to an autopsy and watch the doctors and nurses pulling a body to pieces. One's eyes are not prepared for this sight even if one has watched a butcher chopping up meat. And one's nose can well be assaulted too by the overpowering stench of decay if the corpse is just a few days old. To see this is to experience for oneself some *Dhamma*: how the body is just conditioned and decaying bits and pieces. "As this body is, so that body was; as that body is, so this body will be."

91.

Lists like the following ten stages of the body's decay are often illustrated in traditional Buddhist art, in ancient books and on temple walls, as often seen in Thailand. These are like special prescriptions for the disease of lust:

a bloated corpse (cures attachment to shapeliness)
a discoloured corpse (cures attachment to colour and complexion)
a festering corpse (cures attachment to bodily smell and fine perfumes)
a gnawn-by-animals corpse (cures attachment to greed for fleshy protuberances)
a scattered corpse (cures attachment to gracefulness of limbs)
a bleeding corpse (cures attachment to decoration of the body with ornaments)
a worm-infested corpse (cures attachment to body as one's own)
a skeleton held together by sinews (cures attachment to fine bone structure)
scattered bones (cures attachment to body as "one thing")
rotting and powdered bones (cures attachment to the body as permanent)

92. This Body ...

This body lying in decay
To worms and flies unconscious prey,
Bereft of mind and animation
Portrays man's final situation.
Engendered in a human womb,
A fabric wrought upon the loom
Of sensual lust and will-to-be,
It grew in stature like a tree,
But mind-informed, with fresh desires
Raging within like hungry fires,
Fed by the senses' ample fuel
In an eternal self-renewal.
Self-renewed and self-consumed,
A turbulence forever doomed
To futile striving, hopes and fears,
Alternating through the years:
Childhood, youth, maturity,

Seeking in vain security,
Seeking in vain to quench the fire
By satisfaction of desire.
And day by day with every breath,
Every heart-beat a little death,
Stole from the body's falling source
A fraction of its vital force.
The body undermined by stealth,
Then knew the pangs of failing health.

Francis Story, from *The Buddhist Outlook*

93. Verses of the Arahat Kulla Thera on Seeing a Corpse

Having gone to the charnel-ground
I saw cast there a woman's corpse, discarded in the cemetery,
being gnawn and full of worms.
A rotten congeries, Kulla, see—
diseased it is, impure,
oozing and trickling here and there
wherein fools find delight.
This body I inspected—
inane within and without—
taking the *Dhamma*'s looking-glass
to Knowing and Seeing attained.
As this body is, so that body was;
as that body is, so will this body be.
As foul it is above so foul it is below,
and as it is above so it is below.
As it is by day, so it is by night;
as night, so day the same.
There's no such pleasure even from
a quintet's music as there is
from rightly *Dhamma* seeing
with singleness mind.

Verses of the Elders Bhikkhus, 393–398.

The "Knowing and Seeing"—insight (*vipassanā*)—that this thera saw in himself is first:

Seeing no difference between the living and the dead bodies—only time makes a difference.

Then seeing the dead body as totally foul—not attracted to this (=greed) or repelled by that (=hatred), and applying this to his own body.

Then seeing that all the time, day or night, the body has the same qualities—not that it is desirable at some times but not at others.

The enjoyments that most get from sense-pleasures—here the example of a quintet is given—this thera has found far more abundantly in seeing *Dhamma* rightly.

94.

Spiritual objector:

"All this pondering over corpses and looking into the body's parts is just morbid. One should look at the body as a pure temple of the spirit."

Practical Upāsaka: [20]

"It goes against the grain to gaze at the bits and pieces in this body and see that they have nothing attractive about them. But this way lies Liberation. To glorify the body is to be bound by craving for it."

95.

Doctor:

I cannot understand you when you say that the body is unbeautiful; to me it is such a wonderful machine!

Bhikkhu:

The trouble with that view of the "wonderfulness of the body" is that it is near delight (*nandi*) and delighting in the body is another name for craving, the root of dukkha. Seeing the body's unattractiveness is opposed to craving.

96.

"You're wrong, man, sex is just natural, like breathing—just something you've got to do. Just like eating. It's a beautiful natural function!"

"Not true! Your comparisons are not apt."

"How come? You mean it's not natural?"

---

20. A Buddhist layman keeping five or eight precepts.

"Yes, sex is natural for people with desire, that means sex-desire or lust, in their hearts. But lust is a hindrance to the development of mental-emotional purity. But your comparisons to breathing and eating don't stand examination. Breathing is an automatic body function. No dukkha, good or bad, is made because no intention is needed to decide to breathe!

"Eating is different because, though necessary for the body's life, it is connected with intention, so dukkha is made. When greed for food is present, bad dukkha is made which will fruit as suffering. But when food is eaten mindfully and just to keep the body going, then good dukkha is made—of mindful reflection.

"Sex is different from both these. No sex takes place without desire or lust: this is among the unwholesome mental factors—it can never be karmically wholesome—so unwholesome dukkha is made which has the nature to limit the mind to sensual things."

"That's painting sex too black!"

"No, that's being realistic. Of course, states of mind will vary while one has sex—more or less lust and more or less of loving-kindness. More lust (as when sex is commercial) means more bad dukkha. More loving-kindness, as between two people deeply attached to each other, less bad dukkha and more good dukkha. In the latter case it is called dukkha which is dark and bright, with a dark and bright result."

97. A Manichean and a Buddhist

M. It's all the work of Satan—this foul body. We agree with you Buddhists about that.

B. Well, the body is certainly not pleasant when examined, but we do not say that it has been created, by Satan.

M. But all matter is evil, foul, dragging the soul into darkness, as our Mani says.

B. That's not what the Buddha says, though. Matter is just earth, water, fire, and air elements which are quite neutral, neither good nor evil. They form bodies due to dukkha made by beings; good or evil kammas both lead to the formation of bodies.

M. You must admit, though, that your body is a hindrance to the attainment of spiritual states. You have to feed it and rest it, dose it with medicine when it gets sick. Because of its wretchedness the soul is weighed down.

B. No, I do not admit that. The body is the basis and vehicle for practice so one should take care of it without pampering it. Though it has to eat, sleep, excrete, and gets sick too, at these times we should be mindful, which is possible at all times when not asleep. Even the difficulties of the body can be used in *Dhamma*-practice. And what is this about a soul being weighed down?

M. Well, that is the pure aspirations, the pure thoughts, the still states of contemplation—that is the beginning of discovering the soul.

B. Oh, then the impure aspirations, thoughts and confused states of mind must be not soul! You should investigate all mental states, pure and impure, calm and distracted, and find out whether any of them are substantial or permanent. What would you find, do you think?

M. All right, they're changing. But behind them all is the pure tranquil soul, eternally unchanging.

B. But have you experienced this or are you just telling me some dogma or belief?

M. Yes, I think I have experienced it. Then one is free from the trammels of this body.

B. Really you need to examine all mental states, as I mentioned before, and the body too, in the same light. They're all Anicca, Dukkha, Anattā ...

M. What ...?

B. Sorry! I get so used to using those words that they have slipped off my tongue, unmindfully I am afraid! They mean impermanent, unsatisfactory, and no self. When you look at them like this you neither love the soul nor hate the body. That is, put in a Buddhist way, you don't cling to pure tranquillity and identify it as your soul or self, neither do you reject this body. Don't lay the blame on this poor old body! It's not to blame.

M. But Mani says that it is.

B. Well then, I shall ask you a question. What makes decisions and choices, is it the body or the mind?

M. The mind decides, of course.

B. Then how can the body be blamed? It is not evil, nor is matter darkness. Poor old body just gets dragged along by the decisions the mind makes.

M. But you Buddhists practice contemplation of the body as foul. I have read about it.

B. Yes, but that does not mean it is evil. That kind of meditation is just to break up the attachment to the beauty of bodies. It is the attachment in one's own mind, not any Satan or evil creator, that is responsible for keeping the mind tied down to sensual pleasures. Look inside for the evil creator—his name is attachment, greed, desire, lust—and he is put out of business by contemplating the unattractive. The good creator is in there too, the mind that creates pure mental states, the experience of *jhāna* and so on. But all this creating keeps one in the round of rebirth, you know!

98.

A Hey, man! Why you cut your hair and beard? Hair's natural to have but you monks cut it off. We should keep it; it's natural, it's beautiful.

Bhikkhu: It's cut off for two reasons. First, it decorates this body. You people like decoration. That's what lay life is all about. But bhikkhus like the body plain, without distractions, so that they can see what it's really like.

A. Well, what's it really like?

B. If you like it as it is, "naturally," you should try not washing, not brushing the teeth or cleaning the nails, not combing the hair—and so on. Body and its parts are only beautiful if washing is also "natural."

A. So, you said that hair decorates, what's your other reason?

B. It's a disguise, that beard and moustache—it's something to hide behind, a mask. When you have no hair on the head and face you have no mask behind which to retire. Is it natural or beautiful to hide things? Isn't it better to open up? Who solves problems by hiding them away? Shaving hair and beard is also an outer token of the shaving off of conceit and pride which has to be done steadily and carefully over years of practice.

99. Futility

Mad for pleasure
for fleeting pleasant feelings
clinging to impermanence.
two pulsing bags

clinging together
how pitiful!
clinging to what can't be clung
clinging to changefulness
a fistful of water.
few moments of happiness
found in sex
for which the world is mad.
he burns, on fire inside
for another,
how come he feels no pain?
pain to be assuaged
so he supposes
by making two fires one.
one fire is not enough,
when with another joined
how much more scorching?
scorched and aflame
beings run
from one fire to another.
another fire, another,
as though the fire
by fire could be extinguished.
extinguished, fire gone out
cool peace
no one wants it.
stoke up the furnaces
pile high the blaze
the world's way.
ways to hells and animals
furious fires of desire
burning endlessly.
why do we never tire
of being burnt?
"Hot but sweet" they say.
pleasure like a leper's
picking his scabs
a small relief from pain.
pain, painfulness

how pain-filled indeed
entire Saṃsāra—
filled with pleasure-loving beings
not wanting pain
whose pleasures drive to Dukkha.

100. The Silent Shrine

Where silence reigns the Buddha sits,
He dwells alone, the only face
Has he that one should ever look upon
Deep within the shrine that always is,
The centre of this house—
Where is it found?
Flesh the walls and bones the beams
With windows five to look upon the world,
While wandering, a witless idiot
Roams through the empty rooms;
How slow is he to come upon that shrine,
How faltering his steps unsure!
Distractedly, confused
He fumbles for the door—
Hinges rusty, locked for long, unused,
Swollen wood and jammed the door decayed.
When will he look, this witless one,
When will he see the ancient face of peace?
When will he worship at the shrine?
When will he know the Way and Fruit?
When will he find the silence?
Where the Buddha sits?

Ānanda

The Guardian of the Dhamma

by

Hellmuth Hecker

WHEEL PUBLICATION NO. 273/274

82,000 teachings from the Buddha
I have received;
2,000 more from his disciples;
Now, 84,000 are familiar to me.[1]

Who nothing has heard[2] and nothing understood,
He ages only oxen-like:
His stomach only grows and grows,
But his insight deepens not.

Who has much heard and learned,
But does despise him who is poor in learning,
Is like one blind who holds a lamp.
So must I think of such a one.

Thou follow him who has heard much,
Then what is heard shall not decline.
This is the tap-root of the holy life;
Hence a Dhamma-guardian[3] you should be!

Knowing what comes first and last,
Knowing well the meaning, too,
Skilful in grammar and in other items,[4]
The well-grasped meaning he examines.

Keen in his patient application,
He strives to weigh the meaning well.
At the right time he makes his effort,
And inwardly collects his mind.

Venerable Ānanda, Th 1024–29

---

1. Buddhist tradition has it that there are 84,000 sections of the Teaching (or units of text; *dhammakkhandha*). See "The Expositor" (Commentary to Dhammasaṅgaṇī), vol. I, pp. 22, 34 (PTS).
2. In ancient India, the way of learning and studying was not through books, but by the oral instruction of a teacher. The words "he has heard much (or not)" are, in this context, equivalent to "he is very learned (or not)."
3. Dhamma: literally, the truth, the law. Used for the Buddha's teaching.
4. *Skilful in grammar and in other items.* According to the commentary, this refers to the four "analytical knowledges" (*paṭisambhidā*), of which two are mentioned in these verses, namely "grammar" (or language) and "meaning"; while the words "other items" refer to the remaining two, the analytical knowledges of the law (or conditionality) and of ready wit (perspicuity).

1. Ānanda's Personal Path

The one disciple of the Buddha most often mentioned in his discourses is Ānanda. Amongst all those great monks around the Buddha, he occupies a unique position in many respects, as will be mentioned in these pages. His unique position had already begun before his birth. He came to earth, just as the Buddha did, from the Tusita heaven, and was born on the same day as the Buddha and in the same caste, namely the warrior caste of the royal family of the Sakyas. Their fathers were brothers, so Ānanda was the Buddha's cousin.

He had three brothers, Anuruddha, Mahānāma, and Paṇḍu, and one sister, Rohiṇī. Anuruddha entered the Saṅgha[5] together with Ānanda and became an *arahant*, a fully enlightened one. Mahānāma, the prince of the Sakyas, became a once-returner[6] as a householder. The only thing known about Paṇḍu is the fact that he survived the near-extinction of the Sakya clan during the Buddha's 80th year.

Ānanda's only sister, Rohiṇī, had a skin disease as a result of former jealousy, and lived in seclusion at home until the Buddha talked to her about the kammic cause of her affliction and paved the way to stream-entry for her.[7] Rohiṇī recovered and was later reborn in the "heaven of the gods of the thirty-three" as the wife of Sakka, the king of the gods.

When he was 37 years old, Ānanda joined his brother Anuruddha and his cousin Devadatta and also many other Sakyan nobles to become a "homeless one", a monk (Cv VII.1).

The venerable Belaṭṭhasīsa, an *arahant*—a fully liberated saint, became his teacher in the Saṅgha. Only one verse by the venerable Belaṭṭhasīsa has survived to this day:

Just as the noble buffalo
With hairy neck can pull the plough

5. Saṅgha: the company of monks following the Buddha and his teaching

6. Once-returner: the second stage of enlightenment, which still requires one rebirth in the world of fivefold sense experience.

7. Stream-entry: the first stage of enlightenment, where the first glimpse of Nibbāna is gained, and the first three fetters abandoned.

With little effort, step by step,
So do I let the time flow by
With little effort, day by day,
When joy untainted has been won.

Th 16

Under the guidance of this holy one, Ānanda was introduced into the monk's discipline. He was a willing and diligent pupil and was able to attain the fruit of stream-entry already during his first rains retreat (Cv VII.1).[8]

Later Ānanda told his fellow monks, that the venerable Puṇṇa Mantāṇiputta had also been of great help to him during his learning period. He had taught the Dhamma to the new monks and had explained to them that the "I am" conceit does not arise without a cause—namely, it is brought about through form, feeling, perceptions, mental formations, and consciousness. For a better understanding of this, the venerable Puṇṇa had given a fitting analogy:

> If somebody should want to see his reflection or image, he could do so only through a cause, namely a mirror or a clear body of water. In the same way do the five aggregates[9] reflect the image of "I am." As long as one depends on them and is supported by them, for that long will an "I" be reflected. Only when one does not rely on them any longer will the image of "I" disappear. —SN 22:83

Ānanda thought about this analogy again and again and ever more deeply, until he penetrated the suffering, impermanence and no-self aspects of the five aggregates, and no longer relied upon them as his support. He then began to reap the benefits of monkhood, beginning with the fruit of stream-entry.

8. The Buddha decreed that the monks should stay in one place under shelter during the monsoon rains in India (approximately July–September) and intensify their practice. This is followed to this day.

9. The five aggregates are the aspects of mind and body, which make up what is called a person: form (body), feeling, perceptions, mental formations (volitions, etc.), and consciousness.

During the first years of his life as a monk, Ānanda was fully occupied with the purification of his own mind; he blended easily into the Saṅgha and slowly developed more and more resilience and mental strength. Ānanda was always well content with his life as a monk. He understood the blessings of renunciation and walking upon the Path, which is a joy to tread if one can cross the stream[10] in company with like-minded friends.

When the Buddha and Ānanda were both 55 years of age, the Buddha called a meeting of the monks and declared: "In my 20 years as a monk, as Father of the Saṅgha, I have had many different attendants, but none of them has really filled the post perfectly, as again and again some wilfulness has become apparent. Now I am 55 years old and it is necessary for me to have a trustworthy and reliable attendant." At once all the noble disciples except Ānanda offered their services. But the Buddha did not accept them. Then the great monks looked at Ānanda, who had held back modestly, and asked him to come forward voluntarily. Due to his impeccable behaviour as a monk, he seemed predestined for the post. When he was asked why he was the only one who had not offered his services, he replied that the Buddha knew best who was suitable as his attendant. He had so much confidence in the Blessed One that it did not occur to him to express his own wishes, although he would have liked to become the attendant of the Buddha.

Then the Buddha declared that Ānanda would be pleasing to him and that he wanted him as his attendant. Ānanda was in no way proud that the Master preferred him over his greatest disciples, but instead asked, as a favour, for eight conditions. These were, first of all, that the Master should never pass a gift of robes on to him; second, he should never give him any almsfood which he himself had received; third, having received a dwelling place he should never give it to him; fourth, never to include him in any personal invitation (such as an occasion for teaching Dhamma when a meal would be offered).

Besides these four negative conditions, he also had four positive wishes, namely: if he was invited to a meal, he asked for

10. "Crossing the stream to the other shore" is often used as an analogy for those monks and lay people who have left ordinary reactions and emotions behind, and have purified themselves to the extent of becoming "noble ones."

the right to transfer this invitation to the Buddha; if people came from outlying areas, he asked for the privilege to lead them to the Buddha; if he had any doubts or inquiries about the Dhamma, he asked for the right to present these to the Buddha at any time; and if the Buddha gave a discourse during his absence, he asked for the privilege to have the Buddha repeat it to him privately.

He explained his reasons for these requests in this way: if he did not pose the first four conditions, then people could say that he had accepted the post of attendant only because of material gain; and if he did not express the other four conditions, then it could rightly be said that he fulfilled the duties of his post without being mindful of his own advancement on the Noble Path.

The Buddha granted him these very reasonable requests which were quite in accordance with the teaching. From then on and for twenty-five years, Ānanda was the constant companion, attendant and helper of the Blessed One. In those twenty-five years of his fame, he continued with the same incessant striving for purification as in the first eighteen years of his monkhood as an unknown disciple. He said of himself:

> Through a full 25 years
> As long as I have been in higher training[11]
> I have never had a thought of lust:
> See, how powerfully the Dhamma works.
>
> Th 1039

The subsequent verse expresses the same about thoughts of hate. These verses imply that though he was still a "learner" and "one in the higher training," no thoughts of lust or hate arose in him because his close connection with the Buddha and his devotion to him gave no room to these.

Only such a man could fill the post of a constant companion for the Buddha. Added to that were Ānanda's special positive qualities. How Ānanda attained arahantship and survived the Buddha will be related in due course.

---

11. *Sekha:* lit. "a learner" or "one who trains himself." This denotes a person who has attained one of the three lower stages of sanctity, i.e. a stream-winner, a once-returner and non-returner.

2. Ānanda's Renown

Ānanda is praised on many occasions in the Pali Canon. The greatest recognition for a monk would surely have been when the Buddha asked him to substitute for him as a teacher and then later confirmed that he, himself, would not have presented the teachings in any other way. This praise was given by the Exalted One to both Sāriputta[12] (another famous disciple) and Ānanda.

A similarly high esteem was evident when the monks to whom the Buddha had given a short discourse would ask an experienced monk to explain the teaching more fully. The venerable Mahā Kaccāna was a master in this, and so were Sāriputta and Ānanda (AN 10:115).

Besides the equal status Ānanda had in these respects with Sāriputta, the disciple who was most similar to the Master, there were occasions when the Buddha specially praised Ānanda. He said, for instance, to the monks that King Pasenadi, to whom Ānanda had given a discourse, was very blessed because he had been given the boon of the sight and company of Ānanda (MN 88). Further, just as the multitude of aristocrats, brahmans, ordinary folk and ascetics found joy in seeing a world ruler, equally joyful were the monks, nuns, and male and female disciples about Ānanda. "If a party of these goes to Ānanda to see him, his presence alone gives them joy. When he speaks Dhamma to them, there will be joy for them because of his words. And they are still not satisfied when Ānanda reverts to silence" (DN 16).

In answer to the question of a lay disciple how he could honour the Dhamma, after having honoured the Buddha and Saṅgha, the Buddha's reply was the third praise (of Ānanda): "If you, householder, wish to honour the Dhamma, go and honour Ānanda, the Guardian of the Dhamma"; whereupon the lay disciple invited Ānanda to a meal and gave him a gift of valuable cloth. But Ānanda turned it over to Sāriputta, because he had the greatest mastery of the Teaching; Sāriputta, however, gave it to the Buddha, because he alone was the cause of all bliss (J 296). Another time the Master praised him thus: after Ānanda had answered a question of the Buddha and had left, the Buddha said to the other

---

12. See *The Life of Sāriputta*, The Wheel Nos. 90–92.

monks: "One on the path of higher training is Ānanda, and it is not easy to find one who equals him fully in experience" (AN 3:78).

A layman who had been following another teaching was converted to the Dhamma after a talk with Ānanda. At the end he exulted how amazing it had been that Ānanda had neither elevated his own teaching into the heavens nor dragged the other into the dirt. "Totally straightforward was the exposition of the Dhamma, the inner meaning was explained and he, himself, was not carried away" (AN 3:72).[13] A second time he was praised by King Pasenadi after having given a good explanation to the crown prince of Kosala. "Truly, he looks like Ānanda," because the name means esteemed, lovable, agreeable. And King Pasenadi said that Ānanda's words had been well-founded (MN 90).

In view of this abundance of praise, recognition and privileges, mutterings of envy and resentment could have been expected. But this was not the case at all. He was a man who had no enemies. This rare advantage had not come to him without cause but had been enjoyed by him not only in this life but also in many previous existences.

Ānanda was so much taken up by subordinating his entire life to the Dhamma that fame could not touch him and make him proud. He knew that all that was good in him was due to the influence of the Teaching. When seen in this way, there can be no pride. One who cannot be proud has no enemies, and such a one does not meet with envy. If someone turns inward completely and keeps away from any social contact, as Ānanda's brother Anuruddha did, then it is easy to be without enemies. But if someone like Ānanda, who had daily contact with a large number of people with regard to diverse matters, lives without enemies, without rivals, without conflict and tensions, it borders on a miracle. This quality is truly a measure of Ānanda's uniqueness.

Although Ānanda did experience justified criticism and was occasionally admonished, that was something entirely different. A friendly reminder, a warning or even a substantial reproach to change one's behaviour are aids towards more intense purification. Such criticism, if taken to heart, leads to more inner clarity and higher esteem by others.

13. See *The Roots of Good and Evil*, The Wheel Nos. 251–253, p. 61.

The instances in which Ānanda was admonished were mostly related to points of social behaviour and to points of the Vinaya (the monk's discipline), hardly ever to points of self-purification and were never related to his understanding of the Dhamma. The instances were as follows.

Once, when the Buddha was suffering from wind in the stomach, Ānanda cooked a rice gruel for him, which had helped the Enlightened One when he had previous complaints of this sort. The Buddha admonished him thus: "It is not the proper way for ascetics, it is not proper monk's behaviour, to prepare meals in the house." After the incident, it was decreed an offense for a monk to cook for himself (Mv VI.17). Ānanda adhered to this rule from then on, with full insight into its necessity as a part of true homelessness.

Once Ānanda went on alms-round without his double robe. Fellow monks drew his attention to the rule established by the Buddha, that a monk should always wear his three robes when going to the village. Ānanda agreed wholeheartedly and explained that he had simply forgotten it. Since this and the former case concerned a simple disciplinary rule, the matter was thereby settled (Mv VIII.23). That someone like Ānanda, who had a most extraordinary memory, could also forget something was due to the fact that even a stream-winner is not yet perfect. The Buddha, however, required of the monks that they pay diligent attention to the small, everyday things of a monk's life, and that they base their higher spiritual exertions on the foundation of the discipline. This served to eliminate purely intellectual understanding and conceit.

A different kind of criticism was levelled at Ānanda in two instances by the venerable Mahā Kassapa. Thirty disciples of Ānanda had left the Saṅgha. Kassapa reproached Ānanda that he had not guarded the young men sufficiently. He had gone on walking tours with them without their having the senses well restrained, without having learned to be moderate in eating, and not having trained themselves in wakefulness. Therefore he was a "destroyer of corn,"[14] "a spoiler of the families."[15] His followers

14. By walking about without proper care, he destroyed the "young corn" of the Saṅgha.

15. By allowing unrestrained young monks to come into contact with supporting families, he made the latter disaffected.

crumbled away. "This youngster is still uncontrolled." So did the venerable Mahā Kassapa reprove him (SN 16:11).

To this rather strong reproach, Ānanda only replied that the grey hair had grown on his head in the service of the Saṅgha and yet Kassapa still called him a "youngster." It may be that in this instance Ānanda had overrated his own strength and underrated the worldliness of his pupils. Ānanda did not argue about the objective justification of the censure for his failure. After all he was not yet an *arahant* and was still subject to some defilements. He only objected to the generalization implied by the criticism. One may, however, assume that a saint, an *arahant*, like Kassapa, would have known which form of criticism would be most helpful to Ānanda.

The second incident with Kassapa had a different background. Ānanda had asked Kassapa to accompany him to a nunnery and to teach there. After initial hesitation, Kassapa had agreed. After the discourse was over, a headstrong nun accused Kassapa that only he had talked and he had not let the wise Ānanda utter a single word. It was, she said, as if the needle salesman had tried to sell his wares in the presence of the needle manufacturer. Ānanda begged Kassapa to forgive her. But Kassapa replied that Ānanda should show restraint, lest an inquiry into his behaviour should be initiated (SN 16:10). This was meant by Kassapa to be a reproach that Ānanda had been overzealous in his teaching, and had overlooked the danger of personal attachment. This criticism also will have benefited Ānanda in the future. In any case, Kassapa blamed Ānanda in both instances because of his love for him; there was always an excellent relationship between these two monks.

Another monk, Udāyi, once criticized Ānanda in the following incident. Ānanda had asked the Blessed One how far his voice would reach in the universe. The Lord had answered that the Enlightened Ones were immeasurable and could reach farther than a thousandfold world system (with a thousand suns, a thousand heavens, and a thousand *brahma*[16] worlds), even farther than a three-thousandfold world system. They could penetrate all those worlds with their shining splendour and reach all beings living there with their voice.

16. Brahma: Pali for those gods who enjoy states equivalent to the four deep meditations, or *jhāna* (see later footnote).

Ānanda was delighted with this description, so all-encompassing and transcending all horizons, and he exclaimed: "How fortunate I am, that I have such an almighty, powerful master!" Udāyi objected: "What good does it do to you brother Ānanda, that your master is almighty and powerful?" With these few words, Udāyi strongly reproached Ānanda for looking at the person of the Buddha only, and thereby forgetting his real benefit, namely his own enlightenment. But the Buddha immediately took sides with Ānanda with the following words: "Not so, Udāyi, not so, Udāyi! Should Ānanda die without being fully liberated, he would be king of the gods seven times because of the purity of his heart, or be king of the Indian subcontinent seven times. But Udāyi, Ānanda will experience final liberation in this very life" (AN 3:80).

That the Buddha made this prophecy in the presence of Ānanda showed his confidence in him. He knew that his wide knowledge of the Buddha-word would not make Ānanda negligent in his practice. This utterance also indicated that the Buddha found it useful to shield Ānanda from reproach—self-inflicted and by others—by consoling him that his efforts and strivings would result in the highest attainment still in this lifetime. The *Tathāgata*[17] could make such a declaration only in the case of one who inclined towards being extremely conscientious rather than too negligent.

The only time that the Buddha admonished Ānanda on his own accord was also the most important incident. Previously, the Buddha had instructed Ānanda to oversee the distribution of cloth for robes to the monks. Ānanda had accomplished this task very satisfactorily. The Buddha praised him for his circumspection and told the other monks that Ānanda was very skilled in sewing; he was able to make several different kinds of seams. For a good monk it was necessary that he hemmed his robes, so that they did not fray at the edges, and one could not accuse him of carelessly handling and wasting the offerings of the laity (Mv VIII.12). Later, when the Buddha was residing near his home town he

17. *Tathāgata* (lit. "one who has thus gone" or "thus come") is an epithet of the Buddha, used by him when speaking of himself; generally translated as "the perfect one."

saw numerous seats prepared in a monastery and asked Ānanda whether many monks lived there.[18] Ānanda confirmed this and added, "It is now time to sew our robes, venerable sir." Ānanda was referring to the Buddha's instructions that a monk should care for his robes properly.

However, Ānanda seemed to have arranged a sort of communal sewing circle, maybe to teach his fellow monks that commended art of making seams. Ānanda had not considered that from this a home-like conversational hour would result. Therefore the Buddha gave this very emphatic injunction concerning the danger of mundane gregariousness for the monk:

"A monk does not deserve praise who enjoys socializing, who finds contentment in it, enjoys togetherness, is pleased with it. It is impossible that such a monk should attain at will the bliss of renunciation, the bliss of solitude, the bliss of tranquillity, the bliss of awakening, in their totality.

"Whosoever finds his whole happiness in togetherness has no access to the bliss which exists independent of the desire for togetherness. Even if one who is still attached to others attains meditative absorption, it will not be fully controlled nor will it be complete. Such absorption can in this case only be a result of forceful suppression. Still greater will be the difficulty of attaining final liberation for a person who makes himself dependent on companionship."

The Buddha ends his injunction with the statement that he cannot find any form, the attachment to which would not produce *dukkha*,[19] because of the inherent impermanence in it, even if it were the highest divine form of a *brahma*. This is the universal aspect of the Dhamma.

Subsequently the Buddha expounded the Path of Practice, which he explained solely with reference to Ānanda, not mentioning the first seven steps of the Noble Eightfold Path, but starting with the eighth step. This was because Ānanda had the faculty for deep meditation, and as one in the higher training was as deeply imbued with the Dhamma as anyone outside sainthood

18. See MN 122 in The Wheel No. 87.

19. *Dukkha*: Pali for every kind of unsatisfactoriness, including gross and subtle suffering.

could be. He only needed a few hints to put the right perspective on the community work mentioned above.

Therefore the Buddha expounded here the highest goal—total voidness of concepts, objects and names—and showed the last steps. Furthermore he appealed to Ānanda's love for him as the Master, and emphasized that this love could only be proven if Ānanda followed him into the highest attainment.

Thus one could say that he made use of both approaches, factual and personal, to help Ānanda cut off all remaining worldliness once and for all, and he concluded with this analogy: "Therefore, Ānanda, bear amity towards me, not hostility; long shall that be for your benefit and happiness. I shall not treat you, Ānanda, as the potter treats his unfired pots. Repeatedly admonishing, I shall speak to you, Ānanda, repeatedly testing. He who is sound will stand the test."

This analogy to a potter will be easier to understand if one takes a look at the 405th Jātaka[20] story. It tells of a past life of Ānanda. He had abdicated from a king's throne and had become an ascetic; at that time the Buddha was still the Bodhisatta and was also an ascetic. One day it transpired that the ascetic who later became Ānanda had a small store of salt to flavour his food which went against the ascetic rule of poverty. The Bodhisatta reprimanded him: he had let go of all the riches of his kingdom, but now he had started to store provisions again. The ascetic became ill-humoured because of the reprimand. He replied that one must not hurt the other person when reprimanding him; one must not be rough with one's reproach, as if cutting with a blunt knife. The Bodhisatta replied that, amongst friends, it was not necessary to speak like a potter handling his unfired (i.e. very delicate) pots. A friend could also utter words of blame, because only through repeated exhortation and constant, constructive criticism could one give a person that solidity which was like fired clay. Then the ascetic asked the Bodhisatta's pardon and requested that the Bodhisatta should, out of compassion, always guide him further.

The analogy of the clay pots—easily understandable in those days because it was a common trade—referred to sensitivity and touchiness. For a potter would take the raw, not-quite-dry clay

20. Jātaka tales: 547 stories of the Buddha's past lives.

pot gently and with both hands lest it should break. Then, after firing, he would repeatedly test it for flaws such as cracks or splits, and use it only if it were well-baked. He would tap it again and again, and only a sound pot would stand the test. In the same way, only a sound person, one with excellent qualities, would reach the path and fruit of sainthood.[21]

Just as in that past life the reproach of the Bodhisatta was fruitful and brought the ascetic who was later to become Ānanda to *brahma* realms (J 406), so it was also fruitful this time, because Ānanda accepted the criticism happily, was content with it (MN 122), took it to heart and followed it until he attained the total destruction of suffering in this life.

3. Ānanda as the Buddha's Attendant

One of the virtues of Ānanda, which established his fame, was his conduct as the Buddha's attendant. The Buddha said of him, that he was the best of all attendants, was the foremost of all those monks who had ever filled this post (AN 1:19).

The term "attendant" is actually not comprehensive enough. There is hardly an English word which can do full justice to his position. If we were to choose designations such as "secretary" or "adjunct," then we would not express the most intimate aspects of his attendance, extending to many little items of personal assistance given to the Master. If we called him a "servant," then we would omit the organizational and directing aspects which manifested on many occasions. And if we looked for examples in the world's literature of a confidante of a great man, who accompanied him constantly, we still would not find his likeness.

This loving attention for 25 years consisted of the following services: Ānanda brought water for washing to the Buddha and tooth-wood,[22] he arranged his seat, washed his feet, massaged his back, fanned him for coolness, swept his cell, and mended his robes. He slept nearby at night to be always on hand. He accompanied

21. Reaching path and fruit: this expression means that a person not only knows the Noble Eightfold Path, but becomes the Noble Eightfold Path, and gains the fruits of this attainment, which is holiness.

22. Combines the function of toothbrush and toothpick.

him on his rounds through the monastery (Mv VIII.16) and after meetings he checked to see whether any monk had left anything behind. He carried the Buddha's messages (Cv V.20) and called the monks together, even sometimes at midnight (J 148). When the Buddha was sick, he obtained medicine for him. Once when monks neglected a very sick fellow monk, the Buddha and Ānanda washed him and together carried him to a resting-place (Mv VIII.26). In this way Ānanda performed the many daily tasks and cared for the physical well-being of his enlightened cousin like a good mother or a caring wife.

But above all, he also had the duties of a good secretary, namely the smooth communication between the thousands of monks and the Master. Together with Sāriputta and Moggallāna, he tried to sort out and attend to the manifold problems of human relationships turning up in a community.

In a case of dispute of the monks of Kosambi (AN 4:249), and in the case of a schism in the Saṅgha caused by Devadatta (Ud 5.8 and Cv VII), Ānanda played an important role in clarifying and keeping order. Often he was the go-between for the monks, getting an audience with the Master for them. He brought the Buddha's words to members of other sects. He refused no one and felt himself to be a bridge rather than a barrier.

On several occasions the monks made such a great deal of noise that the Buddha asked Ānanda the reason. Ānanda was always able to explain it fully (MN 67; Pāc 65; Ud 3.3). The Buddha then took care of it accordingly. The last of these three occasions is significant. On behalf of the Buddha, Ānanda called the large group of noisy monks together and reproached them for their behaviour and sent them away. Thereupon the group went into solitude and worked so diligently on the purification of their hearts, that all of them attained the three knowledges[23] during one rains retreat. The Master called them together once more. When they arrived at the Awakened One, he dwelt in imperturbable meditation.[24] The holy monks realized the depth of their master's

23. Three knowledges: knowledge of past lives; knowledge of the arising and passing away of beings according to their *kamma*; exhaustion of the taints. The taints are (a) sensual desire, (b) craving for being, (c) ignorance.

24. *Āneñja-samādhi*: This is the concentration connected with the highest fruit

meditation, sat down and entered in the same absorption. After they had thus passed the first four hours of the night—truly the kind of "greeting" fit for holy ones—Ānanda got up and requested the Buddha to greet the monks who had arrived. Because all of them were in imperturbable meditation, no one could hear him. After a further four hours, Ānanda repeated his request. Again total silence answered him. And a third time, at dawn, Ānanda got up, prostrated before the Buddha, put his hands together and requested a greeting for the monks. Thereupon the Buddha came out of his meditation and answered Ānanda: "If you were able to attain supramundane experiences, then you would have known that all of us had entered into imperturbable absorption, where words cannot penetrate" (Ud 3.3).

This account serves to show Ānanda's unerring patience, as well as his limitations. Such an occurrence may have contributed to Ānanda's determination to practise meditation again and again, despite his many duties. The traditional texts speak of two occasions when he asked the Buddha for a meditation subject, which he could practise in solitude. The Master told him on one occasion, to concentrate on the five aggregates (SN 22:158), and the other time to contemplate the six sense-spheres (SN 35:86).

Among the many things which Ānanda requested from the Buddha for others, the following may be mentioned. When the monk Girimānanda and the monk Phagguṇa were sick, Ānanda asked the Exalted One to visit them and strengthen them by teaching them the Dhamma (AN 10:60; AN 6:58). It was also Ānanda who asked the Buddha—upon Anāthapiṇḍika's suggestion—to have a shrine erected in the monastery (J 479).

In these and many other ways, Ānanda showed himself as a solicitous monk who combined maternal and paternal qualities. His ability for organization, negotiation, and arrangements had already been manifested earlier, when—in a past life—he fulfilled a similar function for the king of the gods, Sakka. In the few instances when Ānanda's past lives in the deva and *brahma* worlds are mentioned, it always related to those lives in which he held the position of a main helper and adjutant of Sakka; for example, as the heavenly charioteer Mātali (in four cases—Jātaka stories

attainment (*arahatta*), based on the fine-material or immaterial absorptions.

31, 249, 535 and 541), and as devas such as the heavenly architect Vissakamma (J 489), the rain-god Pajjunna (J 75), and the five-crested celestial musician Pañcasikha (J 450).

Especially worth mentioning is Ānanda's willingness to sacrifice himself. When Devadatta let loose a wild elephant to kill the Buddha, Ānanda threw himself in front of the Buddha, to die himself rather than to see the Exalted One killed or injured. Three times the Buddha asked him to step back, but he did not comply. Only when the Enlightened One moved gently from the spot through supernatural powers, could he be dissuaded from his intention to sacrifice himself (J 533). This action of Ānanda spread his fame even further. The Buddha told the other monks that already in four former lives Ānanda had shown himself equally willing to sacrifice himself. Even in long bygone times as an animal, as a swan (J 502, 533, and 534) and a gazelle (J 501), he had stayed with the Bodhisatta when he had been caught in a trap. And in three other recorded cases, Ānanda—in his former rebirths—saved the Buddha-to-be's life through his care and skill. In another case the Bodhisatta first sacrificed himself for his monkey mother, and then Ānanda did so (J 222). These stories amplify the virtues of Ānanda and his age-old association with the Buddha.

4. Ānanda as the Guardian of the Dhamma

Amongst the distinctions which gave Ānanda a special place amongst the Buddha's disciples, one of the most noteworthy was that he was the only monk who was not yet an *arahant* amongst those whom the Buddha called pre-eminent in specific abilities. This means that he had qualities which equalled those of the arahants. While others were mentioned because they excelled in one superior quality (except two monks who possessed two such qualities), Ānanda was the one amongst the seventy-five pre-eminent disciples who excelled in five abilities—he was pre-eminent among those who had heard much (of the Buddha's words), who had a good retentive memory, who had mastered the sequential order (or what was remembered), who were energetic, and who attended (on the Master) (AN 1:19).

Upon close examination, one can see that these five qualities belong to the vast complex of virtues which give *sati* (Pali for mindfulness) its strength and power. The quality of mindfulness is power of the mind, power of memory, mastery over recollections and ideas. It is the faculty to use the tool of the mind at any time at will and not be driven by it. In short, mindfulness is circumspection and orderliness, self-restraint, control, self-discipline. In a narrower sense, *sati* or mindfulness is the ability to remember. Ānanda had this ability to a phenomenal degree. He could immediately remember everything, even if he had heard it only once. He could repeat discourses of the Buddha flawlessly up to 60,000 words, without leaving out a single syllable. He was able to recite 15,000 four-line stanzas of the Buddha. It may sound like a miracle to us to be able to accomplish such a feat. But the miracle is solely that we encumber our minds with a hundred-thousand useless things, which hinder us from becoming master over our memory. The Buddha said once that the only reason why one forgets anything is the presence of one of the five hindrances[25] (AN 5:193). Because Ānanda was one in the higher training, he was able to let go of these hindrances at will (if any were still present in him at all) and so could concentrate completely on what he heard.[26]

Because he did not want anything for himself, he absorbed the discourses without resistance or distortion, arranged them properly, knew what belonged together, recognized within different expressions the common denominator, and like a faithful and skilled registrar, could find his way around in his own mind.

This is the quality of "having heard much." He who has heard much in this sense, has discarded wilfulness from his own mind and has become a vessel of truth. He has heard much truth and that means that he has erased all untruth in himself. Such a one is "born from the mouth" of the teacher, is truly trained, because he has let himself be shaped by the teaching of the Exalted One. Hence he who has heard much is the one who is most humble and a most sincere champion of truth. Everything good which he carries in his mind and upon which he acts, he does not ascribe to

25. Five hindrances: sensual desire, ill will, lethargy and drowsiness, restlessness and worry (distraction), and sceptical doubt.

26. Even today in modern Burma there are monks who remember by heart the Discipline, Discourses, and Abhidhamma—the Three Baskets of the Buddhist Scriptures—and can recite them. Printed, they fill forty-five volumes!

his own ability, but to the Dhamma, which he has heard from his teacher. Such a person is truly humble.

> His growth is to be
> The vanquished one of ever greater things.
>
> (Rainer Maria Rilke)

This could rightly be said of Ānanda. When he came to the Buddha he was still ignorant, thinking in a wrong way. Each teaching of the Awakened One forced him to correct his outlook. Constantly losing his old concepts, he totally yielded to the truth.

This quality of listening well and training the mind is named as the first of the five specific abilities of Ānanda and it is recorded that all of his disciples, too, were well versed in this respect (SN 14:5). But the Buddha said it would not be easy to find one who equalled Ānanda in this (AN 3:78). The question as to which monk lent radiance to the Gosiṅga Forest[27], was answered by Ānanda in this way:

> The monk who has heard much, is guardian of the word, treasurer of the teaching, and of what is good in the beginning, good in the middle, and good at the end, and transmits word by word, and in the right way, the completely purified life of the homeless ones: all this he knows, remembers, ably explains, keeps in his heart and understands completely. He gives discourses on the Dhamma to the four kinds of listeners,[28] in completeness, in part and in the right context, to bring them to final eradication of desires.
>
> MN 32

The second quality named is the retention in mind and making use of the discourses heard, and their application to one's own self-inquiry.

---

27. At one time the Buddha was staying in the park of the Gosiṅga *sāla* tree, also described as the Gosiṅga Wood, or Forest, with a number of experienced elder disciples. The venerable Sāriputta mentions that this wood is a delightful place, with the *sāla* trees all in bloom and their scent pervading the air as if in heaven. The Buddha then poses the above question to all the elder disciples and each one answers according to his own "specialty" in Dhamma.
28. Monks, nuns, and male and female lay devotees.

For the third quality (in Pali *gatimanta*), translators have given widely differing renderings. According to the ancient commentary, it refers to Ānanda's capacity to perceive in his mind the internal connection and coherence of a discourse. This he was able to do by understanding well the meaning and significance of the teaching concerned, with all its implications. Hence, even when his recitation was interrupted by a question, he was able to resume the recital where he had left off.

The fourth quality was his energy, his unflagging dedication to his task in studying, memorizing and reciting the Buddha's words and in personally attending on the Master.

The fifth and last quality was that of a perfect attendant, which was described earlier. Furthermore, because of his key position among the Buddha's entourage of monks, Ānanda was naturally the focus of much attention, and he had to deal with a very large number of people. To all those who came into contact with him, he was a model in his blameless conduct, his untiring solicitude for the Master and for the community of monks, his imperturbable friendliness, his patience and his readiness to help. Some potential conflicts did not arise because of his presence, and those which did arise became mitigated and resolved through his influence. Ānanda, as a man without enemies, had a strong and deep impact upon others through his exemplary conduct as well as through his instructions. His image as the Buddha's faithful companion left particularly strong traces in the minds of his contemporaries.

Ānanda was always master of a situation, and, like a king, he had a sovereign comprehension of affairs. Therefore, thanks to his circumspection, he could handle and organize whatever occurred in the daily life of the Buddha and the community. Through the extraordinary power of his memory, he was able to learn from his experiences and never repeat the same mistakes, as most people are liable to do again and again, due to their weak memory. Hence, he could remember people well, even though he may have met them only once, and he could, therefore, deal with them suitably, without leaving the impression that he "manipulated" them. His circumspection accorded with the facts of a situation so naturally that all reasonable people could only agree with him.

If one looks at these five qualities, one receives a vivid picture of Ānanda. The central quality, however, is that of a guardian of the Dhamma, which can be seen even more in the following chapters.

5. Ānanda's Attitude Towards Women

Both brothers, Anuruddha and Ānanda, were no longer in need of female companionship, in any way or form, because of their inner detachment from worldliness and their strong spirit of renunciation. To both, however, the other sex presented a challenge in different ways.

If one has much contact with people, one has to take the difference of the sexes into account. With Ānanda this showed as special care and effort to look after all four kinds of disciples, not only monks and laymen, but also nuns and laywomen. Without Ānanda there would have been only three kinds of disciples, because it was he who was instrumental in the founding of the nun's order. This happened as follows (AN 8:51; Cv X.1).

When many nobles of the Sakya clan had become monks, their wives, sisters, and daughters also wished to live a life of purification under the Awakened One. A large number of Sakyan ladies, under the guidance of the Buddha's stepmother, Mahā-Pajāpatī, followed the Exalted One and tried in vain to gain permission to establish an order of nuns. Ānanda saw the Buddha's stepmother with swollen feet, covered with dust, eyes full of tears at the gate of the monastery of Vesāli. When he asked her compassionately for the reason of her sorrow, she replied that the Master had three times rejected her request for the establishment of an order of nuns.[29]

Ānanda decided out of compassion to intercede himself. He went to the Master, but his request was also denied three times. Then he asked: "Is a woman able to gain the fruit of stream-entry, once-returning, non-returning, and arahantship, if she leaves

29. It seems that the Buddha did not absolutely refuse Mahāpajāpatī Gotami, but perhaps wished to test her determination. It would have been a very difficult thing for aristocratic ladies in those days to do—to become nuns and live a hard life in the forest, subsisting on almsfood. Ladies then had no experience in looking after themselves or organizing anything, as their social scope under Brahmanism was very much restricted.

the household life and enters into homelessness and follows the teaching and discipline of the Exalted One?"

The Buddha affirmed this. Thereupon Ānanda rephrased his request. "If a woman is able to do this, Master—and moreover Mahā-Pajāpatī Gotami has rendered great service to the Master: she is his aunt, his governess and nurse, and nourished the Exalted One with her own milk after his mother died—therefore it would be well if the Blessed One would allow women to leave home for the homeless life, to follow the teaching and discipline of the Master."

Ānanda here brought two arguments to bear. First was the fact that a woman in the Order could gain the highest fruit, become a saint, an *arahant* in this very life, a goal which can be attained only very rarely in the household life. Second, he brought up the very personal element of gratitude for the particularly meritorious services of Mahā-Pajāpatī to the Buddha, which would be a good reason for him to help his stepmother now to gain final liberation. In response to these arguments the Buddha agreed to the establishment of an order of nuns, provided certain cautions and rules were followed.

One might gain the impression from this account, that it needed Ānanda's intense and clever arguments to change the Buddha's mind. But an awakened one's mind cannot be changed, because he is always in touch with absolute reality. What happened here was the same event which all Buddhas encounter, because all of them have established an order of nuns. The whole incident was not meant to prevent the founding of the female branch of the Order, but only to strengthen by that hesitation the message that this brought great dangers with it. For this reason, the Buddha stipulated eight conditions, which were selected so that only the best women would agree to abide by them. They also served to bring about a separation of the sexes in the Order in the best possible manner. In spite of this, the Exalted One declared that because of the founding of the Order of Nuns the dispensation would last only five hundred instead of a thousand years.[30]

30. In the Vinaya (monk's discipline) the Buddha is represented as saying this, but such a prophecy involving time is found only here. There is no other mention anywhere in the whole of the Vinaya (discipline) and the Suttas

Following the Buddha's proclamation of the rules and regulations for nuns, Ānanda asked him about the qualities a monk should have to be a teacher of nuns. The Buddha did not reply that he had to be an *arahant*, a saint, but indicated eight practical and concrete qualities, which also someone like Ānanda, who was not yet an *arahant*, could possess. These eight qualities were: the teacher of nuns must be virtuous; second, he must have comprehensive knowledge of the Dhamma; third he must be well acquainted with the Vinaya, especially the rules for nuns; fourth, he must be a good speaker with a pleasant and fluent delivery, faultless in pronunciation, and intelligibly convey the meaning; fifth, he should be able to teach Dhamma to the nuns in an elevating, stimulating, and encouraging way; sixth, he must always be welcome to the nuns and liked by them—that is, they must be able to respect and esteem him not only when he praises them but especially when there is an occasion for reproach; seventh, he must never have committed sexual misconduct with a nun; and eighth, he must have been a fully ordained Buddhist monk for at least 20 years (AN 8:52).

Since Ānanda had been instrumental in the founding of the Order of Nuns, he now also wanted to help them to advance on the Noble Path. This brought about some difficulties for him. There were two occasions in which nuns stood up for him without justification against Kassapa (SN 16:10–11). One of them was mentioned above in Section 2, "Ānanda's Renown." Both nuns left the Order; they showed thereby that they were no longer able to sustain the necessary impersonal and purely spiritual relationship with their teacher, Ānanda.

Even more extreme was the case of the nun in Kosambi, whose name is not known. She sent a messenger to Ānanda, asking him to visit her as she was sick. In reality she had fallen in love with Ānanda and wanted to seduce him. Ānanda mastered the situation with complete aplomb. In his sermon to her he explained that this body had arisen because of nutrition, craving

(discourses). This makes one suspect an intrusion. The Commentaries, as well as many other later Buddhist writings, have much to say about the decline of the Buddha's Dispensation in five-hundred-year periods, but none of this is the word of the Buddha and only represents the view of later teachers.

and pride. But one could use these three as means for purification. Supported by nutrition, one could transcend nutrition. Supported by craving, one could transcend craving. Supported by pride, one could transcend pride. The monk took in such nutriment as would enable him to lead the holy life. He sublimated his craving and was supported by his longing for holiness. And pride spurred him on to reach that which others had already attained, namely the realization of Dhamma in himself. In this way he could, in due course, transcend nutrition, craving and pride. But there was a fourth cause for the arising of the body, namely sexual intercourse, but this was an entirely different matter. This had been called the destruction of the bridge to Nibbāna by the Blessed One. In no way could its sublimation be used as a path to holiness.

Thereupon the nun got up from the bed, prostrated before Ānanda, confessed her offense and asked for forgiveness. Ānanda accepted the confession and declared that in the Order it was an advantage to confess one's faults and to restrain oneself thereafter (AN 4:159). This incident is an excellent example of Ānanda's great skill to give a suitable Dhamma discourse on the spur of the moment, to find the right word at the right time.

Another incident happened with regard to the wives of King Pasenadi. They had pondered over three things: seldom does a Buddha appear in the world, seldom is one reborn as a human being and seldom is one healthy in mind and body. Yet in spite of the existence of these favourable conditions, they could not go to the monastery and hear the Dhamma. As the king's women they were confined to the harem like birds in a cage, and that was really a disaster for them.

They went to the king and asked him to request the Buddha to send a monk to the palace to teach them the Dhamma. The king promised. The lay disciple praised by the Buddha—a non-returner—declined to do it, because it was a monk's duty. Thereupon the king asked his wives which monk would be most acceptable to them. They discussed it among themselves and unanimously requested the king that he should ask Ānanda, the guardian of the Dhamma, to come and teach them. The Blessed One complied with the request presented to him by the king, and from then on Ānanda taught the Dhamma to the women.

One day during this period, one of the crown jewels was stolen. Everywhere was searched and the women felt very troubled because of the unrest occasioned thereby. Because of this they were not as attentive and eager to learn as usual. Ānanda asked them for the reason and when he heard it, out of compassion he went to the king and advised him. In order to end the anxiety and unrest, he told the king to summon everyone who could possibly be the thief and give them an opportunity to return the jewel unobtrusively. He advised him to have a tent erected in the courtyard of the palace, to put a large pot of water inside and have everyone enter alone. So it was done, and the jewel thief, alone in the tent, let the jewel drop into the pot. Thereby the king regained his property, the thief went unpunished, and peace reigned once again in the palace. This incident increased Ānanda's popularity even more and thereby the popularity of the Sakyan monks. The monks also praised Ānanda, that he had restored peace through gentle means (J 92).

Shortly before the Buddha died, Ānanda asked him a question concerning women: "How shall we relate to women, Master?"—"Do not look at them."—"But if one sees one, Master?"—"Do not address her."—"But if one talks to us?"—"Keep mindfulness and self-control." (DN 16).

This question was posed by Ānanda in view of the imminent death of the Buddha, just before the preparations for the funeral. This problem must therefore have been an important one for him. For himself he did not need an admonition to practise self-control; sensual desire had been overcome by him for 25 years. But during the years he had seen how the problem of the relationship between the sexes again and again stirred the emotions.

The question may have been asked by him for this reason, but also on account of the warning of the Buddha that the Order was endangered through the foundation of the Nun's Order and its lifespan shortened. He wanted to give his contemporaries and his successors a last word of the Buddha on this topic.

6. Ānanda and His Fellow Monks

Of all the monks, Sāriputta was Ānanda's closest friend. There does not seem to have been a close relationship between Ānanda and his brother Anuruddha, because the latter preferred solitude whereas Ānanda was fond of people. Sāriputta was the disciple who most resembled the Master, and with whom he could talk in the same way as with the Buddha. It is remarkable that of all the monks only Sāriputta and Ānanda received an honorary title from the Buddha: Sāriputta was called the Commander-in-Chief of the Dhamma (dhamma-*senapati*) and Ānanda its Guardian. One can see their complementary roles in this. Sāriputta, the lion, was the active teacher; Ānanda more the preserver and treasurer. In certain aspects, Ānanda's methods resembled more those of Mahā-Moggallāna, whose inclinations were also motherly and preserving.

Ānanda and Sāriputta often worked together. They visited the sick Anāthapiṇḍika (MN 153; SN 55:26) together twice, dealt with the dispute of the monks of Kosambi (AN 4:221), and had many Dhamma discussions with each other. When Ānanda received the message one day that Sāriputta had died, he was deeply affected:

All the quarters are bedimmed
And the Dhamma is not clear to me,
Indeed my noble friend has gone
And all about seems dark.

Th 1034

He felt physically quite wretched and even the Dhamma was not alive in him at that moment, such was the impact of the death message. Then the Buddha afforded him great consolation. He asked Ānanda to reflect whether Sāriputta had taken with him virtue or meditation, or wisdom, or liberation, or the purity of liberation? Ānanda had to agree that these, the only important aspects, had not changed. But, he added, Sāriputta had been such a helpful companion and friend for him and others. Again the Buddha directed the conversation onto a higher level by reminding Ānanda of what he, the Buddha, had always taught: that nothing that has arisen can remain forever. The death of Sāriputta was, for the other disciples, like cutting off the main branch of a large tree.

But that should only be another reason for relying on oneself, on no one else, and be one's own light and refuge (SN 7:13).

Many discussions which Ānanda had with other monks are also recorded. Only a few can be related here.

One day the Venerable Vaṅgīsa accompanied Ānanda on his alms round. On the way Vaṅgīsa was overcome by dissatisfaction,[31] the most dangerous illness of ascetics. His heart was flooded by sensual desire. All of a sudden a monk's life seemed senseless and a waste to him, but house and family life attractive and wholesome. The Venerable Vaṅgīsa asked Ānanda for help. When Ānanda became aware of what was going on in his companion, he spoke to him in verse, because Vaṅgīsa, the poet in the Saṅgha, had voiced his request also in verse. Ānanda said:

> Since your perception is distorted,
> Your heart with passion is aflame.
> The marks of beauty should you shun,
> Bound up with lustful longing and desire.
> Your mind, one-pointed and collected,
> In seeing foulness should be cultivated.
> With mindfulness directed on the body,
> Dwell often in disgust concerning it.

Th 1224–25

Ānanda showed him that he constantly refuelled sensual desire because his perception was not controlled, and so he became captivated by feminine charm. When the feeling of deprivation became too strong it would manifest as weariness of mind and dissatisfaction, as a kind of aversion towards the ascetic life. Therefore Vaṅgīsa had to contemplate soberly those things which seemed beautiful and desirable; then he would understand that the body was not beautiful. This would be wholesome practice.

The monk Channa was plagued with doubts about the Dhamma. He understood that the five aggregates are impermanent, but he was afraid of Nibbāna, thought it to be the destruction of the ego. So he came for advice to Ānanda. Ānanda consoled him: he would understand the teaching, he was already beginning to break through the hard shell. Channa was delighted and listened

31. Dissatisfaction with celibacy.

with undivided attention to Ānanda's exposition of the Buddha's discourse on being and not-being (SN 12:15). Thereupon Channa exclaimed how wonderful it was to have such wise brothers as teachers. Now he was firm in the Dhamma again (SN 22:90).

7. Ānanda's Conversations with the Buddha

If one considers conversation as also the silent, inner rapport with a Dhamma discourse, then the whole of the Pali Canon actually consists of Ānanda's conversations with the Buddha. He was almost always present when the Buddha gave a discourse, and not only during the time he was his attendant. And those few discourses which the Blessed One gave in Ānanda's absence, he repeated for him afterwards.[32]

We cannot repeat here all the specific dialogues between the Buddha and Ānanda. The Buddha often addressed Ānanda with a question or teachings, which were either meant for Ānanda's spiritual growth or gave the occasion for a discourse to all the monks present. It is always more stimulating for the listeners when two experts discuss a subject with each other, rather than having only one speaking. In this way many of the conversations between the Buddha and Ānanda are discourses for the instruction of others.

Special occasions for a discourse were when the Buddha smiled when he came to a certain locality. Ānanda knew that a fully enlightened one does not smile without cause, and understood immediately that here was reason for a question. So he asked the Awakened One why he had smiled. Thereupon the Master gave detailed explanations of incidents in past births, Jātaka stories, which had taken place at those localities (MN 81; MN 83; AN 5:180; J 440).

The conversations in which Ānanda asked the question and took the initiative are far more numerous than the ones the Buddha started. For instance, Ānanda asked whether there was a fragrance which went against the wind, different from that of

32. But obviously there are many discourses of the Buddha which were not recorded in full—for instance, the detailed exposition of his "graduated talk" which he gave so many times; and also the many occasions in the account of his last days when only the subject headings are mentioned.

flowers and blossoms. The answer was: the fragrance of him who has taken the triple refuge, is virtuous and generous (SN 3:79).

Another time Ānanda asked how one could live happily in the Order. The answer was: if one is virtuous oneself, but does not blame others for lack of virtue; if one watches oneself, but not others; if one does not worry about lack of fame; if one can obtain the four meditation absorptions without difficulty; and finally if one becomes a holy one, an *arahant*. So here the first step on the path to holiness is mentioned as not criticizing or watching others, but only making demands on oneself (AN 5:106).

Ānanda inquired about many aspects of the Dhamma. For instance, Ānanda asked what were the purposes and blessings of virtue. The answer was: to be free of self-reproach, free of guilt feelings, with a clear conscience. But Ānanda asked further: what were the purposes and blessings of a clear conscience. The Buddha replied that it would bring joy in wholesome thoughts and actions, happiness with progress made and incentive for further striving. And what would result from that? One would experience exaltation in one's heart, being drawn towards the good and perfect bliss; and from that would further result deep calm and insight (AN 10:1).

Sometimes Ānanda reported certain views of his to the Buddha, so that the Buddha could either accept or correct them. For instance he said that good friendship was half of the holy life. Unexpectedly the Buddha disagreed: noble friendship was more than half; it was all of it. What would the holy life be like, if they had not all come to the Buddha, as their best friend, to be shown the right way? (SN 45:2 and SN 3:18; further examples: AN 6:57; MN 121).

Ānanda's best-known remark must surely be the one where he said that causal arising[33] was very profound, but it seemed quite clear to him. Again the Buddha disagreed: it was profound, but very difficult to penetrate. Because it was not properly understood, there was no liberation for beings caught in the wheel of life and death.[34] And then the Buddha explained to Ānanda causal arising

33. Causal arising: dependent origination; see The Wheel Nos. 15, 140, and also 147–149.

34. The wheel of life and death: because each cause has an effect, and ordinary beings cannot see the impact of their cravings, they are caught in rebirth after rebirth, as if in a revolving wheel.

in its manifold aspects (DN 15). At one time, Ānanda saw an archer perform extraordinary feats. When he told the Buddha how he had admired this (Ānanda came from the warrior caste and probably greatly appreciated such skill), the Buddha used his statement to draw an analogy. He said it was more difficult to understand and penetrate the Four Noble Truths[35] than to hit and penetrate with an arrow a hair split seven times.

Another report says that Ānanda once saw the famous Brahman Jāṇussoṇi (MN 4; MN 27; MN 99; AN 2:15; etc.), a disciple of the Buddha, driving along in his glorious white chariot. He heard people exclaim that the chariot of the priest of King Pasenadi's court was the most beautiful and best of all. Ānanda reported this to the Buddha and asked him how one could describe the best chariot according to Dhamma. The Buddha explained in a detailed analogy what the vehicle to Nibbāna had to consist of: the draft-animals had to be faith and wisdom, moral shame the brake, intellect the reins, mindfulness the charioteer, virtue the accessories, *jhāna*[36] the axle, energy the wheels, equanimity the balance, renunciation the chassis; the weapons were love, harmlessness and solitude; and patience was its armour (SN 45:4).

8. Ānanda's Former Lives

A summary of Ānanda's former lives shows that he was only seldom a god, seldom an animal, and mostly a human. His most frequent birth was as a human, while his brother Anuruddha had almost always been a god, and Devadatta very often an animal. His close connection with the Buddha is shown in the fact that he was often his brother.

---

35. The Four Noble Truths; the core of the Dhamma:
    1. the noble truth of dukkha (unsatisfactoriness);
    2. the noble truth of the cause of dukkha, which is craving;
    3. the noble truth of the cessation of dukkha which is Nibbāna;
    4. the noble truth of the path to cessation, which is the Noble Eightfold Path.

36. *jhāna*: four deeply-inward and purified levels of mind at a high degree of concentration, when there is no sense of awareness present but only a brilliant and mindful awareness within. The Pali term may be rendered by "meditative absorption."

The examples of former lives given here will be mainly those which exemplify that he, too, had to exert himself to attain virtue.

Jātaka 498. He and the Bodhisatta were born as cousins among the outcastes or *caṇḍālas*. Their job was the fumigation of malodorous places. In order to escape the contempt they were held in, they disguised themselves as young men of the Brahman caste and went to the University at Takkasilā to study. Their deceit was discovered and they were beaten up by their fellow students. A wise and kindly man ordered the students to stop and advised the two *caṇḍālas* to become ascetics. They followed this advice and, in due course, died; as the consequence for their deceit, they were reborn as animals, namely as offspring of a doe. They were inseparable and died together by the arrows of a hunter. In the next life they were sea hawks and again died together because of a hunter.

With this, their existences below the human level came to an end. Ānanda was born as the son of a king and the Bodhisatta as the son of the priest at court. While Ānanda held the higher position in a worldly sense, the Bodhisatta had more inner abilities because, for one thing, he could remember all the above three lives. But Ānanda could only remember his life as a *caṇḍāla*. At the age of sixteen, the Bodhisatta became a sincerely striving ascetic while Ānanda became king. Later on the Bodhisatta visited the king. He praised the happiness of asceticism and explained the unsatisfactoriness of the world of the senses. Ānanda admitted that he realized this, but that he could not let go of his desires, that he was held fast like an elephant in a swamp. Thereupon the Bodhisatta advised him that even as a king he could practise virtue, such as not levying unjust taxes, and supporting ascetics and priests. But when hot passions arose in him, he should remember his mother. How he had been completely helpless as a baby, and if his mother had not brought him up, he would never have become king. Thereupon Ānanda resolved to become an ascetic, and both attained to the *brahma* realm.

Jātaka 421. The Bodhisatta had been born as a poor labourer and endeavoured to keep the fast days.[37] His longing to be reborn

---

37. *Uposatha:* marking the four phases of the moon when, especially on full moon, devout Buddhist laymen and laywomen observe eight precepts.

as a king in his next life was fulfilled. Ānanda lived in his kingdom as a poor water-carrier. His whole fortune was a coin which he had hidden under a stone in a certain place. When a festival was observed in the city, the water-carrier's wife urged him to enjoy himself too and asked him whether he had any money at all. He said he had this coin but it was twelve miles away. She replied he should get it and that she had saved up the same amount. They could buy garlands, incense and drinks with that. Ānanda set out in spite of the midday heat, happy in the expectation of the festival. When he passed through the courtyard of the king's palace, he sang a song. The king saw him and asked the reason for his joyfulness in such heat. He answered that he did not notice the heat, as he was being driven by hot desire, and told his story.

The king asked how much his treasure amounted to, maybe one hundred thousand pieces? When he finally heard that it was only one coin, he exclaimed that Ānanda should not walk through the heat for he would give him a similar coin. Ānanda replied that he was very grateful because then he would have two coins. The king then offered him two coins but Ānanda said he would fetch his own one nevertheless. The king now became excited and raised his offer to millions, to the post of viceroy, but Ānanda would not let go of his coin. Only when the king offered him half his kingdom did he agree. The kingdom was divided up, and Ānanda was called King One Coin.

One day the two of them went hunting. When they became tired, the Bodhisatta put his head in the lap of his friend and fell asleep. Then the thought came to Ānanda to kill the king and to rule the whole kingdom by himself. He was drawing his sword when he remembered how grateful he—a poor yokel—should be to the king, and how wicked it was of him to have such a wish arise. He put his sword back in its sheath, but even a second and a third time he was overcome by the same desire. Feeling that this thought might rise in him again and again and could lead him on to very evil deeds, he threw away his sword, woke the king, prostrated before him and asked his forgiveness. The Bodhisatta forgave him and said he could have the whole kingdom and he would be satisfied to serve as viceroy under him. But Ānanda replied that he was finished with his lust for power, he wanted to become an ascetic. He had seen the cause of desire and how it grew; now he wanted to pull it out by the roots. He went to the Himalayas and reached perfect insight. The Bodhisatta remained in the world.

Jātaka 282. The Bodhisatta was a righteous king of Benares who practised the ten royal virtues, in that he gave alms, practised the moral rules and observed the sacred days. Now one of his ministers carried on an intrigue in his harem. When he was brought to justice, the gentle king waived the death penalty, only banishing him and allowing him to take his family and fortune along. The minister then went to live at a neighbouring king's court, became his confidant and told him one could easily occupy Benares, because its king was much too gentle. But the neighbouring king, Ānanda, was suspicious, because he was well acquainted with the strength and power of the State of Benares. The minister advised him to experiment. He should destroy one village of Benares. If any of his men were caught, the king would probably even reward the prisoners. True enough, when the marauders were brought before the Bodhisatta, and lamented they had plundered out of hunger, he gave them money.

This served to convince Ānanda of the truth of the treacherous minister's words and he marched into the State of Benares. The commander-in-chief of the Bodhisatta wanted to defend the kingdom, but the king said that he did not want to be the cause of harm for others. If the other king wanted his kingdom, he should have it. He let Ānanda capture him and put him into prison. There he practised loving-kindness meditation towards the rapacious King Ānanda, who was struck down by a fever and plagued by a guilty conscience. Ānanda asked the Bodhisatta's pardon, returned his kingdom to him and swore to be his ally forever. The Bodhisatta returned to his throne and spoke to his ministers about the virtues and rewards of harmlessness, saying that because he had made peace with the invaders, hundreds were spared death on the battlefield. Then he renounced his throne, became an ascetic and attained to the *brahma* realm. Ānanda, however, remained king.

9. The Last Days of Gotama the Buddha

A welcome addition to Ānanda's conversations with the Awakened One is the account concerning the last events in the life of the Buddha in which Ānanda played a leading role. It is the Mahā-Parinibbāna Sutta (DN 16), the discourse on the Buddha's passing away and his ultimate entrance into Nibbāna.[38] These records convey a special mood, namely that of parting, which was especially painful for Ānanda. It is also the first small beginning of the decline of the Dhamma, which will slowly disappear with increased distance from the Buddha's lifetime until a new Buddha arises. This entire text gives, as it were, voice to the admonition to practise Dhamma while there is still a chance. It reflects once more Ānanda's whole character, and therefore we will follow its course, and emphasize those points which are important as far as Ānanda is concerned.

The first section of the Mahā-Parinibbāna Sutta starts at Rājagaha, the capital of the State of Magadha. Devadatta's attempt to create a schism in the Saṅgha had happened seven years earlier. King Ajātasattu reigned in Magadha. King Pasenadi of Kosala had just been overthrown and the Sakya clan had come to its tragic end in which Ānanda's brother, Prince Mahānāma, was killed.

At that time, three famous warrior clans lived north of the Ganges near the Himalayas. They were the Koliyas, the Mallas and the Vajjians, all of which had retained relative independence from the Mahārāja Ajātasattu. Ajātasattu had the intention of destroying the Vajjians and to incorporate their land in his. While the Buddha could not prevent the overthrow of those Sakyans who had not entered the Order because they had to pay a kammic debt, he did help the Vajjians and later indirectly also the Mallas. This is the external "political" background of the last years of the Buddha's life.

In detail, this incident happened as follows:

The king Ajātasattu gave orders to his minister, Vassakāra, to go to the Buddha and announce his intention to go into battle against the Vajjians. While Vassakāra delivered his message, Ānanda stood behind the Buddha and fanned him. The Awakened One turned to Ānanda and put seven questions to him about the lifestyle and conditions of the Vajjians.

---

38. See *Last Days of the Buddha* (*Mahā-Parinibbāna Sutta*), The Wheel Nos. 67–69.

Ānanda declared that they often had council meetings in which they deliberated harmoniously, they did not repeal their old laws, they followed the advice of their elders, did not rape women, honoured their temples and shrines, did not revoke gifts to religious places, and that they gave protection and hospitality to all true priests and ascetics. Some time earlier the Buddha had given these seven rules to them. With these seven qualities, said the Buddha to Vassakāra, one could expect prosperity for the Vajjians, not decline. The king's minister replied that even one of these qualities would be enough for their continued existence as a clan. As long as the Vajjians kept to these seven rules, it would be impossible for the king to conquer them, except through inner dissension or treachery. He left with this conviction in mind and reported to the king that it would be useless to start a war against the Vajjians. Indians in those days had so much confidence in the spiritual strength of a people, that the hint of moral superiority was sufficient to prevent a war. Only much later, after the death of the Buddha, was it possible for the king to overrun the Vajjians, and this was only because they had in the meanwhile forsaken their moral integrity.

This highly political discussion with Vassakāra was used by the Buddha as an occasion to request Ānanda to call all monks of the area together. He then gave them an exhortation about seven things which would serve for the continued existence of the Saṅgha. The monks should: assemble frequently; conduct their affairs amicably; not make new rules but obey the old ones; honour the elders of the Saṅgha and give heed to their advice; resist craving; enjoy solitude; and practise mindfulness at all times, so that like-minded persons would be attracted and those who were already living the holy life would be happy.

After the Buddha had spoken in this way to the monks, he gave them the following terse summary of the teaching, which recurs many times throughout this narrative:

"That is virtue, that is concentration, that is wisdom. Concentration fortified with virtue brings great benefits and great fruits. Wisdom fortified with concentration brings great benefits and great fruits. The mind fortified with wisdom becomes liberated from all taints, namely from the taint of sensual desire, the taint of (desire for) being and the taint of ignorance."

After this exhortation, the Buddha commenced his last journey as described in the second chapter of the sutta. He always went to places where there were people ready to understand Dhamma, or where misunderstandings needed to be sorted out, or where brute force could be prevented. On this last journey he went first in the direction of the Ganges River to Nālandā, which later became a famous Buddhist teaching centre. This town was Sāriputta's birthplace and here he took leave of the Buddha. He wanted to stay there and teach the Dhamma to his mother before he died. When saying farewell, this great disciple voiced once more the Buddha's praise: "It is clear to me, Lord, that there is no one more distinguished in wisdom."[39]

Then the Awakened One went with a large company of monks to Vesāli. This town was the capital of the Vajjians, whose virtue he had praised, and from whom he had averted the threat of King Ajātasattu's attack. Why did the Buddha go to the capital of the Vajjians and spend his last rains retreat in that vicinity? It is not too far-fetched to think that this was meant as a non-aggressive warning to King Ajātasattu to keep the peace, and to the Vajjians to maintain their virtue.

At Vesāli the Awakened One became ill with a deadly disease. He overcame it by will-power, as he did not want to die without having assembled the disciples once more. That a Buddha can become ill is due to the imperfection of the body, but that he can master illness at will is due to the perfection of the Awakened One.

Ānanda was extremely grieved by the Buddha's illness. He was so worried that he could not think properly. He related to the Buddha that he had found consolation in the fact that surely the Awakened One would not attain final Nibbāna without having given regulations about the Community of monks. But the Buddha rejected this. What was there left to pronounce to the disciples? He had taught the Dhamma in all its aspects and kept nothing secret. Only a person who believed that it was he who had to guide the monks, a person who still possessed the "I am" conceit, could conceive himself to be so important. Furthermore the Buddha declared that he was now eighty, had reached old age,

39. See Sāriputta's Lion's roar in *The Life of Sāriputta*, The Wheel Nos. 90–92.

and could move the body only with difficulty, just like an old cart. His body was only at ease when he entered upon and dwelled in the signless deliverance of the mind.[40] With this he implied that a Buddha's body is also subject to the law of impermanence. But he immediately gave Ānanda an antidote for the sadness caused by these words: "So Ānanda, each of you should be an island unto himself, with himself and no other as his refuge; each of you should make the Dhamma his island, have the Dhamma and no other as his refuge."

The third chapter of the Mahā-Parinibbāna Sutta is also located at Vesāli, where the Buddha was dwelling for the rains retreat. One day he requested Ānanda to take a sitting mat and to go with him to the Capala Shrine and pass the day there in meditation. When they were seated, the Blessed One looked at the peaceful landscape before him and reminded Ānanda of the many beautiful spots in the vicinity.

The Buddha said that anyone who had developed the Four Bases to Success[41], had made them his vehicle and his foundation could, if he wished, live out the age. The Exalted One had done all that, and he could, if requested, live to the end of this age.[42] Although Ānanda was given such a plain and broad hint, which certainly coincided with his longing, he did not beg the Buddha to stay alive, out of compassion for all beings. Not only once, but a second and third time, the Buddha addressed Ānanda in this way. But Ānanda did not take these hints; in his confusion he was not

40. *Animitta-cetovimutti*: a deep state of meditation that transcends the "signs," or marks, of conditioned existence.

41. Four bases to success (*iddhi-pada*): will (desire to practise); effort; perseverance (repeatedly applying the mind); and examination (leading to insight).

42. The discussion that follows is based on the commentary's interpretation of *āyukappa*: that the Buddha potentially had the age or lifespan of an *aeon*. The author has followed this interpretation. However, *āyukappa* can also mean one's natural lifespan. In that case the Buddha could perhaps have willed himself to live to a hundred years or even longer (120 is always given in Pali as representing extreme old age), but disease was already upon his body and perhaps he saw that it would be difficult to continue teaching, even though his mind would, of course, remain unaffected.

himself, being ensnared by Māra.[43] Māra had power over him, as he had not yet fully purified himself.

Ānanda, who usually was so circumspect, had lost his mindfulness, which previously had happened only in negligible matters. Otherwise our whole aeon would have taken quite a different turn. Could it be that Ānanda was too much absorbed in the pleasant feeling of being at that moment in so close companionship with the Buddha, in that enchanting evening hour in the peaceful scenic environment of the *sāla* forest? Was it, perhaps, just this very attachment to the Buddha's company that prevented a response which properly should have issued out of that very attachment—a response that would have accorded with his deepest wishes for a longer life for the Exalted One? If Māra had not intervened, Ānanda would have asked the Buddha to accept the burden of a prolonged life, out of compassion for the world. But Māra prevented it, because innumerable beings would have escaped his clutches in such an event.

This scene belongs to the mysteries of the Pali Canon and one could puzzle about it endlessly. One can only accept the fact that it is our own doing which brought us into an age in which the person who could have kept the Awakened One alive to this day was blinded by Māra and remained silent.

Let us continue the account. The Buddha dismissed Ānanda, who seated himself under a nearby tree and started meditating. Then Māra appeared before the Buddha and reminded him of a promise made forty-five years before, immediately after his enlightenment. Māra had then requested the Buddha to enter final Nibbāna and not to teach. But the Buddha had replied that he would not die until he had established and well taught the four kinds of disciples,[44] and until the holy life was well advanced. But now that had been accomplished, Māra declared, and it was time to fulfil his promise. The Buddha replied that he would attain final Nibbāna in three months from that time. One might wonder why the Buddha even gave Māra a promise and also why it was Māra, the Evil One, to whom he first announced the time of his death.

---

43. Māra: the Buddhist "tempter" figure, the personification of evil, passion, and worldliness, obstructing people on their way to liberation.

44. Four kinds of disciples: Monks, nuns, laymen, laywomen.

But just here the supreme detachment of an Awakened One becomes apparent. He considered this mortal body, which he carried around, as belonging to Māra. Immediately after enlightenment, the Awakened One had determined for himself how long he wanted to keep this body. There is no reason for a Buddha to go back on such a resolve, and only Māra would understand it is a "promise," rather than a freely arrived at, voluntary ending.

In any case, the Buddha now dismissed the idea of remaining alive throughout the aeon. He had to specifically let go of this possibility, as it seems to have been the norm for a Buddha to continue living. When the Awakened One relinquished the will to live, there was a great earthquake, and thunder resounded, such was the powerful effect on the natural elements when he renounced them as a basis for life.

When Ānanda became aware of the quake and thunder, he asked the Buddha for their cause. The Buddha replied that there were eight reasons for earthquakes: there are occasions when great forces move, this was the first reason; a monk or Brahman possessing supernormal power may have reached a certain kind of meditation, that was the second reason; the last six concerned the conception, birth, enlightenment, the start of the teaching of the Dhamma, the relinquishing of the will to live, and the final Nibbāna of a Buddha. One can see from this how deeply connected a Buddha, the highest of all beings, is with the whole cosmos.

The expositions that follow on eight kinds of assemblies, eight fields of mastery and eight liberations[45] seem quite unmotivated in this context. It appears to be one of those occasions for a spontaneously arisen discourse. Scholars speak about insertions into the text because at first there were eight reasons for earthquakes, then three other "eights" were brought in. In reality there is a deeper connection, designed to bring Ānanda from the superficial to the profound and to let him know the quickly approaching death of the Buddha in such a way that it would not disturb him.

After the Buddha had helped to direct Ānanda on the path towards enlightenment, he related how he had told Māra forty-five years ago that he would not attain final Nibbāna until the

45. For these groups of "eight," see *The Last Days of the Buddha*, The Wheel Nos. 67–69.

Dhamma was well established. Now Māra had appeared before him and he, the Buddha, had told him he would live only for another three months. Therefore he had now relinquished the will to live. That had been the reason for the earthquake.

Thereupon Ānanda begged the Awakened One three times that he should remain for the whole aeon. But the Buddha replied that the appropriate time for this had lapsed. When Ānanda asked for the third time, the Buddha inquired whether he had faith in the Perfect One's enlightenment. When Ānanda affirmed this, he asked why then was he urging him three times.

Ānanda replied that his reason was because the Awakened One had said he could remain for an aeon due to his practice of the four bases to success. The Buddha asked whether Ānanda had believed this. Ānanda affirmed it. Then the Buddha made it clear to him that he had let the opportunity slip by—"what you missed in this hour, no eternity can return," and told him that, if Ānanda had then requested him, he would have complied the third time. And he also reminded him that not only now, but already fifteen times previously he had made this statement to Ānanda, that due to the four bases to success he could remain for a whole aeon. Five of the places where he had said it were near Vesāli, and it was in this respect that the Buddha had reminded Ānanda of the many beautiful spots in the vicinity at the beginning of this account. But Ānanda had always remained silent.

Finally the Buddha added the admonition that he had always spoken about the impermanence of all phenomena, and that it was unthinkable that a perfect one should go back on his word. In three months time he would attain final Nibbāna. Thereupon he requested Ānanda to assemble the monks of the area. He then addressed the assembly with the exhortation always to practise insight, so that this holy life may endure long for the welfare and happiness of many. At the end of the discourse he made it known that he would pass away in three months. He gave them some stanzas for contemplation; amongst them are these:

> My years are now full ripe,
> the life span left is short.
> Departing, I go hence from you,
> relying on myself alone.

Be earnest, then monks,
be mindful and of virtue pure!
With firm resolve
guard your own mind!

Whoso untiringly pursues
the Teaching and the Rule,
Shall go beyond the round of births,
and make and end of suffering.[46]

The fourth chapter of the sutta tells of the Buddha resuming his journeys after the rains retreat and declaring that he would not return to Vesāli. On the way he spoke to the monks on the same topics he had expounded earlier: that they had to travel through this long round of rebirths because they had not penetrated four things. Previously he had named them as the four truths, but now he spoke on the four stages of the fourth truth: a noble one's virtue, a noble one's concentration, a noble one's wisdom, and a noble one's deliverance. And again, as so often on his last journey, he emphasized concentration fortified by virtue.

At the next resting place he explained to the monks how they should act if someone purported to quote his words. One should remember these quoted sentences and look for their verification in the Vinaya or confirmation in the suttas.[47] If one could not find them there, then one would have to come to the conclusion that it had been wrongly learned by that person, and they should reject it.[48] This admonition was extremely important for the faithful transmission of his words and has been the reason why to this day one can distinguish between the Buddha's own words and post-canonical or unauthentic texts.

After this, the Buddha journeyed to the province of the Mallas, the warrior clan nearest to the Himalayas. It is possible that on the

---

46. Translation of the verses from *Last Days of the Buddha,* The Wheel Nos. 67–69.

47. Sutta: discourse of the Buddha; literally "thread," threading together the gems of the words of the Buddha.

48. For the three remaining of these so-called "four great Authorities," see *Last Days of the Buddha,* The Wheel Nos. 67–69, p. 46

way he had also been in not-too-distant Sāvatthī, because it was there that the news of Sāriputta's death reached him.

In the land of the Mallas, the neighbours of the Sakyas, he became seriously ill, after taking food from the goldsmith Cunda. He had asked the goldsmith to give the mushroom dish[49] only to him and to offer the monks something else. Then he asked that the remainder of the dish be buried, because only a Buddha could digest it and no one else. Also this second illness, dysentry, was borne by the Buddha with equanimity and he was not deterred from his journey. On the way he asked Ānanda to spread his robe as he was exhausted and wished to rest. Ānanda should bring him some water from the nearby stream. Ānanda would have preferred to bring water from the river, because the stream had been churned up by many carts. After the Buddha had repeated his request three times, however, the obedient Ānanda went to the stream and saw that the water had become quite clear in the meantime. He was delighted about his Master's magical powers. A similar incident had happened earlier in the land of the Mallas where a well had been stopped up.

On the way, the Buddha met Pukkusa, a prince of the Mallas, a disciple of Ālāra Kālāma. Pukkusa had been together with that ascetic some fifty years earlier. Pukkusa started his conversation with the statement how astounding it was, what a deep peace those could achieve who had gone forth into homelessness. Once his master had been so deeply concentrated that he did not see nor hear five-hundred carts passing by him and yet there was no question of his being asleep. The Buddha countered this with the question, whether it was more difficult to be so deeply concentrated while there was thunder and lightning, and rain torrents coming down. Pukkusa agreed that it was. Thereupon the Buddha related that he had abided once like that, while all around him oxen and ploughmen were killed by lightning. This account sufficed for

49. It is not quite certain that this was a mushroom dish. See the thorough discussion in *The Last Days of the Buddha*. Arthur Waley also wrote on this subject using Chinese sources (see the volume of collected poetry and articles published to honour his death). It may be assumed that the Buddha instructed Cunda not to give it to the other monks as he knew it would make them ill, while for himself this was not important since death was near.

Pukkusa to declare that the Buddha had thereby expounded the Dhamma in its manifold aspects; he took refuge and became a lay disciple, the last one in the Buddha's lifetime. Then he presented two sets of golden-hued robes to the Buddha. The Buddha asked that he give one to him and the other one to Ānanda. On this occasion Ānanda did not reject the gift. He remarked that the golden hue of the robe was almost without brilliance compared to the bright radiance of the Buddha's skin. The Exalted One said that there are two occasions when the complexion of the Perfect One becomes exceptionally clear and bright: on the day of enlightenment and on the day of his death. In the last hours of the following night he would attain final Nibbāna.

After he had taken a bath in the vicinity, the Buddha turned to Ānanda and said that no one should reproach the goldsmith Cunda that the Buddha had died after taking a meal from him. There were two offerings in the world that are best: the almsfood after which the Bodhisatta becomes enlightened and the almsfood after which he attains final Nibbāna. Cunda would gain much merit from his gift; his life would be prolonged and his well-being heightened. He would gain much influence, fame and a heavenly rebirth.

The fifth chapter starts with the Buddha's request to Ānanda to accompany him to the region of Kusināra, to the *sāla*-tree grove of the Mallas. When they arrived, Ānanda arranged a couch for him, with his head to the north, between two large *sāla* trees. Although it was not the right season, the trees were in flower and sprinkled their blossoms over the body of the Buddha. And blossoms of the heavenly *mandārava* tree fell from the sky, together with heavenly scents, and there was music of the spheres. This peaceful, idyllic picture of the last hours of the founder of Buddhism has been compared with the death of Jesus Christ by a Japanese Buddhist, D.T. Suzuki. In both cases the deaths of the founders have become symbols for those who follow their teachings.

The Awakened One then said that veneration for him through heavenly music, scents, and blossoms was a great honour: yet one who, as a disciple of the Master, enters upon the proper way and practices the Dhamma, honours the Perfect One with the greatest reverence.

At that time, the Venerable Upavana was fanning the Blessed One. Then the Buddha requested Upavana to stand aside. Ānanda asked why Upavana was so summarily dismissed. The Buddha explained that innumerable deities had come from all directions of the world to have a last glance at a fully enlightened one, who so seldom can be seen. But since Upavana, an eminent monk, was standing in front of him, they could not see him. Upavana's spiritual radiance must have been more powerful than the penetrative ability of the gods.

Ānanda inquired further into details about the gods and learned that some were weeping and wailing, but that those free from sense desire were resigned and calm. The Buddha gave Ānanda another directive: there were four places in the world worthy of veneration, which would inspire a faithful follower—the birthplace of the Buddha (near Kapilavatthu), the place of enlightenment (near Uruvela), the place where he taught the Law for the first time (near Benares) and the place of final Nibbāna (near Kusināra). (It is noteworthy that each of these places is in the forest and near a city, but never inside one.) All those who would travel to visit these shrines with confident hearts would attain a heavenly rebirth.

Seemingly out of context, Ānanda asked the question, already narrated, how one should act towards women. Following that, he asked how to deal with the body of the Blessed One. That was a matter for lay people, the Buddha replied; the monks should be concerned with striving for their own deliverance. Then Ānanda wanted to know how the lay people should carry out the funeral ceremony. The Buddha gave detailed instructions about the cremation and the erection of a stupa.[50] There were four beings worthy of a stupa: a perfect Buddha; an enlightened one who does not teach (*pacceka-buddha*); a disciple who is an *arahant*—fully enlightened;

50. Stupa: a reliquary monument used before the Buddha's days and akin to barrows and tumuli in western countries. The remains of the famous would be set in a central place and a great mound raised over them. In India this was surmounted in the case of kings with a parasol. This is the origin of the innumerable stupas, cetiyas, dagobas, and pagodas found now in Buddhist lands, all of which have some precious articles interred there. Not all, of course, hold Buddha relics.

and a universal monarch.[51] He who worships there would also attain good results.

Then Ānanda, overpowered by grief, went aside, clasped the door jamb and wept. He knew he still had to battle and conquer, and the Master, who had compassion for him, would soon be no more. What remained as the fruit of his twenty-five years of service? This famous scene is often depicted in Buddhist art and is reminiscent of the weeping Christians beneath the cross.

When the Buddha did not see Ānanda near him and inquired where he was, he had him summoned and said to him: "Do not sorrow. Have I not told you many times that everything changes and vanishes? How could something that came to being and was formed not be destroyed? For a long time, Ānanda, you have attended the Perfect One, gladly, sensitively, sincerely and without reserve, with bodily acts of loving-kindness, as well as with speech and thoughts. You have made great merit, Ānanda; keep on endeavouring and soon you will be free from all taints."

Following this, he told him an incident of long ago, in which Ānanda already served him and made much worldly merit (J 307).

After the Awakened One had foretold a second time that Ānanda would soon attain arahantship, he turned to the monks and once more proclaimed the praise of Ānanda: all the Buddhas of the past had had such excellent attendants and all Buddhas of the future would have them too. His skill in dealing with people was admirable. Each assembly of monks who were taught by Ānanda were always overjoyed, and everyone wanted to listen to him further. Ānanda had such remarkable, extraordinary popularity, as one otherwise only finds in a universal monarch. Here too, as so often in the texts, one can find the two ways he addressed Ānanda: on the one hand, great praise for him and a summons to the monks to appreciate his greatness; on the other hand, however, always the reminder to overcome the last defilements.

After this praise, Ānanda turned the conversation to another topic. He suggested that it might be better if the Buddha did not die here in the backwoods, but in one of the great capitals, such

51. Universal monarch (*cakkavatti-rāja*): The ideal world ruler of Buddhist texts. He gains power by Dhamma and not by greed and so differs from most who are in authority.

as Sāvatthī, Rājagaha, Kosambi, or Benares. It is noteworthy, that he did not propose the Buddha's hometown of Kapilavatthu. It would have been the most appropriate with respect to distance as well as suitability. But Kapilavatthu had been ransacked and almost destroyed recently by the son of King Pasenadi. So Ānanda did not mention it, just as he did not mention Vesāli, because the Buddha had said that he would not return there. Ānanda thought that the funeral ceremony could be performed better in one of the large cities by the lay followers living there. But the Buddha, lying on his deathbed, explained to him in great detail, why Kusinārā was not an unimportant place at all.

The Buddha had lived there a long time ago as the universal monarch Mahā-Sudassana, and he had left his body there no less than six times as the universal monarch; this was the seventh and last time. The splendour and magnificence of that kingdom had been destroyed, had disappeared and vanished. This, indeed, was enough to make one weary of all conditioned things as one of the most famous stanzas of the Dhamma taught:

> Conditions truly they are transient.
> Their nature is to arise and cease,
> Having arisen, then they pass away,
> Their calming and cessation is true bliss.
>
> Th 1159[52]

The Buddha's discourse about Mahā-Sudassana was the last great teaching he gave. Subsequently he let Ānanda summon the Mallas of Kusinārā, so that they could bid farewell to him. At that time, a wanderer called Subhadda was in Kusinārā and heard about the forthcoming final Nibbāna of the Buddha. He thought that it was rare that a Buddha appeared in the world; therefore it would be well if he could have a doubt resolved by him, before it was too late. He begged Ānanda to let him approach the Buddha. Ānanda refused him, saying that the Master should not be troubled any more. Ānanda refused permission three times out of love for his master. But the Buddha told Ānanda to let the wanderer approach him, because he wanted to inquire for the sake of knowledge and

---

52. These verses are also found in DN 16 (IV); DN 17; SN 15:20; SN 1:11; SN 6:15; SN 9:6; and J 307.

not to cause trouble. Subhadda then asked him a question about which teaching was actually correct, as some of the teachers of different sects contradicted each other. The Buddha replied that he would rather teach him the Dhamma: wherever one follows the Noble Eightfold Path, there one can find the true holy life, there the four fruits of the homeless life would be found. If monks live in the right way, then the world will never be devoid of arahants, or true saints. Over fifty years he has been a monk and had expounded the Dhamma—and apart from adherence to Dhamma there could be no holy life.

This short discourse was sufficient for Subhadda, just as it had been for Pukkusa, to realize the Dhamma in its manifold aspects, and to go for refuge to the Buddha and ask for admission into the order of monks. The Buddha remarked about the rule, according to which wanderers of other sects had to be put on probation for four months. Subhadda agreed readily, he even wanted to be put on probation for four years. Thereupon the Buddha accepted him immediately, making a last exception, and this very last monk disciple of the Buddha soon became an *arahant*.

The sixth and last chapter of the sutta begins with the final instructions of the Buddha. First of all the monks should never think, after his death, that they now did not have a teacher, because now the Dhamma and Vinaya would be their teacher. To this day, the word of the Buddha laid down in the texts is decisive for the followers of his teaching. Second, after his death the monks should no longer address each other indiscriminately as "friend."[53] The senior monks, senior in years in the Order, could address the junior ones as "friend" or with their names, while the junior ones should use "Venerable Sir."[54] This rule also served as an affirmation of the tradition in which the senior monks set an example, and should be honoured just as they had previously honoured the Buddha. This is the way of reverence according to seniority in the Order and does not depend on any qualities that monks or nuns may have.

The third instruction gave the monks permission to abolish the lesser and minor rules and all that they entailed, according to their own judgment. After his death some details would be difficult

53. Friend: Pali *āvuso*, lit. "One of long life," a more respectful word for friend.
54. Venerable Sir: Pali *bhante*, lit. "One who is auspicious."

to understand and might be considered petty. As a guarantee that at least the main rules would be followed, the assembly of monks may decree that minor rules would no longer be binding. Whoever wanted to could keep them, but there would be no compulsion any more. The fourth and last instruction was to impose the higher penalty on the monk Channa. Ānanda asked how that was to be understood. The Buddha explained that Channa was not to be spoken to, or advised, or instructed, no matter what he did.

After these primarily external instructions which Ānanda was to fulfil, the Buddha once more turned to the whole assembly of monks and asked them whether they had any doubt or problem concerning actions or teachings of the Enlightened One, the content and meaning of the Dhamma, the order of monks and, above all, about the Path or the way of practice. Those were the four important points for questions. They should consider them, so that they would not regret it later when the voice of the Teacher had been silenced. But upon being asked three times, the group did not respond.

Thereupon Ānanda said it was amazing that not even one monk had any doubts. The Buddha corrected him once again: you, Ānanda, speak from faith. Only the *Tathāgata* could know for sure that really no one had any doubts. Ānanda, the least one of these five-hundred monks is a stream-winner, incapable of doubt, because the absence of doubt is one of the signs of this attainment. Only with such total knowledge could one speak in this manner. The Buddha showed in this way the difference between Ānanda's confidence and his own, the Perfect One's, insight.

And once more the Master turned to the assembly of monks to give them his final words of farewell. "Now, monks, I declare this to you: it is the nature of all formed things to dissolve. Strive with diligence!"

After the Exalted One had spoken these last words, he entered into the four jhānas and the formless spheres of meditation absorption, until he attained the stage of cessation of perception and feeling. He thus went once more through the whole sequence of meditation states up to that of cessation. While the Master was reclining on the couch and going through the jhānas, Ānanda said to his brother Anuruddha: "The Exalted One has attained final Nibbāna, Venerable Sir." He no longer addressed him as "friend," but as a senior monk, although both had been ordained on the same day. Anuruddha, however, had the divine eye and corrected him: the Buddha was absorbed in the state of "cessation," but had not yet passed away. To recognize this last subtle difference of a state of mind was only possible for an *arahant*, who was—like Anuruddha—skilled in clairvoyance. Subsequently the Buddha entered the nine stages of concentration in reverse order, back to the first *jhāna*. Then he attained again to the four jhānas, and during his absorption in the fourth *jhāna* his body died.

As soon as his body ceased to live, an earthquake and thunder occurred, just as he had predicted. The Brahma Sahampati, who had induced the Buddha to teach and who himself was a non-returner, spoke a stanza, which pointed to the impermanence of even a Buddha's body. The king of the gods, Sakka, also spoke a stanza. He who was also a stream-winner, recited once more the famous lines which the Buddha had proclaimed during his own discourse: Conditions, truly they are transient. As a third, Anuruddha gave voice to two verses: Peaceful had been the death of the Master, without mortal pangs, gentle like a lamp he was extinguished. But Ānanda lamented:

> Then was there terror, and the hair stood up, when he,
> The all-accomplished one, the Buddha, passed away.
>
> Th 1046

And all those of the five-hundred monks who had not yet attained full liberation from passions, lamented like Ānanda. Anuruddha, however, consoled them all. He pointed to the immutable law of impermanence and turned their attention to the presence of invisible deities, amongst whom there were also those who lamented and those who were free of passions, fully enlightened.

Anuruddha passed the rest of the night talking to his brother about the Dhamma. In the forty-three years of their lives as homeless ones, not a single conversation about the Dhamma seems to have taken place between these two very dissimilar brothers. But now Anuruddha devoted himself to his brother who was in need of consolation. Towards morning, Anuruddha asked him to take the message of the final Nibbāna of the Buddha to the Mallas. Out of the circle of close disciples, Anuruddha seems to have naturally taken over the role of the one who gives the directives. And Ānanda went to the town and informed the Mallas.

Thereupon the Mallas gathered all the requisites for a great funeral ceremony, such as flowers and incense, and went in a procession to the *sāla*-tree forest. There they paid homage to the body of the Buddha with festive dance, singing, and music, with banners and flags, with flowers and incense, until the seventh day. One may wonder why they thought of festivities at such a time. But why should they grieve? That would change nothing. They showed respect and veneration for the Master with their dancing and singing. They exulted that a Buddha had appeared in the world, that they had heard more or less of his Dhamma, that he had wandered through India for such a long time teaching the multitudes, and that he had founded the Saṅgha to preserve the Dhamma.

On the seventh day they erected a pyre for the cremation. At this time, Mahā-Kassapa, who had not been with the Buddha during his last days, was on his way to Kusināra with a group of monks. He met a naked wanderer on the road and asked him about the Master. The wanderer replied that he had attained final Nibbāna seven days before. Then the monks in his company who had not become holy ones yet, grieved and lamented. One of the monks present, however, declared that it was a good thing that the stern ascetic had died, because now one could do again what one pleased. So soon the voice of the world, the voice of craving, had made itself heard. This monk, whose name was Subhadda, just as the last disciple of the Buddha was called, expressed what ignoble beings feel towards a Buddha: he is a troublesome reproach for them, a disturber of their superficial ways.

When the Mallas wanted to light the funeral pyre, they were unable to do so. Anuruddha said that the deities were preventing them, because they wanted to wait for the arrival of the venerable Kassapa. The venerable Kassapa soon arrived and, together with his company of monks, he circumambulated the corpse as a last mark of respect towards the "Giver of the Deathless."[55] Then the funeral pyre ignited itself. The corpse burned until only the bones remained; no ashes were to be seen.

55. Giver of the Deathless: an epithet of the Buddha.

When the neighbouring clans heard the news of the Master's death, they all sent messengers to ask for relics so that they could erect stupas for them. However, the Mallas requested the relics for themselves, because the Buddha had died on their land. Only when a Brahman urged them not to argue about the relics of the greatest peace-maker, and suggested that they divide everything unto eight parts did they relent. So it came about that the bones of the Buddha were divided into eight parts. The Brahman asked for the urn, and another clan received the ashes of the coals. In this way ten stupas were erected as memorials.

10. After the Death of the Buddha

Ānanda said in verse about himself:

> The friend[56] has passed away,
> The Master, too, has gone.
> There is no friendship now that equals this:
> The mindfulness directed to the body.
> The old ones now have passed away,
> The new ones do no please me much,[57]
> Today alone I meditate
> Like a bird gone to its nest.

Th 17.3 (vv. 1035–36)

After the funeral ceremonies were over, Ānanda saw only one duty left to him, namely to attain total liberation as prophesied to him by the Buddha. Kassapa advised him to live in the forest in the province of the Kosala, which was near the Mallas and the Sakyans. When it became known that the Buddha's cousin was living in solitude in the forest nearby, he was inundated with visitors. The lay disciples wanted to be consoled about the death of the Buddha and also about the death of Sāriputta and Moggallāna, as well as the death of their just and beloved King Pasenadi. All

---

56. The venerable Sāriputta.

57. "The old ones" means not only the Buddha but also such eminent disciples as Sāriputta and Moggallāna. Some of the newer disciples of the Buddha who were not yet *ariya* (noble ones) and may have caused some trouble in the Saṅgha were doubtless "the new ones."

four had died within the year. Day and night, in the village and in the forest, Ānanda had to console the lay disciples and was never alone. Thereupon a deity who lived in the forest appeared to him. He was concerned about Ānanda's spiritual progress and advised him as follows:

> Now that you're sat at the foot of a tree
> And in your heart, Nibbāna you've placed,
> Meditate, Gotama, do not be negligent,
> What has this hurly-burly to do with you?

SN 9:5

The venerable Ānanda, exhorted by the deity, was stirred again to a sense of urgency.

In the meantime the venerable Mahā-Kassapa had decided to call a council of monks together to strengthen the Teaching and the Discipline. Because of unsafe conditions in the country of Kosala, the council was to take place in Rājagaha under the protection of King Ajātasattu. All living arahants, almost five hundred, were to take part and, in addition, Ānanda, the only one who was not an *arahant*. Ānanda knew most of the discourses of the Buddha and therefore was indispensable to the council.

When the date set for the council came closer, Anuruddha suggested that his brother Ānanda should only be admitted if he had overcome the last taints and had become an *arahant*. He knew the power of such an incentive. When Ānanda heard this, he decided to employ every bit of strength and ability he possessed to realize Nibbāna. He practised the four foundations of mindfulness, a way which came most natural to him according to his tendencies. In the early hours of the morning, when he wanted to rest after his exertion, he knew without a doubt that he had attained release from all passions. The next day the council began. A place had been kept for him. Ānanda appeared through the air by supernatural power and sat down at his place. When Anuruddha and Kassapa became aware that he had become an *arahant*, they expressed their brotherly joy with him and opened the council, which took place during the rains retreat. Other monks could not come to Rājagaha at this time.

During the council, Kassapa questioned the Keeper of the Discipline, Upāli, about each rule and its origin, so that the Vinaya was laid down first. The next item on the agenda was the Doctrine. Kassapa asked Ānanda first about the longest discourses, then about the middle-length discourses, and then the other collections.[58]

After the recitation of the Dhamma and Discipline, Ānanda mentioned those matters which the Buddha had left as a legacy with him to settle. He told the assembly that the Master had allowed the lesser rules to be abolished. The holy monks could not agree what was meant by "lesser rules." Thereupon Kassapa suggested: the lay people would say that the monks had become slothful after the death of the Master if now they abolished rules. Since it was not known which rules were meant, it would be best not to abolish any of them. In that case, one would be sure not to act against the Master's wishes. And so it was done.

The elder monks then said that it had been a breach of the training rules that Ānanda had not asked which rules were meant, and he should confess this as a wrongdoing. Second, he was accused of having sewn a robe for the Exalted One, after having stepped on it. He replied that nothing had been further from his mind than disrespect for the Blessed One. Nevertheless, if the venerable ones considered it a wrongdoing, he would acknowledge it as such. Third, he was criticized for the fact that he had allowed women to salute the remains of the Blessed One first. He replied that at the time of the funeral arrangements, he had thought it would not be an unsuitable time for them (that is, too late) and therefore he had allowed them to pay their homage first. But here too he would accept their verdict. The fourth accusation which the monks levelled at Ānanda, referred to the time when he had neglected to beg the Blessed One to remain for an aeon. Ānanda defended himself by saying he had been possessed by Māra at the time, and therefore had not been responsible for his actions—how could he have otherwise failed to make this request? Ānanda's behaviour in the face of these accusations was exemplary: he submitted to the judgment of the other holy ones, although he, himself, could not see any wrongdoing, a fact which he did not fail to mention.

Ānanda then reported the second instruction which the Buddha had given immediately before his death, namely imposing

58. It is probable that the actual order of the discourses within the various collections was also standardized at this council.

the higher penalty on the monk Channa. The present assembly requested Ānanda to present this decision to Channa himself. Ānanda objected, saying that Channa was a violent and unruly person. The assembly advised him to take a number of monks along. Leading a large group he journeyed to Kosambi where Channa was living, and informed him of the last will of the Buddha, namely that he had been declared dead in the Order.

This penalty had been explained by the Buddha to the horse trainer Kesi. He would use it against monks who could not be changed to wholesomeness either through admonition or discipline. Whoever could not be trained in this way would be considered as dead in the Order: he would not be spoken to, whatever he did. When Channa heard this, he became so horrified that he lost consciousness. When he regained his sense, he was deeply ashamed that the Master had proclaimed this penalty against him as his last instruction given to the Order. This gave him the impetus to put forth his most strenuous effort; within a short time he became an *arahant.* So this penalty showed itself to be the Buddha's last act of compassion for the benefit and happiness of the monk Channa, being effective even after the Buddha's death. When Channa had become a holy one, he went to Ānanda and begged him for a repeal of the penalty. Ānanda replied that as soon as he had attained release from the passions, the penalty was no longer operative in any case.

After the death of the Buddha, the venerable Mahā-Kassapa, as the most respected disciple, had taken over the guidance of the Order. He had however not the status of being a "refuge" as the Buddha had been, nor was he his deputy. He was simply the foremost of the monks with the ten higher qualities.[59] He was, so to say, the symbol for the observance of Dhamma and Discipline.

Everyone turned to him for all questions regarding the Order. In this way he became the Elder of the Saṅgha. After him, Ānanda

59. Ten higher qualities: virtue and restraint as according to the Vinaya—perfection in conduct; much learning, and remembering well; contentment with robes, almsfood, and shelter; ability to attain at will the four jhānas; supernormal abilities with the body as far as the heavenly realms; divine ear; seeing into the mind of other beings; recollection of past lives; divine eye; and exhaustion of the taints.

became the second leading elder, the second most venerated holy one, who was designated to look after the Order. After he had already been a monk for over forty years, he survived the Buddha for another forty. And after having been the personal attendant of the Buddha for twenty-five years, he became the foremost of the holy ones for a similar length of time. At the time of the second council (another assembly of arahants), one hundred years after the final Nibbāna of the Buddha, a personal disciple of Ānanda was still alive. He was a very old monk by name of Sabbakāmi, who—it was said—had been in the Order for one hundred and twenty years (Cv XII).

When Ānanda reached one hundred and twenty years, he felt that his death was near. He went from Rājagaha on a journey to Vesāli, just as his master had done. When the king of Magadha and the princes of Vesāli heard that Ānanda would soon die, they hurried to him from both directions to bid him farewell. In order to do justice to both sides, Ānanda chose a way to die in keeping with his gentle nature: he raised himself into the air through his supernormal powers and let his body be consumed by the fire element. The relics were divided and stupas erected.

The virtuous, wise man,
The hero strong and ever resolute,
The guardian of the word so true,
Ānanda found extinction now.

Th 1049

Buddhism and Christianity: A Positive Approach

(With some notes on Judaism)

by

M. O' C. Walshe

WHEEL PUBLICATION NO. 275/276

Author's Note

This essay, like previous ones by me on *Buddhism and Sex*, and *Buddhism and Death,* simply reflects my personal attempt to find, as a Buddhist, some honest answers to certain problems and questions. In trying to answer these questions for myself, it may be that I can be of some assistance to others who seek to do the same. I am by no means unaware of the magnitude of the task here undertaken, even in this brief outline form, nor of my presumption in undertaking it. Still, it may be of some use, at least as a starting point. I have called this 'a positive approach' because that, I am convinced, is what is needed: an un-polemical approach based on love, respect, and as much understanding as possible, with a willingness to accept as well as offer friendly criticism.

To explain my own approach to Christianity and my qualifications, such as they are, for writing this, it may be as well to state the following. Though of mainly Irish descent, I was not brought up as a Roman Catholic (or any kind of Christian): in fact, like many non-Catholic Irish I grew up (in England) with a certain anti-Catholic bias which it took me long to overcome. At school I attended Church of England chapel services and received a grounding in basic Anglican doctrine of a somewhat conventional nature, for which, however, I am grateful. My subsequent studies have led me into some of the byways of medieval scholasticism among other obscure matters, and have also helped me to realize that things are not always what they seem.

My qualifications for discussing Judaism are even more tenuous, but since some acquaintance with this ancient faith is essential to an understanding of the origins of Christianity, I have done my best. A book I have found very helpful here is *The Authentic New Testament* by Hugh J. Schonfield (London 1955), a rendering by a Jewish scholar which might usefully be consulted side by side with the *Authorized Version* and/or the *New English Bible.* In quoting from the New Testament I have made *ad hoc* renderings based on these three versions, with occasional reference to the Greek.

Finally, and importantly, I sincerely hope that nothing written here will strike any Christian or Jewish reader as either offensive or seriously inaccurate. In any case it is not my purpose to offer a critique of Christian ideas. Modern Christians are no less critical than I am of certain traditional views.

M. O' C. W.

To my Christian and Jewish friends.

Buddhism and Christianity: A Positive Approach

1. The Problem

Most Western Buddhists have some kind of Christian background even if they may themselves never have been professing Christians. Many Eastern Buddhists too may feel the need to have some understanding of the tenets and outlook of Christianity. The typical Western Buddhist (if there is such a creature) is probably someone who has felt the need for an acceptable religion but who, for whatever reason, feels dissatisfied with what Christianity offers, or appears to offer. Such a person's attitude towards Christianity may range from wistful rejection through indifference to a degree, even of actual hostility, and is probably often enough not based on any very firm foundation of knowledge.

Hostility towards Christianity (or any other religion) is not, of course, a proper Buddhist attitude. Those who are aware of such feelings in themselves should seek to discover their roots and thus come to terms with them. Some suggestions about this will be given below. Ignorance is very understandable especially since 'Christianity' is a label that covers many things and a great diversity of attitudes, sometimes mutually contradictory. But in approaching any religion the only fair way to judge it (if we must pass judgement at all) is by considering its best and not its worst manifestations. Intolerance is fairly rare among Buddhists (though not quite unknown), but unfortunately it used to be the besetting sin, indeed the official attitude, of many Christians. All that has changed greatly in recent years. Christians and Buddhists today can and often do meet one another with mutual respect and that brotherly love that both are enjoined to practice, agreeing to differ without acrimony, and perhaps each learning something of value from the other.

Most people would probably agree that the two greatest teachers mankind has ever known were Gotama the Buddha and Jesus of Nazareth (or the Christ). Their teachings, as transmitted, have much in common as well as some significant differences. We shall seek to explore both the differences and the common features, trying as far as possible to avoid being trapped by mere words or entangled in the 'jungle of views.' For example, it is sometimes said that Buddhism is not a religion because it is not theistic, and so conflicts with some dictionary definitions of 'religion.' But this merely shows that dictionary-makers are ignorant and fallible like the rest of us, and bound by the concepts of their own culture. Religion is the quest of the Transcendental which, by definition, cannot be defined. Buddhists consider that for that very reason it cannot have the personal qualities of 'God.' Christians disagree, but still insist that man cannot comprehend the nature of God. As the Athanasian Creed helpfully puts it, regarding the Trinity: 'Not three Incomprehensibles but one Incomprehensible.'

Christianity and Buddhism can both be termed 'religions of salvation,' even if the expression sounds more Christian than Buddhist. In both, there is a supreme goal to be attained, which in Christian terms is sometimes called 'the peace of God which passeth understanding.' Buddhists would omit the words 'of God,' but the rest is perhaps as good a phrase as we can find to describe, or rather designate, Nirvāna. It may be suggested that the fundamental basis of all religions worthy of the name can be found in the famous statement on Nirvāna found in the Udāna:

> There is, monks, an Unborn, Unbecome, Unmade, Uncompounded. If there were not this Unborn, Unbecome, Unmade, Uncompounded, then there would be no deliverance here visible from that which is born, become, made, compounded. But since there *is* this Unborn, Unbecome, Unmade, Uncompounded, therefore a deliverance is visible from that which is born, become, made, compounded.

For most people this is a matter of faith—or scepticism. But there are those for whom it is a fact of experience. Christians would find this statement perfectly acceptable as far as it goes, though they would add certain things to it, most of which would not be acceptable to Buddhists. Still, both would agree that this mysterious, indeed incomprehensible 'Unborn' (to use the Buddhist term) is the guarantee of deliverance. *How* this deliverance can come about is another matter concerning which, indeed, Christians differ among themselves. But in considering—and not minimizing—the differences between Buddhism and Christianity, we should never lose sight of this fundamental agreement at a very deep level—so deep indeed that it can all too easily be overlooked or denied. We can express this agreement schematically thus:

Unborn

Buddhist Nirvāna (impersonal)	Christian God (personal)

Thus, without arguing about who is right, we can say that the terms 'Nirvāna' and 'God' both refer to the Unborn which, being incomprehensible to the ordinary mind, is differently interpreted. It may be objected that the two terms 'Nirvāna' and 'God' are not strictly parallel, since Nirvāna corresponds not so much to God as such, but to the 'peace of God.' However, consideration of at least some types of Christian mysticism may suggest that this is possibly 'a distinction without a difference.'

We should realize, too, that when theistic believers speak of God they may have many different concepts in mind. Thus when Jews and Christians refer to God they certainly mean, in one sense, the same God, yet differently conceived, since the Jewish concept of God's unity excludes (in the Jewish view at least) the Christian Concept of the Trinity. We can also find, especially among modern theologians, a bewildering variety of Christian conceptions of the nature of God, but all have the same ultimate reference. Clearly, to the ordinary way of thinking, not all of these different ideas can be right (though they *could* all be wrong, and must necessarily be inadequate). And yet, as the great Cardinal Cusanus (1401–64) declared, God is 'the coincidence of opposites' wherein all differences are reconciled, and the Hwa Yen (in Japanese Kegon) school of Buddhism seems to teach something very similar, though of course without the theistic reference. Whether or not we think we understand this idea, it may be as well, as we proceed, to bear some such thought in mind.

2. What is Christianity? The Jewish Background

To attempt to 'define' Christianity in all its variety would be a hopeless task. As a short cut, let us take the Apostles' creed, which is familiar to Roman Catholics and Anglicans alike:

> I believe in God the Father Almighty, Maker of heaven and earth, and in Jesus Christ, His only Son our Lord, who was conceived by the Holy Ghost, born of the Virgin Mary, suffered under Pontius Pilate, was crucified, dead and buried. He descended into hell, on the third day rose again from the dead. He ascended into heaven, and sitteth on the right hand of God, the Father Almighty, and thence He shall come again to judge the quick and the dead. I believe in the Holy Ghost, the Holy Catholic Church, the communion of saints, the forgiveness of sins, the resurrection of the body, and the life everlasting. Amen.

This is not of course found in the Bible: it is in the *Book of Common Prayer*, and is recited almost daily by Anglicans throughout the year. As the *Oxford Dictionary of the Christian Church* says, 'it is terse in expression, and lacks theological explanations.' It lacks more than these: it omits all reference to the earthly life and ministry of Jesus. It is the frame without the picture. And it is, too, a highly 'supernatural' or, if we prefer, 'mythical' framework. Very many Christians today would probably defend its retention in the Prayer Book purely on the grounds of tradition, accepting its validity as a genuine statement of their personal belief only with great reservations or qualifications. In any case, it certainly does 'lack theological explanations,' even the very basic one of why the Son of God was born on earth and crucified.

The traditional explanation of this central tenet of Christianity is to be sought in the story of the *Fall of Man*, which is told in 'mythical' form in Genesis, the first book of the Bible. Adam and Eve, our first ancestors, tempted by the serpent (later equated with Satan, or the devil), disobeyed God by eating from the Tree of Knowledge and thus lost the pristine innocence. They were expelled from the Earthly Paradise (the Garden of Eden) and deprived of the eternal life with God which should have been their due. Thus sin and evil came into the world and all men inheriting 'original sin' from their first parents fell into the devil's power and at death all went to hell. Originally the 'eternal life' meant for Adam and Eve may really have been everlasting existence in the Earthly Paradise, and the 'hell' to which they went was not a place of fiery torment, but *Sheol*, 'the pit'—the dismal abode of shades which Jews and Babylonians alike expected as the universal post-mortem lot of all, whether good, bad or indifferent. At any rate, by 'man's first disobedience,' God's original plan was frustrated, and redemption only became possible—in the Christian view—by God's Son taking on human nature and, by the sacrifice on the Cross, vicariously redeeming sinful mankind.

In the Jewish scriptures (the 'Old Testament') the conception of God develops from that of a tribal deity to a universal and omnipotent ruler, the Jews being his chosen people. Thus the Jews developed, for perhaps the first time in history, a true system of monotheism. We find references to a coming saviour or deliverer who is called the Messiah ('the Anointed One'), though opinions differed as to whether the new kingdom he was to establish was to be an earthly or a spiritual one. In any case the Messiah was later interpreted by Christians as the Christ (Greek *Christos*, meaning 'anointed,' being the translation of the Hebrew word). Under Persian influence, Jewish belief about life after death underwent a revolution. God (Yahweh or Jehovah) was opposed by an evil principle of great, indeed almost equal power, which was finally identified with the fallen angel Lucifer (the devil of Christianity). Notions of a final judgement, with a heavenly reward for the virtuous, and hellish punishment for the wicked, evolved. This view, held by the Pharisees, was largely carried over into early Christianity, though the Sadducees denied the existence of an afterlife. There are also slight but definite indications of a belief in some form of reincarnation held in some quarters. The story of Christ's mission and death, and subsequent resurrection, is told in the New Testament. In the Christian view, Christ is the earthly manifestation of the second person of the Holy Trinity (Father, Son and Holy Ghost or Holy Spirit). Whatever many modern Christians, including theologians, may say today, the Apostles' Creed does represent in outline some of the most important things, that most orthodox Christians have believed implicitly, and literally, since very early times. (Many still do.) If we regard it as 'myth' rather than literal fact, we should remember that myths generally conceal profound truths, and therefore deserve to be treated with profound respect.

3. Who Was Jesus?

Central to any consideration of Christianity is the personality of the human Jesus—whoever we may think he really was. For some, his very existence is doubted. They are not likely to be right. But the important thing is this: even supposing for the sake of argument that the man called Jesus, who may or may not have been the Son of God, did not deliver the Sermon on the Mount, somebody did—and that somebody was a very great teacher. There are discrepancies and problems in the gospel narratives about the life of Jesus, but these are really only of secondary importance. We may assume the following: Jesus was born in Palestine a few years before the traditional date, i.e. not later than 4 B.C. The country was under Roman domination but with a native ruler, Herod (37–4 B.C.). It was a time of great unrest and strife, which was destined to end with the destruction of Jerusalem and its great temple in 70 C.E.

This led to the dispersal of the Jewish people, and in fact Jerusalem would not again be in Jewish hands until 1948. The leaders of Jewish society were the Pharisees (who accepted the 'new' Messianic ideas and insisted, not always hypocritically, on purity of life and strict observance of the ritual laws), and their rivals, the influential Sadducees (who rejected such 'new-fangled' notions as an afterlife). In addition there were the ascetic Essenes and various hot-headed nationalist groups such as the Zealots.

Jesus was brought up in Galilee, north of Judea, a region where Messianic hopes ran high, though the Messiah was generally thought of as a military leader who would drive the Romans out and establish an earthly kingdom. We know nothing definite about the life of Jesus prior to the last two or three years before his crucifixion (ca. 30–33 C.E.), though we hear of his being taken to the Temple at Jerusalem (the great national cult-centre) at the age of twelve. The only writings he is likely to have known were the Jewish scriptures, and he probably taught on the Sabbath (Saturday) in his local synagogue or meeting-place at Nazareth before his public career began. It seems that the conviction gradually coalesced in Jesus that he was the coming Messiah, but that this Messiahship was of a spiritual, not a secular and military nature—and this was to lead to much misunderstanding among his friends and foes alike.

His emergence was preceded by the appearance in the Jordan valley of a strange ascetic figure whom some took to be a reincarnation of the prophet Elijah. (This is but one indication that a belief in some sort of reincarnation was not entirely unknown in contemporary Palestine.) This was John the Baptist, perhaps a member of the Essene sect. He proclaimed the coming kingdom of God and called upon the people to repent and wash away their sins in the Jordan. Jesus submitted to baptism by immersion and thereupon had an experience, variously described in the different gospel versions, which finally convinced him and John, that he was indeed the Messiah, as prophesied in the form of the 'suffering Servant of God' in the book of Isaiah.

Immediately after this experience, Jesus withdrew for a period into the desert, where we are told he was subjected to various temptations by Satan. There is considerable general similarity here to the story of how *Māra* tempted the newly enlightened Buddha. At the end of forty days Jesus emerged from the wilderness strengthened in this conviction of his calling, and began his independent ministry. John was shortly afterwards arrested and decapitated. Meanwhile Jesus gathered a group of disciples around him, traditionally twelve in number. They included Matthew the tax-gatherer, the traditional author of the first of the four gospels, the brothers Simon (later called Peter) and Andrew, who were fishermen in the Sea of Galilee, and their associates, James and John, the latter of whom is credited with writing the fourth gospel, which differs markedly from the other three. Among the twelve was also Judas Iscariot, who later betrayed Jesus, and whom Buddhists will compare with Devadatta, though the latter's machinations against the Buddha were less successful.

As Jesus went about from place to place teaching with his disciples, he also healed the sick. We need not today be surprised or sceptical about these so-called miracles, since there are people today with healing powers, and there is no reason to doubt that Jesus had such a gift, quite irrespective of our views about his divinity. Nor shall we quibble here at the use of the traditional word 'miracle,' which after all simply means something wonderful. His most famous sermon is that known as the Sermon on the Mount, which contains the Beatitudes (beginning with 'Blessed are the poor in spirit, for theirs is the kingdom of heaven.') and also the injunction to 'Love your enemies, bless those that curse you, do good to those that hate you, and pray for those who treat you spitefully and persecute you.'

To the Pharisees he said, 'The kingdom of heaven is within you' (Luke 17:21). This saying has been variously interpreted and translated. The Greek words *entos humōn* can also mean among 'you,' but the rendering 'within you' (as in the Authorized Version) is surely right. The Pharisees did not know that the kingdom was to be found within, just as in the well-known Zen *kōan* the dog said 'Wu!' ('no' in Chinese), not knowing that he had the Buddha nature. The Pharisees, of course, expected the coming of a material kingdom. In fairness, it should be stated, however, that there is evidence that some Pharisees at least were better than their biblical reputation.

It is not surprising that Jesus was hated by the establishment. The Pharisees even banded together with their deadly rivals, the Sadducees, to trap him. He was regarded as a dangerous subversive, the more so because, when eventually he openly claimed to be the Messiah, they took him to be a political rebel against the Romans and their Jewish adherents, as indeed did some of his own followers. The result was inevitable. He was betrayed to the Romans with the connivance of one of his own disciples, Judas Iscariot. However, just before the end there came an episode which cannot be passed over in even the most rapid survey because it was to prove of central importance to almost all Christians: the Last Supper. St. Matthew's Gospel says:

> And as they were eating Jesus took bread, blessed it and broke it, and gave it to the disciples saying: 'Take it and eat. This is my body.' And he took the cup, gave thanks and gave it to them, saying: 'Drink from it, all of you, for this is my blood of the covenant, which is shed for many for the forgiveness of sins [Ex.24:8]. But I tell you, I will not drink henceforth of this fruit of the vine until that day when I drink it new with you in my father's kingdom (Matt. 26:26-29).

On this story is based the sacrament of the Eucharist or Holy Communion, in which according to Roman Catholic belief, the bread and wine, on being consecrated by the priest are actually converted into the body and blood of Christ. Since the Reformation, however, the Protestant view has been that the Communion service is a commemoration of the Last Supper but does not involve such a miraculous transformation of the bread and wine (transubstantiation).

After questioning by the Jewish authorities, Jesus was handed over to the Roman governor, Pilate, who yielded reluctantly to strong pressure and sentenced him to death. The horrid ritual of crucifixion took place. According to St. Luke, Jesus uttered the prayer, 'Father, forgive them, for they know not what they do' (Luke 23:34), but this is not mentioned in the other gospels, and even some manuscripts of Luke omit it. The words are surely genuine, but sadly they seem all too seldom to have been remembered, and in fact narrowly escaped deletion from the record. Jesus died relatively quickly, after a very few hours, and that might have seemed the end of the story.

Instead, it was the beginning. Jesus had said that he would rise again from the dead, and so he did. He made a number of appearances to his disciples over a period, it is said, of forty days. As in the case of the so-called healing 'miracles' we need not doubt that such appearances took place, irrespective of our views about his divinity. They had the effect of heartening his dispirited disciples and confirming their wavering faith. The teacher had died and risen again, and the history of Christianity had begun.

Note on Sacrifices. The Eucharist as established by Jesus is regarded by Roman Catholics as a 'bloodless sacrifice' which re-enacts the sacrifice on the Cross and also replaces the Jewish sacrifices in the Temple. It was only in the Temple at Jerusalem that animal sacrifices were made, not in the synagogues, which were not regarded as 'temples.' Hence with the destruction of the Temple in 70 C.E. the practice of such sacrifices ceased in Judaism, while it was never a feature of Christianity. It also never became a feature of Islam. With the virtual disappearance of such sacrifices in India, largely under Buddhist influence, this unpleasant feature of most ancient religions has become rare in the world today.

4. The Christian Church

If St. Paul was not the 'founder' of the Christian Church, he was at least its principal propagator. Originally a Pharisee and persecutor of Christians, he was converted after a vision of Christ, and thereafter wrote, worked and travelled unceasingly to spread the new faith not only among the Jews, but throughout the Roman world, eventually dying as a martyr in Rome under Nero. The Christians were regarded as an intolerable nuisance by the Romans and frequently persecuted, until finally the emperor Constantine (d. 337) himself adopted Christianity, after which the Christians soon began persecuting others. Rome itself soon became a main centre of Christianity, and the Bishop of Rome (the Pope), being regarded as the successor of St. Peter, became supreme head of the Church in the West, and indeed a kind of 'spiritual heir' to the defunct Roman Empire. Thus to Jewish spirituality and Greek philosophy (which has left very obvious traces in St, John's Gospel), was added the Roman concept of authority, though in the East the Orthodox Church centred at Byzantium (now Istanbul), and several smaller churches, maintained an independent existence. Henceforth, till after 1500, the only 'official' faith in the West was what we today know as Roman Catholicism.

The general dogmatic view of medieval Christianity was largely established by St. Augustine (d. 430), and was elaborated by St. Thomas Aquinas (d. 1274). It assumed that this earth is the centre of the universe, and the course of history began with the Creation (dated by the 17th century English Archbishop, Usher, at 4004 B.C.) and will end with the Last Judgement. The time of the Last Judgement is unknown, though it was widely expected to occur in 1000 C.E. until this was disproved by events. Some main points of doctrine, as still taught in the Roman Catholic Church are:

> Through the disobedience of Adam, the first man, all men became sinful ('Original Sin'), and all went to hell until the redeeming sacrifice of Jesus Christ, the Son of God, on the cross. He had two natures, divine and human. Thus he lived a perfect human life, and suffered and died as a man. Redemption is available to all men through grace and by the sacraments which are administered by the appointed ministers

of the Church, who are specially ordained, acknowledge the authority of the Pope, and are bound to celibacy. Those outside the Church, or dying in mortal sin, go to hell, which is everlasting. Those who have committed venial sins for which full penance has not been done go to Purgatory, a place of temporary punishment, until they are sufficiently purified to enter heaven.

Of these articles, most are a matter of faith concerning which there is no arguing. But the doctrine of everlasting hell is a major stumbling-block for many who might be sympathetic to the rest, and voices have from time to time been raised against this teaching. On the face of it the texts do seem to show that Jesus taught the doctrine of an eternal hell. Modern Catholics, however, often stress that we cannot know if any particular person has been assigned to hell, which may, therefore, be empty.

An essential feature of medieval Christianity is the importance of monasticism. Whether there is a historical link with Eastern monasticism of the Buddhist type is a question we cannot enter into, but it is significant that two different cultures should have developed such an institution, which seems to go so much against the grain of human nature. Those who have grown up against a background of Protestantism often scarcely realize the extent to which monasticism still plays a living role not only in the Roman Catholic but also in the Orthodox Church. The ideal of ascetic self-restraint as a way of purification was a fundamental one in early Christianity, and often led to excesses of self-mortification. But in Western Christendom the wise rule established by St. Benedict (529) was a model for all subsequent monastic orders. Here, despite all theoretical differences, Christian and Buddhist *practice* approached each other closely, though it was the mendicant orders ('friars' not 'monks') founded in the early 13th century by St. Dominic and St. Francis of Assisi that came nearest to the *Bhikkhu Saṅgha.* And something of the same ascetic spirit outside the monastic orders is seen in the rule of celibacy for all clergy in the Roman Catholic Church, and for bishops in the Orthodox Church.

By 1500 the Church had become corrupt and worldly, culminating in the flagrant immorality of the Borgia Pope Alexander VI (1492–1503). All previous attempts at reform had been ruthlessly suppressed, but in 1517 Martin Luther, a learned

German monk, aided by the recent invention of printing, led the successful revolt known to history as the Reformation. Luther rejected Papal authority, taking the Bible as the sole source of revelation. He rejected the doctrine of purgatory, and insisted that faith alone was necessary for salvation. The political interests of many of the princes favoured the Reformation, and soon Europe was divided into Catholics and 'Protestants.' In England Henry VIII suppressed the monasteries and made himself head of the Church. Gradually a church of England developed, combining some 'Catholic' features (such as the continuity of bishops) with the new Protestantism. Finally, with the growth of the empire, the Anglican communion became worldwide (in the U.S.A. it became the Protestant Episcopal Church). Another branch of Protestantism was the one instituted at Geneva by Calvin with its sombre insistence on predestination. But the concept of religious freedom was slow to take root. The Calvinists in particular persecuted those they disapproved of almost as fiercely as the Catholics had done.

Catholics and Protestants alike considered missions to the 'heathen' of great importance. While early attempts to spread the religion of peace and love by fire and sword were eventually abandoned, the effort went on by more peaceful means, especially in those parts of the world colonized by Europeans. The reverse process, with the recent introduction of Buddhism and other 'exotic' faiths into the West, may be seen by some as poetic justice.

5. Facing the Dark Side

Regrettably, there are certain dark sides of traditional Christianity which must be squarely faced. The horrific record of the Inquisition, which extorted confessions from 'heretics' by torture and then condemned them to be burnt alive, is something the Roman Catholic Church in particular has had to live down, and no Catholic today would attempt to defend this tragic chapter in the Church's history. Yet the Church *has* triumphed over that grim aspect of its past, while in the present century we have witnessed equal horrors perpetrated in the name of worse causes. We should waste no time in condemning further that which Christians themselves abhor and condemn as strongly as any outsider can. Let us instead seek to understand, if we can, the causes of such ghastly aberrations, causes that are more specific than the general depravity of human nature. Two such causes may perhaps be fairly adduced: the obsession with martyrdom, and the doctrine of hell. These are, of course, interconnected.

Jesus was crucified, and thereby, according to the traditional teaching, redeemed mankind. Christians were frequently persecuted by the Romans and others, and many, by enduring death in various unpleasant guises, came to be venerated as 'martyrs' (i.e. witnesses to the faith). Their cult sometimes assumed morbid forms. Later, Protestants who had suffered under the old Church were similarly revered and lurid accounts of their sufferings were published, such as Foxe's *Book of Martyrs*, a grisly book once considered good reading for Protestant children.

The idea that a loving and almighty Father should cast any of his children, however depraved, into eternal torment is one that most people find unacceptable today. This doctrine greatly exercised the minds of a number of distinguished Victorians, including W.E. Gladstone and the Rev. C.L. Dodgson, better known as Lewis Carroll. If Jesus really taught this doctrine of eternal punishment, he was more rigid than the Pharisees, who held that the wicked would only be condemned to the fire for twelve months. The problem is a grave one. We know that Jesus' words are often quoted differently in different gospels. In some passages this doctrine is ascribed not to Jesus but to John the Baptist. In fact, it is ascribed unambiguously to Jesus only in the gospels of Matthew and Mark. We are thus perhaps justified in attributing this view to the personal prejudices of some of his reporters, or even to mistranslation, for Jesus spoke in Aramaic and the gospels are in Greek. Nevertheless, the belief in eternal punishment passed into orthodox Christian teaching. In fact with the rejection of belief in purgatory the Protestants were left with the stark opposition of Heaven and Hell.

This, then, is the dark side of traditional Christianity. The preaching of hell-fire provoked a moral revulsion that cannot be overestimated. A God, it can be urged, who sinks so disastrously below the moral values he has himself implanted in man, loses all credibility. It must be admitted that this doctrine, or the hangover from it, accounts for a great deal of the hostility to Christianity shown by many people including, it seems, even some Buddhists. Whatever the excuses, such an emotional attitude of violent rejection needs to be examined with care.

In the first place, such an attitude, however 'justified,' is not and can never be a proper Buddhist reaction. Because Buddhists do not share the Christian God-concept, it has been seriously suggested that to 'curse God' is a useful therapeutic exercise. Few Buddhists are likely to feel the need for such a proceeding, though Victorian atheists delighted in it. They thought of it as a splendid shock—therapy—for other people! But a little reflection might suggest the following: either God does not exist, or he does. If he does not, then to curse an empty concept is rather pointless, while if after all he does exist, then either he is an all-loving Father who will overlook and forgive such childishly insulting behaviour, or he is not. In the first case to curse him would be unfair, and in the second case it might be unwise.

Those who seriously harbour any such thoughts are obviously themselves full of *dosa*, the unhealthy root of hate, which may fix itself on a variety of objects. 'God' is unlikely to be the sole target of their aggression. There are, of course, proper Buddhist procedures for dealing with such unhealthy tendencies in oneself: the practice of mindfulness, and the cultivation of the *brahma-vihāras.* Feelings of anger, like other feelings, should be observed dispassionately and not clung to. There is also the more specific practice of developing loving-kindness (*mettā*) and compassion (*karunā*). Those who hate others really hate themselves, and in the practice of *mettā* we first extend loving-kindness to ourselves and then to others. This is in fact a positive technique for carrying out that difficult Christian (and Jewish) injunction: 'Love thy neighbour as thyself.' Christians and Jews put the love of God before this; Buddhists might reflect that, as we have seen, 'God' can be taken as a kind of shorthand symbol for the Unborn which is the guarantee of liberation, and we can surely, with a clear 'Buddhist conscience' extend our love to *that.* Jesus also said: 'Love your enemies,' a precept which many Christians have found singularly difficult even to remember, let alone practice. Unless our response is rather less inadequate than that of such Christians, we have no right to call ourselves Buddhists. And if we *do* see 'God,' or the God-concept, for whatever reason, as some sort of enemy, then this points to some inadequacy in ourselves which calls for investigation.

Perhaps we can find a reason for a concept we find so abhorrent as the hell-fire doctrine. In the Buddhist scriptures too we find descriptions of quite horrific hell-states which, though not eternal, are said to be fantastically long-lasting. While less offensive as being finite and not the creation of a loving father, these too are, to say the least, difficult to believe literally, even though we may well accept that those who have behaved monstrously in this life may encounter as a *karmic* result some very unpleasant conditions in a future state. Fear of retribution is not the best reason for avoiding wrongdoing, but it remains a valid one if we have any conception of justice, human, divine or *karmic*. And even the best of us may be spurred on to greater efforts by fear of the consequences of failure. Thus many who embraced a life of austerity as Buddhist monks or Christian ascetics may have felt the need to frighten themselves as well as others to avoid backsliding. In this way the tendency arose to exaggerate the awful consequences to be expected by those who fail the test. Actually, the Buddhist doctrine of *karma* and rebirth, or the kindred Hindu teaching, provides a more adequate framework for man's long struggle up the ladder to perfection. Many have found such a notion attractive on the grounds of justice, whether they personally accepted it or not, and though it has been officially frowned on by the Christian churches, there seem always to have been some Christians who gave it their assent, including Giordano Bruno in the 16th century and, in modern times, the distinguished Congregationalist Dr. Leslie Weatherhead (d. 1965). There have even been Roman Catholics who have given credence to the idea, such as the 19th century Italian Archbishop Passavalli.

While it cannot be proved from the Bible that Jesus did not teach the existence of an eternal hell, the evidence that he did so is not conclusive, and many who are not Christians find it hard to impute such a doctrine to him. Buddhists should view with sympathy the efforts of Christians to emancipate themselves from a dogma which for too long has cast a deep shadow on their faith. We can regard this, in the sense of C.G. Jung, as the 'shadow side' of Christianity, and meantime profitably devote our own energies to coping with our own shadow or, as Jesus said, the 'beam' in our own eye.

6. Digging a Bit Deeper

Christianity has left its indelible mark on the whole of Western civilization, and in some measure on the whole of the world today, irrespective of whether people accept its teachings or not. There are dedicated atheists today who take a passionate and informed interest in old churches, and every classical scholar knows that but for the devoted labour of generations of Christian monks, inspired by St. Benedict, the whole body of Latin classical literature would have been irretrievably lost. There is indeed a school of thought, largely of Roman Catholic inspiration, which looks back nostalgically to the Middle Ages as the 'Age of Faith' from which we should seek the solution to many of our modern problems. Though this view is exaggerated, it still betrays a genuine perception of an important, if partial, truth. We should not despise the Middle Ages (roughly 560–1500 C.E). Life in medieval times was brutal and squalid for everybody and not, as today, only for some people. To the modern view it was incredibly inconvenient. Yet in some respects it had a richness we have almost completely lost today, and which we still marvel at. It is no accident that surviving medieval cathedrals everywhere can stand comparison as sheer works of art with any modern secular building that can be named. This is quite simply because they were built 'to the glory of God.' And however dim, fitful and even downright contradictory men's vision of what they called God may have been, its inspiration was sufficient to draw them out of themselves. This graphically illustrates the fact that—directly contrary to some trendy theories—the real inspiration of art is at least in a broad sense fundamentally religious. Indeed the very word 'inspiration' implies the idea of a 'breathing into' the artist, whether by the Holy Spirit or by, for instance, Apollo and the Muses. The relation and the parallel between the arts and religion is a matter we shall have to consider briefly later.

Jesus said: 'Man does not live by bread alone.' This fact was realized in the Middle Ages when physical bread was hard-earned and only too liable to fail altogether; after all, a real effort *was* made by the Church—however inadequately sometimes in practice—to provide that spiritual nutriment (out of 'super-substantial bread' as St. Matthew's gospel has it in the Latin version) that was rightly deemed essential. For this reason it is probable that some medieval people, though physically perhaps half-starved, may have still felt more satisfied than their modern descendants who possibly suffer not from too few but from too many 'square meals,' but whose religious sense has atrophied.

The decline in the religious sense can be traced back, with some accuracy, to the period which followed the (inevitable and necessary) break-up of the medieval Church at the Reformation. This coincided for various reasons with man's growing belief that he could 'conquer nature'—meaning of course, not his own unregenerate nature, which he has still so signally failed to conquer, but his physical environment. The course of this process was brilliantly demonstrated recently by the late E. F. Schumacher in his posthumous *Guide for the Perplexed* (1977). The title is taken from a work by the greatest Jewish medieval philosopher, Moses Maimonides (1135–1204). Schumacher showed how modern man's religious sense has increasingly atrophied under the influence of thinking like that of Descartes (1596–1650), a brilliant mathematician who sought to reduce the whole of philosophy to the consideration of what can be weighed and measured, thus eliminating at a stroke all those imponderables which alone give meaning to our existence.

It is precisely on this basis that 'the march of science' developed; but we can now see all too clearly that such a view is inadequate. Despite all the undoubted material benefits and conveniences that 'science' thus understood has brought, it emphatically has not brought the expected millennium, and indeed may yet succeed in destroying the world. Descartes was a Christian who found a place for God in his thinking, but the logical conclusion of his approach led to the systematic rejection of all religious conceptions. For some, this culminated in the view that all history is determined purely by economic forces, and that all man's 'cultural' (including religious) activities and ideas are nothing but a 'superstructure' erected on this materialist basis. The fact that the proponents of this view are now able to impose it officially on a large part of the world, and even to threaten to impose it on the rest of us, no more proves its validity than the fact that the medieval Church was, in its time, similarly able to impose its view on most of Europe. In fact, argument for argument, it could well be claimed that the medieval Church had rather more of truth on its side than its modern atheistic counterpart, whose reactions to any signs of opposition are so depressingly similar.

In fact there is an important, if little known, parallel to the 'superstructure' theory. In his book on the greatest of German mystics, Meister Eckhart, the Japanese Buddhist scholar Shizuteru Ueda (1965) used the expression 'mysticism of infinity with a theistic sub-structure,' following a suggestion by Rudolf Otto (1926). Though scarcely so intended, this neatly reverses the 'superstructure' theory. We might adopt this terminology, replacing 'mysticism of infinity' with 'intuition of the Unborn.' This higher perception is the primary thing for Eckhart, on which the 'theistic substructure' may be said to depend. The wider application of the principle comes with the recognition that what applies in superlative degree to Eckhart applies to a lesser extent also to others whose 'intuition of the Unborn' was feebler than his.

We have seen that monasticism played as large a part in medieval Christianity as it does in Buddhism, and it may well be considered that the abolition of this institution in the Protestant churches was a further contributory factor to the decline of the religious sense. The presence within the community of a group of people who are wholly committed to the religious life to the extent of renouncing worldly pleasures acts in fact as a powerful stimulus to the whole community—a vital leaven which informs the whole lump. Of course monasticism, like everything else, is liable to fall into corruption (often exaggerated by cynics), but as long as there are good monks—and nuns—who are exemplars and teachers to the laity, their influence is profound, going much deeper than the conscious level, a fact that is little appreciated in the West today. At the very least they are a constant reminder that it is possible to live—and even to live happily—without being a slave to one's sense-desires, and that in fact, bread apart, 'man does not live by sex alone.'

7. Christian Mysticism

What is termed 'mysticism' has a long history in the Christian Church. It has frequently been an object of suspicion. The Catholic Church has always sought to control its mystics lest they slip into heresy, while the Protestants have often rejected it partly for its 'Catholic' associations, and partly because of its alleged 'pagan' origins in Neoplatonism, as well as its affinities to various Oriental schools of thought, including Buddhism. In the author known as 'Dionysius the Areopagite' (ca. 500), we find notions of that negative theology expressed in the 14th century English *Cloud of Unknowing*, as well as the classical threefold way of the mystic's progress, the way of 'purgation, illumination, and union.' The word 'mysticism' comes from a Greek root meaning to close the eyes or mouth, and has associations with the ancient Greek mysteries. One definition is 'an immediate knowledge of God attained in this present life through personal religious experience.' If we equate this with a true 'intuition of the Unborn,' we can assert that it is in fact the indispensable basis of the religious life. Any 'religion' is dead, or sterile, if *no* such intuition informs it. Let us glance briefly at one of the greatest of Christian mystics, the German Meister Eckhart (ca. 1260–1328).

Eckhart was a prominent member of the Dominican order, who taught at the University of Paris and held high office until he was accused by the Archbishop of Cologne of spreading heretical doctrines among the common people. His case was referred to the Pope, and in 1329, after his death, twenty-eight of his propositions were condemned. His case has remained controversial to this day, though the majority view now is that he remained—if only just—within the bounds of orthodoxy. About a hundred of his German sermons have been preserved, in which he constantly pursues the theme of the 'birth of the Son (i.e. Christ) or the Word, in the soul.' This birth takes place in the peak (or spark, or castle) in the soul, and the man in whom it takes place is said to be deified, 'just as the bread and wine at the Eucharist become God.' The way to achieve this birth is by radical detachment from all earthly things, for 'all things are pure nothing,' since God alone has being. The 'power of the soul' by which, through divine grace, this is achieved is the 'higher intellect.' It may be fairly urged that those who condemned Eckhart's views as heretical did so because they were unable to rise to his level of consciousness.

Eckhart said, 'To get at the kernel, you must break the shell.' We may compare Eckhart with Nāgārjuna, the great Buddhist philosopher and founder of the Mādhyamika ('Middle Way') school, who 'broke the shell' of traditional Buddhist formulations. In the freer atmosphere of ancient India he was able to get away with this as Eckhart was not. Yet much of what Eckhart had said was put a little differently by the great Cusanus (Nikolaus von Cues, 1401–64), who nearly became Pope. One of the most learned men of his age, Cusanus took a prominent part in the (not very successful) efforts to reform the Church after the scandals of the Avignon papacy. His work *De docta ignorantia* uses mathematical symbolism to show how man can never attain by finite means to a perfect knowledge of God who is infinite, and who is called by him in a famous phrase 'the coincidence of opposites.' In the same spirit he strove for unity within the Christian world and even beyond it, boldly declaring, 'Hence there is a single religion and a single creed for all beings endowed with understanding, and this religion is presupposed behind the diversity of rites.' If only the spirit of Cusanus had prevailed, the religious history of Europe would have taken a decided turn for the better.

8. Contrasts

It would not be honest to pretend that there are no differences between Buddhism and Christianity, and before going further we should once more consider these. In doing so, we are at once confronted with the question of 'level.' Obviously, at the 'fundamentalist' level the differences are greatest, and it is fair to point out that at this level Buddhism may claim an advantage: it really is pretty difficult in the present age to maintain a fundamentalist view of Christianity based on a literal interpretation of the sources (i.e. the Bible), whereas the difficulties of accepting Theravada Buddhism in this way are very much less. The Pāli Canon, despite its enormous length, is remarkably self-consistent and it contains very little which a modern Western-trained mind (unless conditioned to reject *all* religious ideas) would find totally unacceptable, though much may be unfamiliar.

Let us consider briefly the difference between the founders of Buddhism and Christianity as seen by their respective followers. Each was in a sense a man—a perfect man—and at the same time more than a man. Each was in a sense unique: Jesus as Christ absolutely so, the Buddha at least relatively 'unique' in the sense that Buddhas appear only at vast intervals of time, so that Gotama was the only Buddha for this age. They attained their particular status, however, as it were from opposite directions. The Christ was God—or an aspect of God—who had descended from heaven in order to be born as a man; the Buddha had attained his status—in the course of this life—as the culmination of innumerable human lives of unexampled effort, in order to rise decisively above human (or any kind of 'relatively' superhuman) status and become the supreme 'Teacher of gods and men.' In modern jargon we might say they represent two different 'models' of the Transcendental in man—the 'God-man' and the '*Dhamma*-man.' Jesus said: 'I and my Father are one' (John 10:30).

The Buddha declared: 'He who sees me sees the *Dhamma*.' Each taught a Way to be followed, and in some sense *was* that 'Way.' Each is an exemplar to be followed, and indeed one of the most influential books of Christian devotion ever written was *The Imitation of Christ* by Thomas a Kempis (d.1471); yet still there is a difference. The Buddha is an exemplar and teacher to be followed; the Christ is *also*, and most importantly, a sacrificial victim by whose death on the Cross mankind may be saved. This sacrifice is repeated (in the Catholic view) or commemorated (according to the Protestants) in the sacrament of the Eucharist.

Man, in the Christian view, can never *become* God: the creature is eternally distinct from the Creator. In Buddhism, a man *can* become a Buddha by following the almost inconceivably difficult path of the Bodhisattva (in the Theravada school as well as in Mahayana Buddhism). Christianity offers no real parallel to this. Both religions grew up against a background of original polytheism, which they transcended in different ways. Buddhism did not formally reject the gods of an earlier pantheon, but devalued them; before the rise of Christianity, Judaism had long since elevated the one time tribal god to the status of Creator of heaven and earth, and Christianity incorporated the Jewish concept of the Messiah as an aspect of Deity.

Just as Buddhism differs at its apex from Christianity, by having no God-concept, so too at the human level it differs similarly by having no soul-concept. It is not the place here to discuss the intricacies of the *anattā* doctrine in Buddhism, but there is a sharp contrast here between the Christian emphasis on the importance of the human soul and the Buddhist view of the impersonality of all things including our 'selves.' In the next section it will be indicated that even this difference is perhaps less total than appears, but it would be wrong to pretend that no difference exists.

Other consequences flow from the difference between a theistic and a non-theistic religion. Thus there are different attitudes towards the question of good and evil, and the rule of justice. Medieval theologians could even spend their time debating whether a thing is good because goodness is an absolute principle, or simply because God just decided that certain things are good. And too, with the virtual collapse for many of the traditional Christian concepts of heaven and hell modern Christians are left with a largely unresolved dilemma as to what they should believe about an afterlife, and the rewards and punishments for their actions. The gradually growing uncertainty about this contributed, along with the development of an increasingly materialist scientific outlook, with all its obvious practical successes, to the tremendous decline in the religious sense which is so notable today—even though it looks as if a reaction has now set in.

9. Points of Contact

It was necessary to stress the differences before discussing the very real points of contact between the two religions. These are at various levels which call for discrimination. Superficially, a surprising number of resemblances can be found: celibate monks or clergy with shaven heads; the gesture with palms together which in Buddhism (as in India generally) denotes veneration or greeting and, in Christianity, prayer (and hence can be misleading); the use of incense, anointing and holy water; rosaries; the representation of saints or divine persons with a nimbus or halo (really an aura)—these are some of the most obvious features. And since Buddhism shares some of these things with Hinduism, we may also note the striking resemblance between the Hindu practice of bathing in a sacred river to wash away one's sins, and the activities of John the Baptist. Some of these resemblances may be coincidental or due to cultural transference, but they may too point to some deeper affinity.

In attempting a serious comparison of concepts and terms in the two religious systems, we are faced with many difficulties—both superficial resemblances and superficial differences can turn out to be misleading. There is also the problem of language: those who cannot read the texts in the original are at the mercy of translators whose competence may vary. The difficulty can be vividly illustrated by comparing two or three of the thirty-odd English translations of the Dhammapada. One might be forgiven for not realizing that all were meant to be renderings of the same work! Only when we have avoided these elementary pitfalls can we begin to attempt a true comparison.

We have considered the differences between the conceptions of the respective founders in Buddhism and Christianity, among which is the fact that the Buddha is a teacher but not a saviour. Yet we do find something similar to the saviour-figure in (especially but not exclusively) Mahayana Buddhism: the Bodhisattva. Of course, the figure of Christ cannot be wholly equated with that of a Bodhisattva without falsification, but there is a considerable resemblance. Likewise, the emphasis in Lutheran Christianity on the necessity of faith in the saving power of Christ has been compared to the similar stress laid in the Pure Land schools of Buddhism (such as the Shin school of Japan), on the need for faith in Amitābha Buddha, who is held to represent the *Dharmakāya* or Ultimate Truth. However, here too caution is necessary, and it would be misleading to attempt too close an equation of the Christian *Trinity* with the *Trikāya* ('Three Bodies') of Mahayana Buddhism (even though there is perhaps a certain parallel between the *Nirmānakāya*—the human manifestation of the Buddha-principle—and the human Christ).

Probably the most fundamental difference between Christianity and Buddhism concerns the twin questions of 'God' and the 'soul.' And it is perfectly true that the two systems cannot be entirely reconciled on these points. Nevertheless, the difference can to a certain extent be legitimately 'relativised.' As regards the God-concept, this has already been referred to in connection with the Udāna statement about the Unborn (see section above subtitled: '1. The Problem'). It need only be added here that in some Christian thinking today little more is said about God than is said there about the Unborn.

In discussing such matters, and especially the idea of the 'soul,' we have to bear in mind the very important question of levels of truth, which is very clearly stated in Buddhism in terms of the distinction between *paramatthasacca* or 'ultimate truth' and *sammutisacca* or 'conventional truth.' Thus the *anattā* doctrine certainly denies the reality of an enduring 'soul' or 'self' according to ultimate truth, but in terms of conventional truth such a thing exists. In fact, for the Buddhist, 'salvation' (to use the Christian term) consists precisely in the realization of this *ultimate* truth, whereby the relative truth is transcended. Some Christian mystics come close to this idea: thus Eckhart declared that 'all creatures are pure nothing.' He meant that only God gave them being, which is not, of course, identical with the Buddhist conception.

In fact, the ordinary 'unenlightened' person whether Buddhist, Christian or anything else, lives by the light of 'conventional' truth which, in daily life, is extremely important. In Buddhism, one characteristic of the *arahant* or enlightened being is that he creates, no fresh *karma*, though he may still be subject to the results (*vipāka*), painful or pleasant, of past *karma*. So *karma* is only produced by those whose thinking is still determined by 'conventional truth.' Such beings are said to be 'owners of their karma, heirs of their karma.' This brings us to the field of ethics, and here we find a great similarity between the precepts of Buddhism, Judaism and Christianity, even though the reasons given for moral behaviour differ. For those who suppose that religion consists of 'living a good life' in the sense of behaving decently, there might seem little to choose between Buddhism, Christianity, Judaism and perhaps even Humanism. But there is rather more to it than that.

The opposite of moral behaviour is called 'sin' by English-speaking Christians and Jews, and *akusala kamma* or 'unskilled action' by Buddhists. In the Judeo-Christian view the sinner will be punished by God, while Buddhism holds that his unskilled action will bring its own retribution. Of course, Jews and Christians regard sin as above all an offence against God; nevertheless, we find that the words used in both Hebrew and Greek for sin mean literally 'missing the mark,' which is after all not far from the Buddhist idea. The basic moral code for Jews and Christians is given in the Ten Commandments (Ex. 20:2-17), all of which are prohibitions ascribed to God. For the lay Buddhist there are the Five Precepts which are not prohibitions, but undertakings to refrain from: 1. killing, 2. theft, 3. sexual misconduct, 4. wrong speech, and 5. intoxication. The first four of these agree closely with some of the Ten Commandments; the fifth has an equivalent prohibition in Islam but not in the Judeo-Christian code, though obviously drunkenness is not looked on with favour. It is possible to argue about the detailed interpretation of all these Precepts or Commandments, but Buddhists, Christians and indeed most people would agree that some such code is an absolute necessity for any kind of decent living, and would utterly reject the idea that there are no absolute moral standards at all. (Any idea that Zen Buddhism rejects morality is based on a total misunderstanding.)

St. Paul said: 'There now remain faith, hope and love (or 'charity'): these three. But the greatest of these is love' (1 Cor. 13:13), and elsewhere it is said: 'God is love' (1 John 4:16). The Greek word used in these passages is *agape*, which is close in meaning to the Pāli *mettā*, meaning essentially pure love without sensual or other emotional attachment. It is scarcely necessary to point out that Buddhists and Christians alike are well aware of the ambiguities of the word 'love,' and that slogans of the type 'Make love not war' are a falsification of either teaching. Taken in isolation, the words 'God is love' might seem to depersonalize God by equating him with an abstract quality, but the context shows that this is not intended. But it is interesting to note that in Buddhism *mettā* is the first of the four *brahma vihāras*, the practice of which is said to lead to rebirth in the Brahma-world. And it has already been pointed out that the practice of this represents a Buddhist way of carrying out the difficult Judeo-Christian injunction: 'Love thy neighbour as thyself.'

10. Conclusion

The position of religion in the world today is a peculiar one. Despite persecution and repression in some parts, and confident predictions of its forthcoming disappearance in others, not only has it not vanished, but it has begun to display a vitality and resilience which have astonished and dismayed its critics. True, extraneous factors such as nationalism have often played a part in this. Nevertheless, there can no longer be any doubt that there has in recent times been a real resurgence of what can at least broadly be called 'religion,' though its manifestations have been many and varied, ranging from fundamentalist Christianity through a variety of nationalist-coloured forms (Christian, Islamic and even Buddhist), to the wave of occultism and the subcultures of 'hippydom' and drugs now happily past their peak. Not all of these manifestations are desirable, and the dangers of some are obvious. But all point to a disillusionment and dissatisfaction with the apparently triumphant materialist values whether these appear in a 'communist' or a 'capitalist' guise. The fact is that this dissatisfaction goes far deeper than a mere emotional reaction against the shoddy values and the general mental and spiritual impoverishment which are the inevitable concomitants of a purely materialist outlook.

The materialist world-view implicit, until recently, in most scientific thinking is demonstrably inadequate to the task of explaining the world, as a growing number of scientists are coming to realize. ESP phenomena are being studied with increasing seriousness, if sometimes for the wrong reasons, while the actual evidence for survival of bodily death and even for some kind of reincarnation or rebirth is now so strong that it is gradually but inevitably forcing recognition in some unlikely quarters. Even things like astrology are being regarded with something less than the total disdain which was the standard reaction until only yesterday. All this belongs, admittedly, only to what may be termed the lower reaches of 'religion.' Its main importance is that it breaches the bastion of materialism, thus removing, for a significant number of people, a serious obstacle to faith in something higher. To put it crudely, many educated people now feel able to admit openly that after all, Darwin, Marx and Freud did not know all the answers.

For some, this is a new exhilarating experience, and perhaps rather frightening. But the inevitable question arises: What now?

What the new knowledge actually does, in the first place, is to disprove once and for all that basic and yet so improbable assumption of materialistic science (or 'scientism' as it has been called): inanimate matter by pure chance, by some incredible series of flukes, 'contrived' to teach itself to think. We now have *proof*, or as near proof as makes no difference, that what we call 'mind' is autonomous, and that if either member of the pair we call mind-and-matter is subordinate or illusory, it is matter and not mind. So far, so good. The worrying thing is that this recognition seems at one fell swoop to bring back chaos in the place of science's carefully-ordered cosmos. The attraction of materialism to the scientific mind was that it produced a neat and tidy, ultimately finite system. Actually it still does—as far as it goes. The difference is merely that the mind (*whatever* 'mind' may be) that can grasp such a system is itself outside of that system—which ought logically to have been obvious all along. A stone cannot perceive itself, though a dog can perceive it, while a man can not only perceive the stone but—to some extent at least—'understand' it.

The chaos which this recognition brings can look at first sight almost total. It is like a dreamworld in which anything can happen, in which what we yesterday dismissed as superstition can easily turn out to be fact, in which the very criteria of what is probable and improbable cease to be clearly discernible. Once we accept spoon-bending, the result is mind-bending! The temptation to retreat even into the bleak orderliness of materialism may be strong, and what before looked so unbearable may seem comforting by comparison. If we resist this temptation we may find it necessary to come to terms with what used to be called the 'supernatural' (and is better termed the paranormal)—though that does not mean becoming obsessed with it. But some modern Christians may well find that, 'blinded by science,' they have perhaps rejected too much of their traditional beliefs, without being too sure of how to find the way back.

The traditional Buddhist view of the 'three worlds' may be helpful here. Human existence as normally experienced is in *kāmaloka* or the realm of sense-desires. Beings normally visible to us here are human beings and animals, but there are others:

the inhabitants of various 'states of woe,' as well as some happier beings. Some are mischievous, some neutral or benevolent, but all are more or less ignorant, and they pass into, or out of, these various states according to their *karmic* deserts. Other, definitely happier beings also exist, under the same basic *karmic* conditions, in *rūpaloka* and *arūpaloka,* the realm of form and the formless world, where consciousness is related to that of the *jhānic* states attainable in this life. These beings are the *devās,* the highest of whom are like the gods of polytheistic religions. But though very long-lived they are not immortal. Likewise they may be wise but are not enlightened. Beyond all these worlds is the *lokuttara* or Transcendental, the Secure Refuge on the 'other shore,' or the Unborn. This is beyond all imagining but not beyond the possibility of realization in this life.

If we compare this outline with that of traditional Christianity the differences are less great than might have been supposed. One difference is that in the Christian view the various non-visible beings in the different realms are eternally 'fixed' in their present state of woe or bliss; and of course those in the higher realms are termed 'saints' or 'angels and not 'gods.' The only serious Buddhist objection to this scheme in principle would be its total rigidity. It is like trying to capture the film of the eternal flux in a single 'still.' The other main difference is, of course, that for Christians the 'transcendental' realm is occupied by a personal God, who is creator of the whole. It can, however, be urged that on the basis of our present empirical knowledge something rather like the Buddhist view of the 'inhabited' cosmos is beginning to emerge. It will be the task of future scientists, and philosophers of science, to explore it—a challenging task that few as yet have embarked upon.

What is *not* the field of 'science' but of 'religion' is the realm of the Unborn. And here we can usefully distinguish between the 'higher' religions (including both Buddhism and Christianity), and what we may term the 'lower' religions. In these latter, there may indeed be genuine contact of some kind with the invisible denizens of the 'three worlds' (perhaps even the highest), but no 'breakthrough' to the Transcendental. To such faiths as these—often perfectly 'genuine' as far as they go—the traditional term 'paganism' may fittingly be applied. The Old Testament may possibly be read as the record of the development of 'Judaism' from a lower to a higher religion in this sense, and it seems that in ancient Greece, too, we can catch this very act of 'breaking through' with the emergence of philosophers like Plato, who had a genuine 'intuition of the Unborn.' Both these streams, of course, contributed to the growth of Christianity.

The Unborn cannot be defined, or imagined, or reached by any ratiocinative process. It can, however, be *realized*. But long before this full realization is attained, it can be more or less dimly intuited. To such an intuition it is 'felt' to be an ultimate refuge in a world of flux. Christians call it God and give it the attributes of a loving Father. For Buddhists this is illegitimate: the Ultimate is 'signless.' This has absurdly led some learned Buddhist book-scholars, finding nothing 'graspable' about it, to equate Nirvāna with total extinction indistinguishable from that postulated by the materialists, only postponed, improbably, to the death of the *Arahant*. They should know better. But Christians too know that they should not try to imagine God. As a Romanian priest, speaking of the Orthodox 'Jesus Prayer,' told Ronald Eyre, 'The first law, when we begin to pray, is not to "fancy" anything or imagine anything, because God Himself does not come under the sway of the imagination. Fantasy is a stumbling block to our union with God' (*The Long Search*, p. 162.)

True religion is not 'the opium of the people' (rather the reverse, it is the 'awakener'!), nor is it any kind of shallow escapism. It is the way out of *saṃsāra*, the 'world of flux,' to the true and abiding (not 'everlasting' but rather, 'timeless') refuge of the Unborn. And it represents a fundamental human need which we repress at our peril. There are many surrogate religions, and there are even genuine 'lower religions' which actually can lead to a happier life than most people know, but yet stop short of the real goal. Such, for instance, were the systems which Gotama himself found and tried out in the course of his own Great Search. And some of these can be taken today in the form of popular 'meditation schools' and the like. The level attainable by such means probably varies considerably, though it may well he doubted whether most of them attain the heights reached by Gotama's teachers, Ālāra Kālāma and Uddaka Rāmaputta. The arts, too, can be a surrogate religion (possibly the only one readily available to some), though they can perhaps, too, sometimes function as a genuine 'way' capable of leading to—or at least towards—the real goal. Great art is fed from unconscious channels which may stem from a true 'intuition of the Unborn.' Lesser forms of art are perhaps fed from sources related to the 'higher worlds,' and so on—right down the scale to a point where the sources of inspiration become distinctly dubious. There might be less confusion about the nature of 'art' if this were clearly recognized. But to discuss this subject adequately would require a separate study.

This essay is written in an ecumenical, not a polemical spirit. It is in no sense a 'critique' of Christianity. There is a shallow view abroad today which claims that the new spirit of ecumenism between churches and even between religions is merely a defensive measure due to the general decline in religious belief. This view has begun to lose the plausibility it at first enjoyed. It is more reasonable to ascribe the new attitude to a deepening religiosity (however vague its outlines may sometimes seem to be) which sees the old polemical spirit as nothing short of a scandal. Of course religion *is* threatened in the world today, but from without far more than from within. From within, there are very evident signs of renewal. In fact, as we have seen, it is the very materialistic values themselves, still outwardly so triumphant, that are being steadily undermined from within. It may be literally true that only through the reassertion of religious values (perhaps partly through new forms) can mankind be saved from physical as well as spiritual catastrophe.

There are doubtless some irreducible differences in the ways whereby Buddhists, Christians and others would *explain* the world, and still more perhaps that which lies *beyond* the world (and is, therefore, strictly inaccessible to 'explanation'). There is far less difference between their views on how we should live and act *in* the world. The spirit of pure, disinterested love, no matter whether it bears a 'Christian,' a 'Buddhist' or any other label, is the solvent for all our problems, and the only certain recipe against impending disaster, whatever form this may take. It thus makes good sense to pool our 'spiritual' resources in seeking solutions for the common problems of mankind. This is in no sense a call to any form of overtly 'political' action. But if those with specific political commitments are sufficiently imbued with this spirit of love, they will not go far wrong.

The Buddhist doctrine of *anattā* or 'not-self' is a difficult one even for some Buddhists to grasp, but if we think of it in the ethical sense of utter selflessness we can see its practical application. True 'detachment' as preached by Christian mystics and many others, means being 'detached' not from other people's problems and sorrows (or indeed from those of the various other beings with which we share this life on earth), but from our own worldly impulses: sense-desires, greed for power and influence and self-assertion, anger and hatred. It is, not only, not incompatible with 'love'. It is in fact the only way in which real love—loving one's neighbour as oneself—can find full expression.

Bibliographical Note

Here only a handful of books will be mentioned (out of a vast number of possibilities) in addition to the versions of the Bible mentioned in the *Author's Note.* I have omitted books on Buddhism, and have deliberately referred, as far as possible, to paperbacks of the Penguin type as these are convenient and cheap. Even out-of-print Penguins can often be found.

The Life of Jesus by C. J. Cadoux (Penguin 1948) is useful if it can be found; the old and famous *Life of Jesus* by Ernest Renan (1863), though obviously dated, is also still worth reading. To these might be added the four volumes of *Penguin Gospel Commentaries,* particularly perhaps that by John Marsh on *St. John.* There are also Penguin volumes on Roman Catholicism, The Orthodox Church, and Judaism by recognized authorities. Another relevant Penguin volume is *How the Bible Came to Us* by Canon H.G.G. Herklots.

For Meister Eckhart my own translation of his *German Sermons* in two volumes (Watkins) is now available, and there is also the Harper paperback selection by R.B. Blakney (1941, but still in print). There is an English translation of the *Of Learned Ignorance* (*1440*) of Nicholas of Cusa (Cusanus) by Fr. G. Heron (Routledge 1954). On Archbishop Passavalli (1820–97) see *Reincarnation: The Phoenix Mystery* by J. Head and S. L. Cranston (New York 1977), p. 179.

The contribution of C.G. Jung to the psychology of religion should not be overlooked. *Jung and the Story of Our Time* by Laurens van der Post (Penguin 1978) provides the best possible introduction.

For a stimulating view of the varieties of living religions *Ronald Eyre on the Long Search* (Collins 1979), based on his TV series of that title, can be recommended. Those who are still worried by the idea of some fundamental conflict between 'science and religion' could read with profit E. F. Schumacher's *A Guide for the Perplexed* (Fontana 1977), going on from there to Lyall Watson's *Supernature,* in which the attempt to expand the frontiers of science beyond its materialist limits is made. This book (1973) and its successor *The Romeo Error* (1974), with useful bibliographies, have both appeared in Coronet Paperbacks. On the theme of the latter, see also my *Buddhism and Death* (The Wheel 261, Kandy 1978).

Transcendental Dependent Arising

A Translation and Exposition of the Upanisa Sutta

by

Bhikkhu Bodhi

WHEEL PUBLICATION NO. 277/278

Preface

Tucked away in the Saṃyutta Nikāya among the "connected sayings on causality" (*Nidānasaṃyutta*) is a short formalized text entitled the *Upanisa Sutta*, the "Discourse on Supporting Conditions." Though at first glance hardly conspicuous among the many interesting suttas in this collection, this little discourse turns out upon repeated examination to be of tremendous doctrinal importance. Its great significance derives from the striking juxtaposition it makes of two applications of "dependent arising" (*paṭiccasamuppāda*), the principle of conditionality which lies at the heart of the Buddha's doctrine. The first application is the usual one, setting forth the causal sequence responsible for the origination of saṃsāric suffering. Apart from a slight change it is identical with the twelve-factored formulation recurring throughout the Pali Canon. The change—the substitution of "suffering" for "ageing-and-death" as the last member of the series—becomes the lead for the second application of dependent arising. This application, occurring only sporadically in the Pali Canon, shows the same principle of conditionality to structure the path leading to deliverance from suffering. It begins with faith, emerging out of the suffering with which the first series ended, and continues through to the retrospective knowledge of liberation, which confirms the destruction of the binding defilements. By linking the two series into a single sequence, the sutta reveals the entire course of man's faring in the world as well as his treading of the path to its transcendence. It shows, moreover, that these two dimensions of human experience, the mundane and the transcendental, the dimensions of world involvement and world disengagement, are both governed by a single structural principle, that of dependent arising. Recognizing this broader range of the principle, the *Nettipakaraṇa*, a Pali exegetical treatise, has called the second application "transcendental dependent arising" (*lokuttara-paṭiccasamuppāda*).

Despite the great importance of the *Upanisa Sutta*, traditional commentators have hardly given the text the special attention it would seem to deserve. Perhaps the reason for this is that, its line of approach being peculiar to itself and a few related texts scattered through the Canon, it has been overshadowed by the many other suttas giving the more usual presentation of doctrine. But whatever the explanation be, the need has remained for a fuller exploration of the sutta's meaning and implications. We have sought to remedy this deficiency with the following work offering an English translation of the *Upanisa Sutta* and an exposition of its message. The exposition sets out to explore the second, "transcendental" application of dependent arising, drawing freely from other parts of the Canon and the commentaries to fill out the meaning. Since full accounts of the "mundane" or saṃsāric side of dependent arising can be readily found elsewhere, we thought it best to limit our exposition to the principle's less familiar application. A similar project has been undertaken by Bhikshu Sangharakshita in his book *The Three Jewels* (London, 1967). However, since this work draws largely from Mahayanist sources to explain the stages in the series, the need has remained for a treatment which elucidates the series entirely from the standpoint of the Theravada tradition, within which the sutta is originally found.

—Bhikkhu Bodhi

* * *

Note on References

References to the Dīgha Nikāya (DN) and the Majjhima Nikāya (MN) refer to the number of the sutta. References to the Saṃyutta Nikāya (SN) refer to the number of the chapter followed by the number of the sutta within that chapter. References to the Aṅguttara Nikāya (AN) refer to *nipāta* (numerical division) followed by the number of the sutta within that *nipāta.*

Upanisa Sutta

While staying at Sāvatthī the Exalted One said:

"The destruction of the cankers, monks, is for one who knows and sees, I say, not for one who does not know and does not see. Knowing what, seeing what does the destruction of the cankers occur? 'Such is material form, such is the arising of material form, such is the passing away of material form. Such is feeling ... perception ... mental formations ... consciousness; such is the arising of consciousness, such is the passing away of consciousness'—for one who knows and sees this, monks, the destruction of the cankers occurs.

"The knowledge of destruction with respect to destruction has a supporting condition; I say, it does not lack a supporting condition. And what is the supporting condition for the knowledge of destruction? 'Emancipation' should be the reply.

"Emancipation, monks, also has a supporting condition; I say, it does not lack a supporting condition. And what is the supporting condition for emancipation? 'Dispassion' should be the reply.

"Dispassion, monks, also has a supporting condition; I say, it does not lack a supporting condition. And what is the supporting condition for dispassion? 'Disenchantment' should be the reply.

"Disenchantment, monks, also has a supporting condition; I say, it does not lack a supporting condition. And what is the supporting condition for disenchantment? 'The knowledge and vision of things as they really are' should be the reply.

"The knowledge and vision of things as they really are, monks, also has a supporting condition; I say, it does not lack a supporting condition. And what is the supporting condition for the knowledge and vision of things as they really are? 'Concentration' should be the reply.

"Concentration, monks, also has a supporting condition; I say, it does not lack a supporting condition. And what is the supporting condition for concentration? 'Happiness' should be the reply.

"Happiness, monks, also has a supporting condition; I say, it does not lack a supporting condition. And what is the supporting condition for happiness? 'Tranquillity' should be the reply.

"Tranquillity, monks, also has a supporting condition; I say, it does not lack a supporting condition. And what is the supporting condition for tranquillity? 'Rapture' should be the reply.

"Rapture, monks, also has a supporting condition; I say, it does not lack a supporting condition. And what is the supporting condition for rapture? 'Joy' should be the reply.

"Joy, monks, also has a supporting condition; I say, it does not lack a supporting condition. And what is the supporting condition for joy? 'Faith' should be the reply.

"Faith, monks, also has a supporting condition; I say, it does not lack a supporting condition. And what is the supporting condition for faith? 'Suffering' should be the reply.

"Suffering, monks, also has a supporting condition; I say, it does not lack a supporting condition. And what is the supporting condition for suffering? 'Birth' should be the reply.

"And what is the supporting condition for birth? 'Existence' should be the reply.

"What is the supporting condition for existence? 'Clinging' should be the reply.

"What is the supporting condition for clinging? 'Craving' should be the reply.

"What is the supporting condition for craving? 'Feeling' should be the reply.

"What is the supporting condition for feeling? 'Contact' should be the reply.

"What is the supporting condition for contact? 'The sixfold sense base' should be the reply.

"What is the supporting condition for the sixfold sense base? 'Mentality-materiality' should be the reply.

"What is the supporting condition for mentality-materiality? 'Consciousness' should be the reply.

"What is the supporting condition for consciousness? 'Kamma formations' should be the reply.

"Kamma formations, monks, also have a supporting condition; I say, they do not lack a supporting condition. And what is the supporting condition for kamma formations? 'Ignorance' should be the reply.

"Thus, monks, ignorance is the supporting condition for kamma formations, kamma formations are the supporting condition for consciousness, consciousness is the supporting condition for mentality-materiality, mentality-materiality is the supporting condition for the sixfold sense base, the sixfold sense base is the supporting condition for contact, contact is the supporting condition for feeling, feeling is the supporting condition for craving, craving is the supporting condition for clinging, clinging is the supporting condition for existence, existence is the supporting condition for birth, birth is the supporting condition for suffering, suffering is the supporting condition for faith, faith is the supporting condition for joy, joy is the supporting condition for rapture, rapture is the supporting condition for tranquillity, tranquillity is the supporting condition for happiness, happiness is the supporting condition for concentration, concentration is the supporting condition for the knowledge and vision of things as they really are, the knowledge and vision of things as they really are is the supporting condition for disenchantment, disenchantment is the supporting condition for dispassion, dispassion is the supporting condition for emancipation, and emancipation is the supporting condition for the knowledge of the destruction (of the cankers).

"Just as, monks, when rain descends heavily upon some mountaintop, the water flows down along with the slope, and fills the clefts, gullies, and creeks; these being filled, fill up the pools; these being filled, fill up the ponds; these being filled, fill up the streams; these being filled, fill up the rivers; and the rivers being filled, fill up the great ocean—in the same way, monks, ignorance is the supporting condition for kamma formations, kamma formations are the supporting condition for consciousness, consciousness is the supporting condition for mentality-materiality, mentality-materiality is the supporting condition for the sixfold sense base, the sixfold sense base is the supporting condition for contact, contact is the supporting condition for feeling, feeling is the supporting condition for craving, craving is the supporting condition for clinging, clinging is the supporting condition for existence, existence is the supporting condition for birth, birth is the supporting condition for suffering, suffering is the supporting condition for faith, faith is the supporting condition for joy, joy is the supporting condition for rapture, rapture is the supporting condition for tranquillity, tranquillity is the supporting condition for happiness, happiness is the supporting condition for concentration, concentration is the supporting condition for the knowledge and vision of things as they really are, the knowledge and vision of things as they really are is the supporting condition for disenchantment, disenchantment is the supporting condition for dispassion, dispassion is the supporting condition for emancipation, and emancipation is the supporting condition for the knowledge of the destruction (of the cankers)."

Transcendental Dependent Arising

An Exposition of the Upanisa Sutta

Dependent arising (*paṭiccasamuppāda*) is the central principle of the Buddha's teaching, constituting both the objective content of its liberating insight and the germinative source for its vast network of doctrines and disciplines. As the frame behind the four noble truths, the key to the perspective of the middle way, and the conduit to the realization of selflessness, it is the unifying theme running through the teaching's multifarious expressions, binding them together as diversified formulations of a single coherent vision. The earliest suttas equate dependent arising with the unique discovery of the Buddha's enlightenment, so profound and difficult to grasp that he at first hesitated to announce it to the world. A simple exposition of the principle sparks off the liberating wisdom in the minds of his foremost disciples, while skill in explaining its workings is made a qualification of an adroit expounder of the Dhamma. So crucial is this principle to the body of the Buddha's doctrine that an insight into dependent arising is held to be sufficient to yield an understanding of the entire teaching. In the words of the Buddha: "He who sees dependent arising sees the Dhamma; he who sees the Dhamma sees dependent arising."[1]

The Pali texts present dependent arising in a double form. It appears both as an abstract statement of universal law and as the particular application of that law to the specific problem which is the doctrine's focal concern, namely, the problem of suffering. In its abstract form the principle of dependent arising is equivalent to the law of the conditioned genesis of phenomena. It expresses the invariable concomitance between the arising and ceasing of any given phenomenon and the functional efficacy of its originative conditions. Its phrasing, as terse as any formulation of modern logic, recurs in the ancient texts thus: "This being, that exists;

1. MN 28.

through the arising of this, that arises. This not being, that does not exist; through the ceasing of this, that ceases."[2]

When applied to the problem of suffering, the abstract principle becomes encapsulated in a twelve-term formula disclosing the causal nexus responsible for the origination of suffering. It begins with ignorance, the primary root of the series though not a first cause, conditioning the arising of ethically determinate volitions, which in turn condition the arising of consciousness, and so on through the salient occasions of sentient becoming down to their conclusion in old age and death:

> "With ignorance as condition, the kamma formations; with kamma formations as condition, consciousness; with consciousness as condition, mentality-materiality; with mentality-materiality as condition, the sixfold sense base; with the sixfold sense base as condition, contact; with contact as condition, feeling; with feeling as condition, craving; with craving as condition, clinging; with clinging as condition, existence; with existence as condition, birth; with birth as condition, ageing-and-death, sorrow, lamentation, pain, grief, and despair arise. Such is the origination of this entire mass of suffering."
>
> —SN XII, *passim*

The corollary of this formula, which constantly accompanies it, describes the conditioned cessation of suffering. It shows how, when ignorance ceases, all the following conditions successively cease, down to the cessation of the "entire mass of suffering."

Though the principle of dependent arising is applicable to any situation where an origination of phenomena takes place, the Pali Buddhist tradition has focused upon the doctrine almost exclusively in terms of its twelvefold formulation. So much has this been the case that the two have tended to be blankly identified with each other, dependent arising being equated simply with the twelvefold series and the twelvefold series being regarded as an exhaustive treatment of dependent arising. This exclusiveness of emphasis doubtlessly poses a certain danger of rigidity; but even despite this danger it is not without its justification. For the aim of

---

2. *Imasmiṃ sati idaṃ hoti, imassa uppāda idaṃ uppajjati. Imasmiṃ asati idaṃ na hoti, imassa nirodha idaṃ nirujjhati.* MN 79, MN 115 etc.

the Buddha's teaching is not abstract and theoretical, but concrete and soteriological. Its goal is liberation from suffering, understood in its deepest sense as the unsatisfactoriness of sentient existence indefinitely repeated in the wheel of becoming, the cycle of births and deaths, called *saṃsāra.* The twelve-term nexus contributes to this liberative thrust by bringing the principle of dependent arising to bear directly on the condition which it is the doctrine's overriding concern to ameliorate. If suffering is produced by causes, these causes and the way they can be stopped must be uncovered and exposed. The twelvefold application accomplishes precisely this. In its positive or direct aspect (*anuloma*) it makes known the causal chain behind suffering, demonstrating how the round of existence arises and turns through the impulsions of craving, clinging, and karma, working freely behind the shielding screen of ignorance. In its negative or reverse side (*paṭiloma*) it reveals the way to the cessation of suffering, showing that when ignorance is eliminated by the rise of true knowledge all the factors dependent on ignorance likewise draw to a close.

However, as a consequence of this constriction of attention, sight has tended to be lost of the broader range of exemplifications the principle of dependent arising might have, even within the limits of the soteriological direction of the teaching. Dependent arising cannot be reduced to any single one of its applications. Any application is only a pedagogical device framed from the standpoint of the teaching's practical orientation. Above and beyond its specific instances, dependent arising remains an expression of the invariable structural relatedness of phenomena. It is a principle to which all phenomena conform by the very nature of their being, the principle that whatever comes into existence does so in dependence on conditions. From the perspective this teaching affords, things are seen to arise, not from some intrinsic nature of their own, from necessity, chance or accident, but from their causal correlations with other things to which they are connected as part of the fixed order obtaining between phenomena. Each transient entity, emerging into the present out of the stream of events bearing down from the past, absorbs into itself the causal influx of the past, to which it must be responsive. During its phase of presence it exercises its own distinctive function with the support of its conditions, expressing thereby its own immediacy of being. And then, with the completion of its actuality, it is swept away by the universal impermanence to become itself a condition determinant of the future.

When this law of inter-connected becoming, of conditionality and relatedness, is extracted from its usual exemplifications and explored for further doctrinal bearings, it can be found to have other ramifications equally relevant to the realization of the teaching's fundamental aim. One particular exemplification of dependent arising, found with minor variations in a number of suttas, shows the basic principle to serve as the scaffolding for the course of spiritual development issuing in final emancipation.[3] It figures in these suttas as the architectonic underlying the gradual training, governing the process by which one phase of practice conditions the arising of the following phase all the way from the commencement of the path to the realization of the ultimate goal. To be sure, the application of dependent arising to the achievement of deliverance is already covered from one angle by the reverse or cessation side of the twelvefold formula, according to which the cessation of ignorance sets off a series of cessations culminating in the cessation of suffering. Thence in itself such an application is not a unique feature of these suttas. What gives these suttas their distinctive quality and value is the positive form in which they cast the sequential pattern of the liberative venture. Whereas the series of cessations presents the achievement of liberation logically, in strict doctrinal terms as the consequence following upon the annulment of saṃsāric bondage, the present sequence views the same chain of events dynamically, from the inner perspective of living experience.

As living experience, the advance to emancipation cannot be tied down to a series of mere negations, for such a mode of treatment omits precisely what is most essential to the spiritual quest—the immediacy of inner striving, growth, and transformation. Parallel to the demolition of old barriers there occurs, in the quest for deliverance, a widening of vistas characterized by an evolving sense of maturation, enrichment, and fulfilment; the departure from bondage, anxiety, and suffering at the same time means the move towards freedom and peace. This expansion and enrichment

3. SN XII.23; AN X.3–5.

is made possible by the structure of the gradual training, which is not so much a succession of discrete steps one following the other, as a locking together of overlapping components in a union at once augmentative, consummative, and projective. Each pair of stages intertwines in a mutually vitalizing bond wherein the lower, antecedent member nurtures its successor by serving as its generative base, and the higher, consequent member completes its predecessor by absorbing its energies and directing them on to the next phase in the series. Each link thus performs a double function: while rewarding the efforts expended in the accomplishment of the antecedent stage, it provides the incentive for the commencement of the consequent stage. In this way the graduated training unfolds organically in a fluid progression in which, as the Buddha says, "stage flows over into stage, stage fulfils stage, for crossing over from the hither shore to the beyond."[4]

All the factors comprised in this sequence come into being in strict subjection to the law of conditioned genesis. The accidental, the compulsory, and the mysterious are equally excluded by the lawful regularity governing the series. The stages of the path do not emerge fortuitously or through the operation of some inscrutable power, but originate conditionally, appearing spontaneously in the course of training when their requisite conditions are complete. Thus the course of spiritual development these suttas reveal is a dependent arising—a coming into being in dependence on conditions. But this dependent arising differs significantly from its mundane counterpart. The mundane version, with its twelve links, describes the movement of *saṃsāra*, which revolves in a perpetually self-regenerating circle leading from beginning to end only to find the end lead back to the beginning. The mechanism of this process, by which defilements and renewed existence mutually kindle one another, is fuelled by the hope that somehow some solution will yet emerge within the framework of laws set for the turning of the wheel, a hope repeatedly disappointed. The present version of dependent arising delineates a type of development that only becomes possible when this hope has been dispensed with. It hinges on the prior recognition that any attempt to eliminate suffering through the gratification of craving

4. AN X.2.

is doomed to failure, and that the only way to stop it is to cut through the vicious nexus at its base. Though the movement it describes is still cyclic, it is not the circular revolution of *saṃsāra* it is concerned with but a different kind of rotation that only comes into play when the essentially defective nature of the ordinary human condition has been clearly perceived and the urge towards liberation from it made the dominant motive of the inner life. The present sequence depicts the movement towards release. It sets forth a drive which, in contrast to the pointless repetition of *saṃsāra*, evolves up and outwards in an unbroken spiral ascent—a pattern in which each turn supports and strengthens its successor's capacity for liberation, enabling the series as a whole to pick up the momentum needed to break the gravitational pull of the mundane sphere. Since all the phases in this progression arise in dependence on their antecedents, the series represents a dependent arising. But unlike the familiar version of dependent arising, the present version leads, not back to the round of becoming, but to the overcoming of *saṃsāra* and all its attendant sufferings. Hence the *Nettippakaraṇa* calls this sequence "transcendental dependent arising" (*lokuttara paṭiccasamuppāda*)—a dependent arising that leads to the transcendence of the world.[5]

The sutta we will investigate here for an account of "transcendental dependent arising, is the *Upanisa Sutta* of the *Nidānasaṃyutta* (SN XII.23). In addition to giving a clear, explicit account of the conditional structure of the liberative progression, this sutta has the further advantage of bringing the supramundane form of dependent arising into immediate connection with its familiar saṃsāric counterpart. By making this connection it brings into prominence the comprehensive character of the principle of conditionality—its ability to support and explain both the process of compulsive involvement which is the origin of suffering and the process of disengagement which leads to deliverance from suffering. Thereby it reveals dependent arising to be the key to the unity and coherence of the Buddha's teaching. When the Buddha declares, "I teach only suffering and the cessation of suffering,"[6]

5. Sec. 388, see Ñāṇamoli, transl., *The Guide* (*Nettippakaraṇaṃ*) (London: Pali Text Society, 1962), p. 97.

6. MN 22, SN XXII.86.

the bond which unites these two terminals of the doctrine as complementary sides of a single, internally consistent system is simply the law of dependent arising.

The *Upanisa Sutta* gives three expositions of "transcendental dependent arising." The first expounds the sequence in reverse order, beginning with the last link in the series, the knowledge of the destruction of the cankers (*āsavakkhaye ñāṇa*), and tracing the chain backwards to the first link in the liberative sequence, namely, faith. At this point it crosses over to the mundane order, explaining faith as arising through suffering, suffering as conditioned by birth, birth as conditioned by existence, and so on back through the familiar links to ignorance as the first member of the chain. After completing the reverse exposition, the Buddha then expounds the same series in forward order, beginning with ignorance and following through to the knowledge of destruction. This he does twice, in exactly the same way, once before and once after the striking simile comparing the sequential origination of the factors to the gradual descent of rainfall from a mountain, through the graded ponds, lakes, streams, and rivers to the great ocean at the mountain's base. Thus the series of conditions presented in the sutta can be mapped out in the abstract as follows:

Mundane Order

Ignorance (*avijjā*)
Kamma formations (*saṅkhārā*)
Consciousness (*viññāṇa*)
Mentality-materiality (*nāmarūpa*)
Sixfold sense base (*saḷāyatana*)
Contact (*phassa*)
Feeling (*vedanā*)
Craving (*taṇhā*)
Clinging (*upādāna*)
Existence (*bhava*)
Birth (*jāti*)
Suffering (*dukkha*)

Transcendental Order

Faith (*saddhā*)
Joy (*pāmojja*)
Rapture (*pīti*)
Tranquillity (*passaddhi*)
Happiness (*sukha*)
Concentration (*samādhi*)
Knowledge and vision of things as they are (*yathābhūtañāṇadassana*)
Disenchantment (*nibbidā*)
Dispassion (*virāga*)
Emancipation (*vimutti*)
Knowledge of destruction of the cankers (*āsavakkhaye ñāṇa*)

For ease of explanation we will examine the links of transcendental dependent arising in direct order. However, before doing so, it is instructive to note that there is special significance in the initial presentation of the series in reverse. Such a presentation serves to throw an important spotlight on the nature of the causal relation obtaining between the path to liberation and its goal. It shows that the type of causal development displayed by this progression is quite different from the pattern of blind efficient causality which involves the incidental emergence of an effect out of its causal matrix, as for example when a series of geological changes triggers off an earthquake or a number of atoms combine to form some new molecule. The relationship between the path and the goal belongs to a more complex order of causality, one which can perhaps be pictured as a set of prior causes giving rise to an effect but can never be adequately and correctly comprehended in terms of this model. What we have here is not an instance of simple, one-directional causality proceeding forward unmodified in a straight line; we have, rather, a species of teleological causality involving purpose, intelligence, and planned striving simultaneously projected towards and refracted from the aimed at effect in a process of reciprocal determination. In the workings of this relationship not only does the path facilitate the achievement of the goal, but the goal as well, already present from the outset as the envisaged aim of striving, itself bends back to participate in the shaping of the path. Starting from man's awareness of the painful inadequacies of his existence, and his intuitive groping towards a condition where these are allayed, the formula proceeds to trace back, in terms derivative from and constantly checked against the goal, the series of alterations he must induce in his cognitive and emotive makeup to bring the goal into his reach.

We see this pattern illustrated in the traditional account of prince Siddhartha's great renunciation.[7] When the future Buddha leaves his palace, he goes forth in the confidence that beyond the perishable, defective, and substanceless things of the world there is accessible to man an unperishable and self-sufficient state which makes possible deliverance from suffering. What he needs to discover, as the objective of his "holy quest," is the path bridging the two domains. This he does by pursuing backwards from the goal of striving the obstructions to its attainment and the steps to be taken to remove those obstructions. One line of exploration begins with ageing and death as the fundamental manifestation of the suffering which weighs upon the world, and follows its chain of conditions back to ignorance as the underlying root.[8] Another, complementary line starts with the defilements as the principal obstruction to emancipation. It then finds the defilements to be sustained by ignorance, ignorance by the distracted mind, and the distracted mind by a causal nexus going back to lack of faith in the true Dhamma.[9] From this the conclusion follows, as shown in the *Upanisa Sutta*, that to achieve deliverance the defilements must be removed through dispassion, to reach dispassion ignorance must be overcome by correct understanding, to arouse understanding the mind must be concentrated, and so on through the counter-conditions down to the gain of faith in the true Dhamma.

In both cases the reverse direction of the sequential logic reveals the peculiar nature of the path-goal relationship. The two stand together in a bond of reciprocal determination, the path leading to the achievement of the goal and the goal giving form and content to the path. In addition to the forward thrust of the path, there is thus a basic feedback emanating from the goal, so that the goal can, in a sense, generate out of itself, through the

7. MN 26.
8. See SN XII.4–10.
9. See AN X.61, 62.

circuit system of man's constitutional capacities, the series of measures needed to bring about its actualization. This relationship is analogous to the relation between a guided missile and its mobile target. The missile does not reach its target merely through its own initial thrust and direction. It finds it precisely because it is being controlled by signals the target is itself emitting.

* * *

Faith (Saddhā)

"Suffering is the supporting condition for faith": After asserting as the last step in the mundane sequence that birth is the supporting condition for suffering, the sutta switches over to the transcendental series with the pronouncement that suffering is the supporting condition for faith. With respect to both assertions the present formulation diverges from the usual version of twelve-factored dependent arising. In the usual version the forward sequence ends with the statement that birth is the condition for ageing-and-death, sorrow, lamentation, pain, grief, and despair. With this it concludes, leaving unstated the implied aftermath—that this "mass of suffering" will generate anew the fundamental ignorance at the head of the whole series, thus beginning another run through the cycle. The fact that suffering here replaces ageing-and-death as the last member of the saṃsāric part of the series therefore has a special importance. It cautions us to the impending change, signalling that we are about to witness, in the progression of links to follow, not just one more turn of the wheel but an interruption of its forward spin and a struggle to reverse its natural direction of movement.

The Buddha's declaration that suffering is the supporting condition for faith points to the essential backdrop to the awakening of the religious consciousness. It reveals that spiritual awareness and the quest for enlightenment do not arise spontaneously in harmony with our natural modes of world-engagement, but require a turn "against the current," a break away from our instinctual urges for expansion and enjoyment and the embarkation in a different direction. This break is precipitated by the encounter with suffering. Suffering spurs the awakening of the religious consciousness in that it is the experience of suffering which first tears us out of our blind absorption in the immediacy of temporal being and sets us in search of a way to its transcendence. Whether in the form of pain, frustration, or distress, suffering reveals the basic insecurity of the human condition, shattering our naïve optimism and unquestioned trust in the goodness of the given order of things. It throws before our awareness, in a way we cannot evade, the vast gulf stretching between our ingrained expectations and the possibilities for their fulfilment in a world never fully susceptible to domination by our wills. It makes us call into question our schemes of values built upon the bedrock of personal expedience. It leads to a revaluation of all values and a new scale of worth indifferent to the claims of self-concern. And it opens us to confidence in an unseen order of relations and inter-connections, an order in which the values that emerge, so often in forceful opposition to the old, will find their proper justification and reward.

Yet for suffering to become an effective spur to spiritual awakening it is not enough merely to encounter it. For the religious consciousness to be aroused suffering must be not only met as a constant liability of our existence, but confronted and grappled with in the arena of thematic reflection. As long as we engage suffering simply in its superficial modes, as felt pain and sorrow, we will react to it in one of two ways, both of which operate at a purely psychological level. In the first case we will react to suffering in an unhealthy manner, as when we arouse resentment against the source of our displeasure and seek relief by annihilating it, ignoring it, or running away in pursuit of some easy escape. In the second case we will react to suffering in a mentally healthy way, as when we fortify our minds with patience and courage, strengthen our capacities for endurance, and seek to resolve the problem in a realistic manner. But though the second approach is definitely to be preferred to the first, in neither case does that inward revolution take place which awakens us to our extreme need for deliverance and compels us to set off in a new direction previously unknown and unexplored. The urge for liberation can only set in when pain and sorrow have been confronted with reflective awareness and recognized as symptoms of a deeper ailment demanding a radical therapy. The quest for a conclusive solution to the problem of suffering begins with an act of understanding, not with mere tribulation. It starts from the realization that suffering is more than a chance encroachment upon a state of affairs otherwise felicitous, that it is a malady which infects our being upwards from its very root. We must come to see that the breeding ground of suffering lies not so much in the outside world as at the base of our own being, and that any cure that is to be permanently effective must uproot it at this inward source.

The arising of such a realization depends upon the adoption of a new perspective from which the fact of suffering can be faced in its full range and universality. Though single in its essence, suffering or *dukkha* yet divides into three stages or tiers in accordance with the level of understanding from which it is viewed.[10] At the most elementary level suffering appears as physical pain and oppression, manifest most clearly in the events of birth, sickness, ageing and death, as well as in hunger, thirst, privation, and bodily discomfort. At a higher level it comes to be seen as a psychological fact—as the sorrow and frustration springing from our separation from what is desired, our meeting with what is disliked, and the disappointment of our expectations. And at the third and highest level suffering becomes manifest in its essential form, as the inherent unsatisfactoriness of the saṃsāric round in which we turn without purpose on account of our ignorance and attachments. These three tiers are not mutually exclusive. In each case the lower level serves as basis for the higher, by which it is absorbed and comprehended. Thus, though the penetration of the highest stage, the essential suffering comprised in the "five clinging aggregates" (*pañcupadānakkhandhā*), represents the climax of understanding, this realization comes as the fruit of a long period of preparation grounded upon the first flash of insight into the basic inadequacy of the human condition. Such an insight usually dawns through particular experiences typical of the first two stages of suffering—through sudden pain, loss or disappointment, or through chronic anxiety, confusion, and distress. But in order to become the stimulus to a higher course of development, our vision must be capable of rising from the particular to the universal. It is only when we see clearly for ourselves that we are "sunk in birth,

10. See Lama Anāgārika Govinda, *The Psychological Attitude of Early Buddhist Philosophy* (London, 1969), pp. 49–52.

ageing, and death, in sorrow, lamentation, pain, grief, and despair, sunk in suffering, overcome by suffering" (MN 29), that we are really ready for the means to bring this unsatisfactory condition to an end.

Since it is suffering that impels us to seek the way to liberation, suffering is called the supporting condition for faith. By itself, however, the confrontation with suffering even at the level of mature reflection is not sufficient to generate faith. For faith to arise two conditions are required: the first is the awareness of suffering, which makes us recognize the need for a liberative path; the second is the encounter with a teaching that proclaims a liberative path. Thence the Buddha says that faith has for its nutriment hearing the exposition of the true Dhamma.[11] *Saddhā*, the faith that comes into being as a result of hearing the exposition of the true Dhamma, is essentially an attitude of trust and commitment directed to ultimate emancipation. In order for such faith to arise and become a driving force of spiritual development, it must meet with an objective ground capable of eliciting its forward leap into the unknown and of prompting its inner urge towards liberation. From the Buddhist perspective this objective ground is provided by the three objects of refuge—the Buddha, the Dhamma, and the Saṅgha, that is, the enlightened Teacher, his teaching, and his community of noble disciples. The faith to be placed in them must not be blind and uncritical. Though initially requiring consent born out of trust, it also must be based on critical scrutiny—the Teacher tested to determine his trustworthiness, his doctrine examined to decide on its cogency, and his disciples interrogated to ascertain their reliability.[12] As a result of such examination, conducted either through personal confrontation whenever possible or through scrutiny of the scriptural records, faith becomes settled in the Buddha as the Perfectly Enlightened One, the unerring guide on the path to deliverance; in the Dhamma as his teaching and the path leading to deliverance; and in the Saṅgha as the community of the Buddha's disciples who have verified his teaching through their own direct experience, and hence may be relied upon for guidance in our own pursuit of the goal.

11. AN X.61. *Ko cāhāro saddhāya? Saddhammassavanan-ti 'ssa vacanīyaṃ.*
12. See MN 47, MN 95.

As the first requisite of spiritual development, faith is compared to a hand, in that it is needed to take hold of beneficial practices, and to a seed, in that it is the vitalizing germ for the growth of the higher virtues.

Beneath its seeming simplicity it is a complex phenomenon combining intellectual, emotional, and conative elements. Intellectually faith implies a willingness to accept on trust propositions beyond our present capacity for verification, propositions relating to the basic tenets of the doctrine. Through practice this assent will be translated from belief into knowledge, but at the outset there is required an acceptance which cannot be fully corroborated by objective evidence. Emotionally faith issues in feelings of confidence and serene joy, coupled with an attitude of devotion directed to the objects of refuge. And at the level of volition faith reinforces the readiness to implement certain lines of conduct in the conviction they will lead to the desired goal. It is the mobilizing force of action, stirring up the energy to actualize the ideal.

* * *

Joy (Pāmojja)

"Faith is the supporting condition for joy": Faith functions as a support for the next link in the series, joy or gladness (*pāmojja*), by permitting an outlet from the pent-up tensions of an existential impasse brought on by the reflective encounter with the problem of suffering. Prior to the discovery of the true Dhamma two alternatives present themselves to the thoughtful individual as he struggles to work out a viable solution to the problem of suffering once it has emerged into the open in its full depth and universality. One alternative is compliant submission to a justification of suffering developed along traditional theological lines—that is, a theodicy which sees evil and suffering as detracting from the goodness of the created order only superficially, while ultimately contributing to the total perfection of the whole. This solution, though generally aligned with the higher ethical values, still appears to the sensitive thinker to be a facile answer constantly provocative of a gnawing sense of doubt and disbelief. The other alternative is resignation to suffering as a brute fact unintelligible to man's moral sense, an incidental offshoot of a universe totally indifferent to any structure of spiritual or ethical values. This solution, though not internally inconsistent, clashes with our basic moral intuitions so sharply that the result, for the sensitive thinker, is often a turn to nihilism in one of its two forms—as reckless license or ineffectual despair.

Neither the theological nor the materialistic answers can show the way to an actual escape from suffering. Both, in the last analysis, can only hold out a choice between resignation and rebellion. The gain of faith in the true Dhamma spells the end to this quandary by pointing to a solution which can admit the pervasive reality of suffering without needing to justify it, yet can give this suffering a cogent explanation and indicate an escape. Suffering, from this perspective, is traceable to distinct causes endowed with ethical significance; it is the inevitable result of our own immoral actions returning to ourselves. Our actions, when viewed from the standpoint of the Dhamma, are neither threads in some invisible handiwork of divine perfection, nor meaningless pulsations of nerves and brain, but expressions of ethically significant decisions having an integral place in a morally intelligible world. They are seen as choices for which we bear full responsibility before an impersonal universal law that ensures the preservation of an equilibrium between deeds and their results, so that virtuous deeds bring forth happiness and evil deeds suffering. The round of becoming in which we are immersed—where we are born, grow old, suffer, and die—this round is created by ourselves, fashioned out of our own blindness and craving. We build the round ourselves and we can bring it to an end by ourselves, by eradicating this world-sustaining ignorance and desire. The path to liberation is revealed in all its practical details with full precision and clarity. It is a path of conduct and insight each man must tread for himself, success being dependent entirely on his own diligence, sincerity and energy, and on his capacities for renunciation and understanding.

The gain of faith in the true Dhamma thus points to an outlet from the contention of opposed alternatives, neither of which can be happily embraced. It exhausts the pressures of an apparent dead-end, and as the stress and tension fall away there springs up a surge of joy conditioned by the acquisition of faith. This incipient swell of joy grows by degrees as the aspirant's contemplation focuses more sharply upon the objects in which confidence has been reposed. Sustained reflection on the Buddha, Dhamma, and Saṅgha gradually dispels the darkness of doubt and indecision. It issues in an effusion of light, of peace and inner clarity, when as a result of such reflection the defilements are attenuated and the mind's impulsion towards the elevating qualities the refuges represent gains in forward momentum. For this reason faith is compared to a miraculous water-clearing gem. According to Indian legend, there is a special gem possessed by the mythic universal monarch which, when thrown into a stream of turbid water, immediately causes it to become clear. The strands of vegetation float away, the mud settles, and the water becomes pure, serene, and sweet-tasting, fit to be drunk by the monarch. Similarly, it is said, when the gem of faith is set up in the heart it causes the hindrances to disappear, the defilements to settle, and the mind to become clear, lucid, and serene.[13]

The strengthening of confidence in the objects of refuge becomes the incentive for a firmer dedication to the practice of the teaching. Thence the texts ascribe to faith the characteristic of "leaping forward."[14] Faith leaps forward in that "when the yogin sees that the hearts of others have been set free, he leaps forward, by way of aspiration, to the various fruits of a holy life, and he makes efforts to attain the yet unattained, to find the unfound, to realize the unrealized."[15] This aspect of faith is illustrated by a courageous hero who lunges across a turbulent river to escape from danger, saving himself thereby and inspiring others by his example.

At this stage, in particular, the aspirant's faith creates a readiness to undertake the basic rules of moral training. Through his settled faith in the Buddha, Dhamma, and Saṅgha he is prepared to enter the path of practice, which requires at the start that he train in the foundation of the path, the observance of moral discipline (*sīla*). For this reason the acceptance of moral

13. *Milindapañhā.* See Edward Conze, *The Way of Wisdom* (The Wheel No. 65/66), (Kandy: Buddhist Publication Society), pp. 30–31.

14. *Ibid. Pakkhandanalakkhaṇā saddhā.*

15. *Ibid.*, p. 31.

restraint is said to be undertaken out of faith.[16] Moral restraint is taken up by accepting rules of discipline designed to inculcate an inner disposition of virtue by controlling bodily and verbal actions. The codes of rules vary in scope from the five basic precepts of the Buddhist layman to the more than 227 training rules undertaken by the bhikkhu or fully ordained monk, but all share the common characteristic of disciplining behaviour. Each of the basic precepts involves an explicit principle of abstinence requiring to be observed and an implicit mental attitude to be cultivated through such abstinence. The former consists in abstention from the unwholesome actions of taking life, stealing, sexual abuse, false speech and partaking of intoxicants; the latter calls for a persistent effort to develop a mind of compassion, honesty, purity, truthfulness, and sobriety. The immediate result of living in conformity with these guidelines to right action is the arising of a sense of freedom from remorse (*avippatisara*). Remorse, a feeling of regret over moral transgression and neglect, tends to provoke guilt, agitation, and self-recrimination. When, through close adherence to the precepts, the mind is freed from remorse, an ease of conscience and "bliss of blamelessness" set in born of the knowledge that one's actions are beyond reproach. Thence the Buddha declares wholesome rules of conduct to have freedom from remorse as their benefit and reward.[17] The joy that comes through realizing one's purity confirms the confidence originally placed in the teaching. Thereby it arouses still stronger faith and a desire for further application to the practice.

* * *

Rapture (Pīti)

"Joy is the supporting condition for rapture": Though for certain individuals serene faith in the objects of refuge and a clear conscience are sufficient to transform joy into rapture, such cases are the exception rather than the rule. Generally, in order for the emotional tone of the spiritual life to be lifted to that pitch of intensity

16. *Visuddhimagga*, I.98. Bhikkhu Ñāṇamoli, trans. *The Path of Purification*, 3rd ed. (Kandy: Buddhist Publication Society, 1975), p. 36.
17. AN X.1.

suggested by the term "rapture" (*pīti*) a further commitment to the training is necessary. This commitment takes the form of deliberate application to the practice of meditation. Methods of meditation contributing to the attainment of liberation are classified into two systems—serenity meditation (*samathabhāvanā*) and insight meditation (*vipassanābhāvanā*). Serenity meditation aims at the creation of a state of calm concentration by unifying the mind in focus on a single object. Insight meditation aims at insight into the nature of phenomena by directly contemplating the bodily and mental processes as they occur on the successive moments of experience. Though there is a system which employs mindfulness as a direct means to the awakening of insight, in the usual pattern serenity is cultivated first as a preliminary measure, since the unification and purification of consciousness effected by concentration facilitate correct penetration of the nature of things through contemplative insight. This is the sequence utilized by the present sutta, the stages from "rapture" through "concentration" covering the systematic development of serenity; the two following stages, the development of insight.

Serenity meditation is cultivated on the basis of a single object selected from a standard set of objects reserved exclusively for the development of concentration. These objects, traditionally numbered at forty, include the coloured and elemental circles called *kasiṇas,* the cemetery contemplations, the recollections of the three refuge objects, meditation on the sublime abodes of love and compassion, mindfulness of breathing, etc. After taking up one of these objects as his field of work, the yogin strives to unify his mind by fixing his attention on his object to the exclusion of all sense data, concepts, thoughts, memories, projections, fantasies, and associative thinking. His aim is to make his mind one-pointed, and this forbids at once its dispersal among a multiplicity of concerns. Success in the practice depends on the harmonization of the mental faculties in the work of concentration. Through mindfulness (*sati*) the yogin bears the object in his field of awareness and prevents it from slipping away; through discernment (*sampajañña*) he maintains a cautious watch upon the mind, noting its tendencies to stray and swiftly correcting them; and through energy (*viriya*) he strives to dispel the impediments to mental unification, and to maintain his awareness at a pitch which is simultaneously taut but relaxed.

The impediments to meditation are classified into a group of five factors called the "five hindrances" (*pañcanīvaraṇa*). These are sensual desire, ill-will, stiffness and torpor, restlessness and regret, and doubt. The Buddha calls these five hindrances "corruptions of the mind" and "weakeners of wisdom." He says they are conducive to pain, blindness, and ignorance, and compares them respectively to a debt, a disease, imprisonment, slavery, and the dangers of a desert journey. Their removal by unremitting exertion is the first task facing the meditator. As he proceeds in his practice, striving with patience and diligence, there come suddenly momentary breaks in the course of his efforts when the hindrances fall away, the flow of inner verbalization stops, and the mind abides one-pointedly on the object. The achievement of this momentary concentration, brief as it is, gives immense satisfaction. It is a powerful experience unleashing spurts of mental energy which flood up to the surface of consciousness and inundate the mind with waves of joyous refreshment. It brings an elating thrill bordering on ecstasy, crowning the yogin's previous endeavours and inspiring further effort.

This experience marks the arising of rapture. The distinguishing feature of rapture is a strong interest and delight directed to the object of attention. Its function is to give refreshment to the body and mind. It can assume both wholesome and unwholesome forms, depending on whether it is motivated by attachment or detachment with respect to its object, but on occasions of meditative consciousness it is always wholesome. The commentaries distinguish five degrees of rapture which make their appearance in the successive stages of mental unification.[18] "Minor rapture," the lowest on the scale, is said to be able to raise the hairs of the body. "Momentary rapture," the next degree of development, rushes through the body with an intensity likened to streaks of lightning flashing forth in the sky at different moments. "Showering rapture," the third degree, breaks over the body again and again with considerable force, like the waves on the seashore breaking upon the beach. "Uplifting rapture" is so-called because it is credited with the ability to cause the body to levitate, and the *Visuddhimagga* cites several cases where this literally occurs. And

18. Vism. IV.94–98, Ñāṇamoli, pp. 149–150.

"pervading rapture," the highest on the scale, is said to completely fill the whole body as a huge inundation fills a rock cavern. Since the commentary to our sutta defines joy (*pāmojja*), the prior link in our sequence, as weak rapture, we may assume this to signify the delightful interest preceding the deliberate development of meditation, that is, in the stages when faith in the Dhamma was just acquired and the purification of moral discipline commenced. The five degrees of rapture presented here would then pertain exclusively to the rapture found in meditative consciousness. And since the last degree of rapture only gains ascendancy with the attainment of full absorption, which does not come until later, it seems that the degrees of rapture which are distinctive of the present stage of progress are the four beginning with minor rapture and reaching their peak with uplifting rapture.

* * *

Tranquillity (Passaddhi)

"Rapture is the supporting condition for tranquillity": While the appearance of rapture indicates a definite advance in the work of concentration, its coarser modes still contain an element of exuberance which is in constant danger of slipping out of control and spilling over into unwholesome states of mind dominated by restlessness and agitation. For rapture involves an intense delight in the object coupled with an anticipation of even greater delight to come. The experience of present delight can often be accompanied by an underlying worry that this pleasure will disappear, while the expectation of further delight can stimulate a subtle grasping at the future. Both states, the anxiety and the grasping, bring along an excitation inimical to the centering of the mind in one-pointed calm. For this reason, as the yogin progresses in his practice, a point is reached where the ecstatic exultation sparked off by rapture becomes felt as an obstruction to the development of mental unification, a corruption of the training which must be pacified and stilled.

Rapture itself will remain as a factor of meditative development up to the third absorption, but to permit further progress its detrimental tendencies have to be sublimated. Through continued application to the practice rapture becomes more refined, shedding the heated zest of its initial forms. With its refinement it increasingly evokes along with itself another quality called "tranquillity" (*passaddhi*). Tranquillity is characterized by the quieting down of mental disturbances. It removes agitation and restlessness, imparting to the mind a soothing calm comparable to the cool shade offered by a tree to travellers oppressed by the sun's heat. Tranquillity operates in two co-occurrent forms, "tranquillity of body" and "tranquillity of mind," where "mind" signifies the aggregate of consciousness and "body," not the physical organism, but the group of consciousness-adjuncts included in the aggregates of feeling, perception, and mental formations.[19] Thence the arising of tranquillity results in the subsiding of disturbances throughout the full extent of the psychodynamic system. It allays the propensity towards excitement, soothes the innervations brought on by rapture, and casts over the meditative endeavour a profound stillness paving the way for deeper states of concentration to follow.

Tranquillity further induces in both consciousness and its adjuncts the qualitative factors of lightness, malleability, wieldiness, proficiency, and rectitude. These factors, present to some extent in every wholesome state of consciousness, perform the respective tasks of eliminating sluggishness, rigidity, unwieldiness, disability, and insincerity. By holding at bay these mental corruptions destructive to moral and spiritual progress, they enhance the functional efficiency of the mind, rendering it a more tractable instrument for application to the higher stages of the path.

* * *

Happiness (Sukha)

"Tranquillity is the supporting condition for happiness": As the yogin's psychosomatic system is brought to a state of

19. Vism. XIV.144, Ñāṇamoli, p. 525. The "five aggregates" (*pañcakkhandhā*) are the basic categories into which Buddhism analyzes the sentient organism. The aggregate of material form covers the physical body; the aggregates of feeling, perception, mental formations and consciousness cover the mind. Of these four, the first three are considered the adjuncts or concomitants of consciousness, the primary factor of mental life.

tranquil composure, a feeling of inner happiness or bliss (*sukha*), unobtrusively present from the start, gains in prominence until it emerges in its own right as a salient feature of the training. Though closely associated with rapture, happiness is not identical with the latter and can arise in its absence. Rapture denotes a mental factor belonging to the fourth of the five aggregates into which Buddhism classifies the psycho-physical organism, namely, the aggregate of mental formations (*saṅkhārakkhandha*). It is a conative rather than affective phenomenon, which fuses zestful interest with a sense of joyous delight. Happiness, on the other hand, is a purely hedonic factor belonging to the second aggregate, the aggregate of feelings (*vedanākkhandha*). It is pleasurable feeling, here, as the happiness conditioned by tranquillity, the pleasure which springs up in meditation as disturbances subside.

Rapture is relatively coarse in quality and happiness subtle. Thence, though rapture is always accompanied by happiness, in the higher meditative attainment of the third *jhāna* happiness can remain even after rapture has faded away. The *Atthasālinī*, a commentary to the *Abhidhamma-piṭaka*, illustrates the difference between them with a vivid simile:

> A man who, travelling along the path through a great desert and overcome by the heat is thirsty and desirous of drink, if he saw a man on the way, would ask, "Where is water?" The other would say, "Beyond the wood is a dense forest with a natural lake. Go there, and you will get some." He, hearing these words, would be glad and delighted. Going onwards, be would see men with wet clothes and hair, hear the sound of wild fowl and pea-fowl, etc., see the dense forest of green like a net of jewels by the edge of the natural lake, he would see the water lily, the lotus, the white lily, etc., growing in the lake, he would see the clear transparent water, he would be all the more glad and delighted, would descend into the natural lake, bathe and drink at pleasure and, his oppression being allayed, he would eat the fibres and stalks of the lilies, adorn himself with the blue lotus, carry on his shoulders the roots of the *mandalaka*, ascend from the lake, put on his clothes, dry the bathing cloth in the sun, and in the cool shade where the breeze blew ever so gently lay himself down and say:

> "O bliss! O bliss!" Thus should this illustration be applied: The time of gladness and delight from when he heard of the natural lake and the dense forest till he saw the water is like *piti* having the manner of gladness and delight at the object in view. The time when, after his bath and drink be laid himself down in the cool shade, saying, "O bliss! O bliss!" etc., is the sense of *sukha* grown strong, established in that mode of enjoying the taste of the object.
>
> —Maung Tin, trans. *The Expositor* (*Atthasālinī*), (London 1920), Vol. I, pp. 157–58.

Despite the simile's suggestion, rapture and happiness are not necessarily asynchronous, and are in fact only sundered with the attainment of the third *jhāna*. The presentation of happiness as arising subsequent to rapture only means that happiness becomes the salient feature of the path after rapture has already made its own distinctive contribution and settled back to a subsidiary place. In the present stage rapture still persists, only its exuberance has now been toned down by the prevailing quiescence developed in the stage of tranquillity.

The subcommentary to the *Upanisa Sutta* explains *sukha* as the happiness of the access to absorption. The term "access" (*upacāra*) denotes the stage in the cultivation of serenity immediately preceding full absorption, the intended goal of serenity meditation. Access is characterized by the abandonment of the five hindrances and the arising of the "counterpart sign," the self-luminous object of interior perception which is the focal point for the higher stages of concentration. The abandoning of the hindrances began already with the gain of faith, which conferred a serene lucency suspending their turbulence, and each ascending rung along the path marked their attenuation to a further degree. Since the hindrances are the principal obstructions to both serenity and insight, the early stages of the path are primarily concerned with their debilitation and elimination.

The elimination of the hindrances prior to attaining access is brought about by means of two methods, one specifically directed to each hindrance separately, the other applicable to all at once. The former is to be employed when a particular hindrance obtrudes itself with persistent force, the latter on other occasions when no one hindrance seems especially conspicuous. The specific method involves the reversing of the causal situation out of which the hindrance develops. Since each defiling factor is a conditioned phenomenon coming into existence through distinct causes, the key to its elimination lies in applying the appropriate antidote to its causal base. Thus sensual desire arises on account of unskilful attention to the attractive features of things, to alluring objects and physical bodies. It is attenuated by considering the impermanence of the objects of attachment, and by reflecting on the repulsive nature underlying the attractive appearance of the bodies which arouse desire. Ill-will or anger also springs up from unskilful attention, in this case to the unpleasant aspects of persons and things; it is reversed by developing loving kindness towards disagreeable people and patience in the face of unfavourable circumstances. Stiffness and torpor become prominent by submitting to moods of sloth and drowsiness; they are dispelled by the arousal of energy. Restlessness and regret arise from attending to disturbing thoughts and are eliminated by directing the mind to an object conducive to inner peace. And doubt, grounded upon unclarity with regard to fundamental points of doctrine, is dispelled by clear thinking and precise analysis of the issues shrouded in obscurity.

In contrast to these techniques, which counter the hindrances separately, the practice of concentration on one of the prescribed objects of serenity meditation inhibits them all simultaneously. Though only effective so long as no particular hindrance impedes the meditative progress, this method, drawing upon the power of mental unification, is capable of bringing tremendous force to bear upon the struggle against their supremacy. Since the latent defilements can crop up into the open only so long as the mind is driven by discursive thinking, the unification of the mind upon a single object closes off the portal through which they emerge. As the mind descends to increasingly deeper levels of concentration, the hindrances are gradually made to subside until, with the attainment of access, their suppression becomes complete. Held at bay in the base of the mental continuum, the latent defilements are no longer capable of rising to the surface of consciousness. For as long as the suppressive force of concentration prevails, their activity is suspended, and the mind remains secure in its one-pointed stabilization, safe from their disruptive influence. This abandonment of the hindrances through the power of suppression brings a feeling of profound relief accompanied by a blissful effusion born from the newly accomplished purification. The Buddha compares the happiness of abandoning the hindrances to the happiness a man would experience if he were unexpectedly freed from debt, cured of a serious illness, released from prison, set free from slavery, or led to safety at the end of a desert journey.[20]

* * *

Concentration (Samādhi)

"Happiness is the supporting condition for concentration": The attainment of access signals a major breakthrough which spurs on further exertion. As a result of such exertion the bliss generated in the access stage is made to expand and to suffuse the mind so completely that the subtlest barriers to inner unification disappear. Along with their disappearance the mind passes beyond the stage of access and enters into absorption or full concentration (*samādhi*). Concentration itself denotes a mental factor present in both the attainments of access and absorption. Its salient feature is the wholesome unification of the mind on a single object, and it brings about a harmonization between consciousness and its concomitants to a degree sufficient to free them from the distraction, vacillation, and unsteadiness characterizing their normal operations. The mind in concentration, fixed firmly on its object, is like the flame of a candle shielded from the wind or the surface of a lake on which all the waves and ripples have been stilled.

However, although both access and absorption partake of the nature of concentration, an important difference still separates them, justifying the restriction of the term "full concentration" to absorption alone. This difference consists in the relative strength in the two attainments of certain mental concomitants called the "factors of absorption" or "*jhāna* factors" (*jhānaṅgāni*)—namely, applied thought, sustained thought, rapture, happiness, and mental one-pointedness. These factors, aroused at the very beginning of serenity meditation and gradually cultivated through the course of its progress, have the dual function of inhibiting

20. DN 2.

the hindrances and unifying the mind on its object. According to the commentaries, the factors are aligned with the hindrances in a direct one-to-one relation of opposition, such that each *jhāna* factor has the specific task of countering and occluding one hindrance. Thus applied thought counteracts stiffness and torpor, sustained thought doubt, rapture ill-will, happiness restlessness and regret, and one-pointedness sensual desire.[21] At the same time the factors exercise a consolidating function with respect to the object, applied thought directing the mind to the object, sustained thought anchoring it there, rapture creating an interest in it, happiness experiencing its affective quality, and one-pointedness focusing the mind on the object.

In the access attainment the *jhāna* factors are strong enough to keep the hindrances suppressed, but not yet strong enough to place the mind in absorption. They still stand in need of maturation. Maturation comes as a result of continued practice, which gives them the power to lift the mind beyond the threshold plane of access and plunge it into the object with the unshakeable force of full absorption. In the state of absorption the mind fixes upon its object with such a high intensity of concentration that subjective discriminations between the two no longer occur. The waves of discursive thinking have at last subsided, and the mind abides without straying even the least from its base of stabilization. Nevertheless, even full concentration admits of degrees. At the plane of absorption concentration is divided into four levels called the four jhānas. These are distinguished by the aggregation of factors present in each attainment, the order of the four being determined by the successive elimination of the comparatively coarser factors. In the first *jhāna* all five *jhāna* factors are present; in the second applied and sustained thought are eliminated, in the third rapture is made to fade away; and in the fourth the feeling of happiness is replaced by equanimity, the peaceful feeling-tone which veers neither toward pleasure nor toward pain. One-pointedness remains present in all four jhānas, the one constant in the series. To rise from the first *jhāna* to the second, the yogin, after emerging from the first *jhāna*, must reflect upon the coarseness of applied and sustained thought and the first *jhāna*'s inadequacy due

21. Vism. IV.86, Ñāṇamoli, p. 147.

to the proximity of the hindrances. Then he must consider the second *jhāna* as more peaceful and sublime, arouse the aspiration to attain it, and exert his energy to achieve a stronger degree of mental unification. Similarly, to rise from the second to the third *jhāna* he must repeat the same procedure taking rapture as the coarse factor needing to be eliminated, and to rise from the third to the fourth *jhāna* he must reflect on the coarseness of happiness and the superiority of neutral, equanimous feeling.

Beyond the fourth *jhāna* lie four even subtler stages of concentration called the four formless attainments (*arūpasamāpatti*). In these attainments the luminous counterpart sign serving as the object of the jhānas is replaced by four successively more refined formless objects, which give their names to their respective attainments—the base of infinite space, the base of infinite consciousness, the base of nothingness, and the base of neither perception nor non-perception. At the peak of this scale of meditative equipoise consciousness arrives at a point of unification so fine that, like the geometric point, it eludes detection, and its presence can be neither affirmed nor denied.

* * *

Knowledge and Vision (Ñāṇadassana)

"Concentration is the supporting condition for the knowledge and vision of things as they really are": Despite the loftiness and sublimity of these exalted attainments, immersion in deep concentration is not the end of the Buddhist path. The unification of consciousness effected by serenity meditation is only a means to a further stage of practice. This stage, ushered in by the next link in the series, "the knowledge and vision of things as they really are" (*yathābhūtañāṇadassana*), is the development of insight (*vipassanā bhāvanā*).

Through his deep concentration the yogin is able to suppress the defilements, to bring them to a state of quiescence where they no longer invade the active processes of thought. But beneath the surface stillness the defilements lie latent, ready to spring up again if provoked. As long as the defilements remain present, even if only in dormant form, release from suffering has yet to be achieved, for the latencies of the defilements lying quietly in the mental continuum can still regenerate the saṃsāric round of continued birth and death. The latent tendencies are the seeds of renewed existence, which bring about a re-arising of the stream of consciousness and thence of all the remaining links in the saṃsāric chain. To end the round and attain deliverance the defilements must be completely destroyed; it is not enough merely to suppress them. The destruction of the defilements cannot be brought about by concentration alone, for concentration, even at its deepest levels, can only effect the suspension of their activity, not their eradication. To destroy the defilements down to their bottommost stratum of latency something more is needed—*paññā*, the wisdom which penetrates the true mark of phenomena. Concentration gains its place in the Buddhist discipline in so far as it induces the mental one-pointedness of at least the access level required as the support for wisdom. Thus the Buddha enjoins his disciples to develop concentration, not as an end in itself, but because "one who is concentrated understands things as they really are."[22] Only a mind which has been rendered pure and calm can comprehend things in accordance with actuality, and the discipline of concentration, by suppressing the hindrances, engenders the required purity and calm. The actual work, however, of extricating the defilements is performed exclusively by wisdom.

Wisdom is "the one thing needed" to cut off the defilements because the most fundamental of all the mental depravities is ignorance (*avijjā*). Ignorance is the kingpost upon which all the other defilements converge and the lynchpin which holds them all in place. While it remains the others remain, and for the others to be destroyed it must be destroyed. Doctrinally defined as nescience with regard to the four noble truths, ignorance signifies not so much the lack of specific pieces of information as a basic non-comprehension regarding the true nature of things as expressed in the four truths. Since the eradication of the defilements depends upon the eradication of ignorance, the one factor capable of abolishing the defilements is the factor capable of abolishing their fundamental root, and that is the direct antithesis of ignorance—wisdom or "the knowledge and vision of things as they really are." For this reason, at the beginning of our sutta, the Buddha

22. SN XXII.5.

proclaims: "The destruction of the cankers is for one who knows and sees, I say, not for one who does not know and does not see." The defilements, epitomized in the "cankers," are only destroyed for one who overcomes ignorance by the wisdom which knows and sees things as they are.

The compound expression "knowledge and vision," indicates that the kind of knowledge to be developed is not mere conceptual understanding, but knowledge which in its directness and immediacy is akin to visual perception. Conceptual understanding is often needed to clear away the intellectual obstructions to a correct perspective, *but it must eventually yield to the light of direct experience.* To achieve this experiential understanding it is necessary to enter upon the practice of the second system of Buddhist meditation, the development of insight. The practice of insight meditation aims at dislodging the defilements by eradicating the ignorance at their base. Ignorance is overcome by generating, through mindful observation, a direct insight into things as they really are. The material upon which insight works is precisely the sphere where ignorance is concealed, our own psycho-physical experience. Its method is the application of mindfulness or discerning awareness to this sphere without interruption and in all activities.

In the discourse the Buddha states that what must be known and seen as they are is the five aggregates—their nature, their arising, and their passing away. The five aggregates—material form, feeling, perception, mental formations, and consciousness—are the basic categories structuring the Buddha's analysis of experience. Each experiential occasion, from the Buddhist perspective, is a complex process involving a number of factors functioning in unison. To normal, non-analytical consciousness this unified complex appears as a uniform mass, a false appearance which, when accepted at face value, leads to the assumption of a simple solid self as the permanent subject of cognition. The assumption of permanent selfhood Buddhism holds to be the basic conceptual error dominating our mental horizon. It is the outermost shell of egoistic projection shielding the pre-conceptual ignorance, and thus the first of the ten fetters to be broken along the path to liberation.

To dispel the illusion of independent selfhood the experiential process must be submitted to searching scrutiny which rectifies the false perceptions contributing to its formation. The first phase in this examination is the dissection of the cognitive fabric into the distinct threads entering into its make-up. These "threads" or components are the five aggregates. The aggregate of material form covers the physical side of experience, comprising both external material objects and the body together with its sense faculties. The other four aggregates constitute the mental side of experience. Feeling is the affective quality of pleasure or pain, or the neutral tone of neither pleasure nor pain, present on any occasion of mental activity. Perception is the selective faculty, which singles out the object's distinctive marks as a basis for recognition. The formations aggregate is a comprehensive category incorporating all mental factors other than feeling and perception; its most conspicuous member is volition. And consciousness is the faculty of cognition itself, which sustains and coordinates all the other factors in the task of apprehending the object. These five aggregates function in complete autonomy, entirely through their reciprocal support, without need for a self-subsistent unifying principle to be identified as a self or subject.

In order to develop the knowledge and vision of things as they really are with respect to the aggregates, the yogin must first emerge from his state of deep concentration, for the analytical faculty—silenced in the folds of serenity—has to be brought into play to effect the required dissection. With his mind made clear and pliant as a result of concentration, the yogin attends to the diverse phenomena coming into range of his awareness. The phenomena are attended to as they become manifest to determine their salient characteristics; then, on this basis, they are assigned to their appropriate place among the aggregates. Whatever is physical belongs to the aggregate of material form; whatever registers affective tone is feeling; whatever notices the object's marks is perception; whatever wills is a mental formation; and whatever cognizes is consciousness. The aggregates may further be grouped into a simpler scheme by placing material form on one side and the four mental aggregates on the other, the two being coupled as mentality-materiality (*nāma-rūpa*). They are then correlated with their causes and conditions to expose their dependently arisen nature. The analytic procedure generates the realization that experience is just a double stream of material and mental events without a subsisting self. The synthetic procedure makes it clear that all these events are conditioned phenomena which arise when their conditions are present and cease when their conditions disappear.

This last realization becomes the portal to the next major stage in the development of understanding, the contemplation of rise and fall. As the yogin attends to the states that appear, he sees how each undergoes the same process of coming into being, altering, and passing away: "Such is the arising of material form, feeling, perception, formations, and consciousness. Such is the passing away of material form, feeling, perception, formations, and consciousness." The contemplation of rise and fall brings into focus three marks common to all conditioned phenomena— their impermanence, unsatisfactoriness, and selflessness. Impermanence is generally the first characteristic to be discerned, as it becomes clear through the immediate attention given to rise and fall. The perception of impermanence leads directly to insight into the other marks, which follow naturally from the first. The notion of "happiness," or "pleasure," at the level of philosophical understanding rather than mere feeling, hinges upon an implicit notion of permanence. If something is to be truly a source of happiness it must be permanent. What is impermanent is incapable of yielding lasting happiness and security, and therefore turns out, under examination, to be really unsatisfactory, a potential source of suffering. The notion of selfhood in turn rests upon the two pillars of permanence and pleasure. What is impermanent and unsatisfactory cannot be identified as a self, for it lacks any solid unchanging core upon which the notion of selfhood can be grounded. Thus the impermanent, unsatisfactory phenomena comprised in the five aggregates turn out to have a third characteristic, the aspect of selflessness. The realization of these three characteristics—impermanence, unsatisfactoriness, and selflessness—through unmediated insight is the knowledge and vision of things as they really are.

* * *

Disenchantment (Nibbidā)

"The knowledge and vision of things as they really are is the supporting condition for disenchantment": As the yogin contemplates the rise and fall of the five aggregates, his attention becomes riveted to the final phase of the process, their dissolution and passing away. This insight into the instability of the aggregates at the same time reveals their basic unreliability. Far from being the ground of satisfaction we unreflectively take them to be, conditioned things are seen to be fraught with peril when adhered to with craving and wrong views. The growing realization of this fundamental insecurity brings a marked transformation in the mind's orientation towards conditioned existence. Whereas previously the mind was drawn to the world by the lure of promised gratification, now, with the exposure of the underlying danger, it draws away in the direction of a disengagement. This inward turning away from the procession of formations is called *nibbidā*. Though some times translated "disgust" or "aversion," the term suggests, not emotional repugnance, but a conscious act of detachment resulting from a profound noetic discovery. *Nibbidā* signifies in short, the serene, dignified withdrawal from phenomena which supervenes when the illusion of their permanence, pleasure, and selfhood has been shattered by the light of correct knowledge and vision of things as they are. The commentaries explain *nibbidā* as powerful insight (*balavā vipassanā*), an explanation consonant with the word's literal meaning of "finding out." It indicates the sequel to the discoveries unveiled by the contemplative process, the mind's appropriate response to the realizations thrust upon it by the growing experiences of insight. Buddhaghosa compares it to the revulsion a man would feel who, having grabbed hold of a snake in the belief it was a fish, would look at it closely and suddenly realize he was holding a snake.[23]

As our rendering implies, disenchantment marks the dissipation of an "enchantment" or fascination with the kaleidoscopic pleasures of conditioned existence, whether in the form of sense enjoyments, emotions, or ideas. This fascination, resting upon the distorted apprehension of things as permanent, pleasurable,

23. Vism. XXI.49–50, Ñāṇamoli, p. 761.

and self, is maintained at a deep unverbalized level by the hope of finding self identity in the conditioned. As the enchanted mind presses forward seeking explicit confirmation of the innate sense of selfhood, everything encountered is evaluated in terms of the notions "mine," "I," and "my self," the principal appropriative and identificatory devices with which the inherent sense of personal selfhood works. These three notions, imputed to phenomena on account of ignorance, are in actuality conceptual fabrications woven by craving, conceit, and speculation, respectively. The insight into impermanence, unsatisfactoriness, and selflessness cuts the ground out from underneath this threefold fabrication, reversing the mode in which phenomena can be viewed. Whereas before the development of insight the aggregates were regarded as being "mine," "I," and "self," now, when illuminated with the light of insight knowledge, they are seen in the opposite way as "not-mine," "not I," and "not self." Since the fascination with phenomenal existence is sustained by the assumption of underlying selfhood, the dispelling of this illusion through the penetration of the three marks brings about a de-identification with the aggregates and an end to their spell of enchantment. In place of the fascination and attraction a profound experience of estrangement sets in, engendered by the perception of selflessness in all conditioned being. The suttas present this sequence thus:

> Material form, monks, is impermanent, suffering, and non-self. Feeling, perception, mental formations, and consciousness are impermanent, suffering, and non-self. What is impermanent, suffering and non-self, that should be seen with correct wisdom as it really is: "This is not mine, this am I not, this is not my self." So seeing, the instructed noble disciple becomes disenchanted with material form, disenchanted with feeling, disenchanted with perception, disenchanted with mental formations, and disenchanted with consciousness.
>
> —SN XXII.15–17

* * *

Dispassion (Virāga)

"Disenchantment is the supporting condition for dispassion": In the trail of disenchantment there arises a deep yearning for deliverance from the round of saṃsāric becoming. Previously, prior to the arrival at correct knowledge and vision, the mind moved freely under the control of the impulses of delight and attachment. But now, with the growth of insight and the consequent disenchantment with conditioned existence, these impulses yield to a strong detachment and evolving capacity for renunciation. Whatever tends to provoke grasping and adherence is immediately abandoned; whatever tends to create new involvement is left behind. The old urges towards outer extension and accumulation give way to a new urge towards relinquishment as the one clearly perceived way to release. Every motion of the will becomes subordinated to the newly ascendant desire for liberation: "Just as a fish in a net, a frog in a snake's jaws, a jungle fowl shut into a cage ... just as these are desirous of being delivered, of finding an escape from these things, so too this meditator's mind is desirous of being delivered from the whole field of formations and escaping from it."[24]

The desire for deliverance leads to a quickening of insight. The capacity for comprehension picks up new speed, depth, and precision. Like a sword the mind of insight-wisdom cuts through the net of illusions fabricated on account of ignorance; like a light it illuminates phenomena exactly as they are. As the power of insight mounts, driven by the longing for liberation, a point is eventually reached where a fundamental turnabout takes place in the seat of consciousness, effecting a radical restructuring of the mental life. The beam-like radiance of insight expands into the full luminosity of enlightenment, and the mind descends upon the supramundane path leading directly and irreversibly to final deliverance.

This transformation, signified by *virāga* or dispassion, is the first strictly supramundane (*lokuttara*) stage in the progression of transcendental dependent arising. The earlier links in the sequence leading up to dispassion are all technically classified as mundane (*lokiya*). Though loosely called "transcendental" in the sense that

24. Vism. XXI.46. Ñāṇamoli, p. 760.

they are directed to the unconditioned, they are still mundane in terms of their scope since they operate entirely within range of the conditioned world. Their objects of concern are still the five aggregates, or things derivative upon them. But with the attainment of dispassion consciousness passes clear beyond the mundane level, and for a fleeting moment realizes as its object the unconditioned state, *nibbāna.*

The shift in standpoint comes about as the immediate consequence of the preceding stages of development. Through insight into the three marks the basic distortions covering over the true nature of phenomena were exposed; with the uncovering of their true nature there set in a disengagement from phenomena. This disengagement led to an attitude of relinquishment and a fading out of desire. Now, having released its grip on the conditioned, the mind turns to the unconditioned, the deathless element (*amata dhātu*), focusing upon it as the only state fully adequate to itself:

> Whatever is there of material form, feeling, perception, mental formations, and consciousness—he beholds these phenomena as impermanent, suffering, as a disease, a boil, a dart, a misfortune, an affliction, as alien, as decomposing, as empty, as selfless. He turns his mind away from these phenomena; and when he has turned his mind away from them, he focuses his mind on the deathless element, thinking: "This is the peaceful, this is the sublime, that is, the stilling of all formations, the relinquishing of the foundations, the destruction of craving, dispassion, cessation, nibbāna."
>
> —MN 64

Though the realization of the unconditioned requires a turning away from the conditioned, it must be emphasized that this realization is achieved precisely through the understanding of the conditioned. Nibbāna cannot be reached by backing off from a direct confrontation with *saṃsāra* to lose oneself in a blissful oblivion to the world. The path to liberation is a path of understanding, of comprehension and transcendence, not of escapism or emotional self-indulgence. Nibbāna can only be attained by turning one's gaze towards *saṃsāra*, and scrutinizing it in all its starkness. This principle—that the understanding of the conditioned is the way to the unconditioned—holds true not only in the general sense that an understanding of suffering is the spur to the quest for enlightenment, but in a deeper, more philosophical sense as well.

The path to nibbāna lies through the understanding of *saṃsāra* for the reason that the experiential realization of the unconditioned emerges from a prior penetration of the fundamental nature of the conditioned, without which it is impossible. The states of mind which realize nibbāna are called liberations (*vimokkha*), and these liberations are threefold according to the particular aspect of nibbāna they fix upon—the signless (*animitta*), the wishless (*appaṇihita*), and emptiness (*suññata*). The signless liberation focuses upon nibbāna as devoid of the "signs" determinative of a conditioned formation, the wishless liberation as free from the hankering of desire, and the emptiness liberation as devoid of a self or of any kind of substantial identity. Now, these three liberations are each entered by a distinct gateway or door called "the three doors to liberation" (*vimokkhamukha*).[25] These three doors signify precisely the contemplations of the three universal marks of the conditioned—impermanence, suffering, and selflessness. Insight into each mark is a different door leading into the realization of the unconditioned. The profound contemplation of impermanence is called the door to the signless liberation, since comprehension of impermanence strips away the "sign of formations" exposing the markless reality of the imperishable to the view of the contemplative vision. The contemplation of suffering is called the door to the wishless liberation, since understanding of the suffering inherent in all formations dries up the desire that reaches out for them. And deep contemplation of selflessness is called the door to the emptiness liberation, since it exposes the voidness of substantial identity in all phenomena and hence the unviability of the self-notion in relation to the unconditioned. In each case the understanding of the conditioned and the realization of the unconditioned are found to lock together in direct connection, so that by penetrating the conditioned to its very bottom and most universal features, the yogin passes through the door leading out of the conditioned to the supreme security of the unconditioned.

---

25. See Vism. XX1.66–73, Ñāṇamoli, pp. 766–769.

The supramundane consciousness that realizes nibbāna directly penetrates the four noble truths, illuminating them all at once with startling clarity: "Just, O monks, as a man in the gloom and darkness of the night, at the sudden flashing up of lightning, should with his eyes recognize the objects; just so the monk sees, according to reality: 'This is suffering, this is the origin of suffering, this is the cessation of suffering, this is the path leading to the cessation of suffering.'"[26] The penetration of the truths simultaneously performs four functions, one with respect to each truth. It fully understands (*parijānāti*) the first noble truth, the truth of suffering, since by taking nibbāna as its object it acquires a perspective from which it can directly see that in contrast to the unconditioned every thing impermanent, defiled, and conditioned is marked with suffering. It abandons (*pajahati*) the second noble truth, the truth of the origin, since it eradicates the craving and defilements which originate suffering so that they can never arise again. It realizes (*sacchikaroti*) the third noble truth, the truth of cessation, by apprehending nibbāna in which all the suffering of *saṃsāra* is permanently cut off. And it develops (*bhāveti*) the path, the fourth noble truth, since at the moment of penetration the eight mental factors comprised in the noble eightfold path concurrently arise performing the task of realization. Right view sees the unconditioned; right thought directs the mind upon it; right speech, right action, and right livelihood eradicate their opposites; right effort invigorates the mind; right mindfulness fixes attention on the unconditioned, and right concentration unifies the mind in absorption on the unconditioned. The ancients compare the mind's ability to perform this fourfold function to the burning of a lamp. Just as a lamp simultaneously burns the wick, dispels the darkness, creates light, and uses up the oil, so the supramundane knowledge simultaneously understands suffering, abandons craving, realizes nibbāna, and develops the path.[27]

The breakthrough to the unconditioned comes in four distinct stages called the four supramundane paths. Each momentary path-experience eradicates a determinate group of defilements ranked in degrees of coarseness and subtlety, so that the first path eliminates

26. AN III.25.

27. See Vism. XXII.92, Ñāṇamoli, p. 808.

the coarsest defilements and the fourth path the most subtle. The defilements cut off by the paths are generally classified as ten "fetters" (*saṃyojana*), receiving this designation because they fetter sentient beings to *saṃsāra*. With the first path the yogin eradicates the first three fetters—personality view, doubt, and misapprehension of rules and observances. Thereby he becomes a "stream-enterer" (*sotāpanna*), one who has entered the stream of the Dhamma and is bound for final deliverance in a maximum of seven more lives passed in the human or heavenly worlds. The second path weakens all the remaining fetters to the point where they no longer arise frequently or obsessively, but cuts off none completely; with its attainment the yogin advances to the stage of a "once-returner" (*sakadāgāmi*), one who is due to return to the sense sphere world only one more time. By eliminating sensual desire and aversion by means of the third path, he attains the state of a non-returner (*anāgāmi*), no longer bound to the sense sphere but heading for rebirth in a pure divine abode, where he will reach the final goal. The fourth path cuts off the remaining five fetters—desire for existence in the fine material and immaterial planes, conceit, restlessness, and ignorance. With its attainment the yogin becomes an *arahat*, who has destroyed all the defilements and reached the state of perfect purification.

* * *

Emancipation (Vimutti)

"Dispassion is the supporting condition for emancipation": Each of the supramundane path-moments is immediately followed by several moments of a different kind of supramundane experience called "fruition" (*phala*). Fruition marks the enjoyment of the realized degree of release effected by the path's work of eradicating defilements. Whereas the attainment of the path is an extremely intense exhilarating experience requiring the expenditure of a tremendous quantum of energy, the attainment of fruition is characterized by its peacefulness, relaxedness, and blissful quiescence. If the path-attainment be illustrated by a captive's sudden bursting of the chains that hold him in captivity, fruition may be compared to his savouring the taste of freedom that lies beyond the captive state.

The completion of the fourth path and fruition results in full emancipation (*vimutti*): "With the destruction of the cankers, he directly realizes for himself, enters, and abides in that emancipation of mind, emancipation of wisdom, which is cankerless."[28] The subtlest and most tenacious fetters have been broken, and there is nothing now that makes for further bondage. Having destroyed the mental corruptions at their basic level of latency, the yogin has completed his task. There is nothing more to do, and nothing to add to what has been done. He abides in the living experience of deliverance.

The emancipation realized by the *arahat* has a twofold aspect. One aspect is the emancipation from ignorance and defilements experienced during the course of his lifetime, the other the emancipation from repeated existence attained with his passing away. Through his complete penetration of the four noble truths, the *arahat* has eradicated ignorance and released his mind from the grip of the passions. The fading away of the passions issues in a stainless purity called emancipation of mind (*cetovimutti*); the fading away of ignorance issues in a radiant awareness called emancipation of wisdom (*paññāvimutta*). The mind of the *arahat* is at once impeccably pure through the absence of attachment and radiantly bright through the luminosity of wisdom. Endowed with this emancipation of mind and of wisdom, he can move and act in the world without being soiled by the mire of the world. He chooses, thinks, decides, and wills free from the compulsion of egoistic habits. The grasping of "I" and "mine" has ceased, the inclination to conceit can no more obsess him. Having seen the egoless nature of all phenomena he has cut through the tangle of egoistic constructs and become "a sage who is at peace" (*muni santo*).

Since he has destroyed the defilements, whatever disturbances might assail a person on their account no longer assail him. Even though sublime and striking sense objects come into range of his perception they cannot overwhelm his mind: "His mind remains untouched, steadfast, unshakeable, beholding the impermanency of everything."[29] In the *arahat* greed, hatred, and delusion, the

28. MN 6, MN 12, MN 40, etc.
29. AN VI.55.

unwholesome roots which underlie all evil, have been totally abandoned. They are not merely suppressed, but withered up down to the level of their latencies, so that they are no longer able to spring up again in the future. This destruction of greed, hatred, and delusion is called the nibbāna realizable during lifetime; it is nibbāna visible here and now. "In so far as the monk has realized the complete extinction of greed, hatred, and delusion, in so far is nibbāna realizable, immediate, inviting, attractive, and comprehensible to the wise."[30] Because in this attainment the five aggregates continue to function, sustained by bodily vitality, it is also called "the nibbāna element with a residue remaining."[31]

But though for the *arahat* disturbances due to the defilements do not arise, he is still subject to "a measure of disturbance" conditioned by the body with its six sense faculties.[32] Though he cannot be overcome by greed and aversion he still experiences pleasure and pain; though he cannot generate kamma binding to *saṃsāra* he must still choose and act within the limits set by his circumstances. Such experience, however, is for the *arahat* purely residual. It is merely the playing out of his stored up kamma from the past, which can still fructify and call forth responses so long as the body acquired through prior craving stands. But because craving has now been inwardly exhausted, there lies ahead for him no renewal of the round of birth and death. All feelings, being experienced with detachment, not being delighted in, will become cool. They arouse no new craving, provoke no new expectations, lead to no new accumulations of kamma; they merely continue on devoid of fecundity until the end of the life span. With the break-up of the body at his passing away, the *arahat* makes an end to the beginningless process of becoming. This is the second stage of his emancipation—emancipation from renewed existence, from future birth, ageing, and death: "The sage who is at peace is not born, does not age, does not die, does not tremble, does not yearn. For him there does not exist that on account of which he might be born. Not being born, how can he age? Not ageing, how can he

30. AN III.55.

31. *Sa-upādisesa nibbānadhātu.* See *Itivuttaka* 38.

32. See MN 121.

die?"[33] Because, with the emancipation from continued existence, no residue of the aggregates persists, this attainment is called "the nibbāna element without residue remaining."[34]

* * *

The Knowledge of Destruction (Khaya-ñāṇa)

"Emancipation is the supporting condition for the knowledge of destruction": Following each of the four paths and fruits there arises a retrospective cognition or "reviewing knowledge" (*paccavekkhana ñāṇa*) which reviews the defilements that have been abandoned by the particular path and the defilements remaining to be eliminated. In the case of the last path and fruition, the path and fruition of arahatship, the reviewing knowledge ascertains that all defilements have been eradicated and that there are none left to be destroyed. This knowledge certifying the abandonment of the defilements arises immediately after the mind has been liberated from their grip by the full penetration of the four noble truths:

> He understands as it really is: "This is suffering, this is the origin of suffering, this is the cessation of suffering, this is the path to the cessation of suffering. These are the cankers, this is the origin of the cankers, this is the cessation of the cankers. This is the path to the cessation of the cankers." As he is knowing and seeing thus, his mind is liberated from the canker of sensuality, from the canker of existence, and from the canker of ignorance. When it is liberated, the knowledge arises in him: "It is liberated."
>
> —MN 39

As the text indicates, this cognizance of the mind's liberation is direct and personal, without dependence on others. Just as a keen sighted man can look into a pool of clear, limpid water and see for himself the shells, pebbles, gravel and shoals of fish. The

33. MN 140.

34. *Anupādisesa nibbānadhātu.* See *Itivuttaka* 38.

liberated person can look into himself and see that his mind has been set free from the cankers.[35]

The retrospective cognition of release involves two acts of ascertainment. The first, called the "knowledge of destruction" (*khaya-ñāṇa*), ascertains that all defilements have been abandoned at the root; the second, the "knowledge of non-arising" (*anuppāde ñāṇa*), ascertains that no defilement can ever arise again. The two together are also called the "knowledge and vision of emancipation" (*vimutti-ñāṇadassana*), the use of the word "vision" again underscoring the perceptual immediacy of the cognition by which the mind verifies its own release from the defilements. By possessing this knowledge, one who has destroyed the defilements not only experiences the freedom that results from their destruction, but acquires as well an inner certitude with respect to their destruction. If a liberated individual only enjoyed liberation from the defilements without also enjoying indubitable knowledge that he is liberated, his attainment would always be haunted by an inner suspicion that perhaps, after all, some area of vulnerability remains. Even though no defilement ever came to manifestation, the shadow of uncertainty would itself mar the attainment's claim to completeness. However, because the attainment of arahatship automatically generates a retrospective cognition ascertaining the final abandonment of all defilements, there is no room for such a suspicion to arise. Like a deer in a remote forest far from the reach of hunters, the one who has crossed over attachment to the world walks in confidence, stands in confidence, sits down in confidence, and sleeps in confidence.[36] He is out of reach of the defilements, and knows he is out of their reach.

Though the knowledge of the destruction of the cankers is not always set up in the *arahat*'s awareness, it is permanently available to him, and awaits only his advertence to make itself present. Since the cankers have been eradicated, whenever the *arahat* looks into his mind he can see at once that they have been cut off. The suttas illustrate this with a bold simile:

---

35. Ibid.

36. MN 26.

> Sandaka, it is like a man whose hands and feet have been cut off; whether he is walking or standing still or asleep or awake, constantly and perpetually are his hands and feet as though cut off; and moreover while he is reflecting on it, he knows: "My hands and feet have been cut off." Even so, Sandaka, whatever monk is a perfected one, the cankers destroyed, who has lived the life, done what was to be done, laid down the burden, attained his own goal, the fetters of becoming utterly destroyed, freed by perfect profound knowledge, for him whether he is walking or standing still or asleep or awake, the cankers are as though destroyed; and moreover while he is reflecting on it, he knows: "My cankers are destroyed."
>
> —MN 76 (trans. I.B. Horner)

The *arahat* understands that the defilements he has eradicated brought bondage to the round of existence. He sees them as "defiling, conducive to renewed existence, afflictive, resulting in suffering, leading to future birth, ageing, and death."[37] Thence, by witnessing their utter eradication in himself, he gains certainty of his emancipation from the round: "Unshakeable is my emancipation. This is my last birth. There is now no renewal of existence."[38] Such knowledge remains an inalienable part of the *arahat*'s spiritual inheritance. It is the basis for his assurance of immunity from future becoming. By reason of this knowledge he sounds the lion's roar with which he seals his triumph over the cycle of repeated births: "Destroyed is birth, lived is the holy life, the task has been completed, there is no returning to this state."

37. MN 36.
38. MN 26.

Inspiration from the Dhammapada

by

Dr. N. K. G. Mendis

WHEEL PUBLICATION NO. 279

Inspiration from the Dhammapada

Namo Sammāsambuddhassa!
Homage to the supremely Enlightened One!
Namo Saddhammassa!
Homage to the sublime teaching!
Namo Buddhasaṅghassa!
Homage to the Buddha's community of monks!

In the pages that follow it is hoped to draw attention to the inspiration and guidance we can obtain from the Dhammapada as we model our way of living in accordance with the Noble Eightfold Path. It is not suggested that actual practice can be replaced by reciting the scriptures, but the scriptures can and do help us by stimulating enthusiasm; also, the scriptures provide material for us to investigate the Dhamma, which investigation is the second factor of enlightenment; furthermore, in times of need when we are being assailed by unwholesome thoughts, we can repel these by recalling relevant portions of the sayings of the Enlightened One.

The Dhammapada is a collection of utterances of the Buddha made at various times to suit different occasions. These utterances were rehearsed at the first council of Arahats, convened three months after the *Parinibbāna* of the Buddha, and took the form of a collection of verses, bearing the name Dhammapada and forming part of the Pali Canon. In that form, which comprises 423 verses in 26 sections, the Dhammapada has come to us through all these years for our guidance.

The Noble Eightfold Path

The Noble Eightfold Path is also referred to as the mundane path (*lokiya*), when pertaining to those still unliberated. When followed diligently it leads to the supramundane path (*lokuttara*) and the final extinction of suffering. Here we are concerned with the mundane path and the difficulties we may encounter as we tread this path and how we can look to the Dhammapada as a fountain of encouragement. There are eight factors in this path which are traditionally described as belonging to three groups:

Wisdom	=	Right view and right thought.
Morality	=	Right speech, right action and right livelihood.
Concentration	=	Right effort, right mindfulness and right concentration.

When one follows this path one does not go step by step according to the sequence given. If that were the case one would be able to gain wisdom and concentration before morality is established, which is not possible. Morality is an essential prerequisite for concentration which in turn promotes wisdom. In actual fact, as one progresses along this path there is a simultaneous association of the different links in varying degrees.

At this stage it would, perhaps, be relevant to discuss who will want to follow the Noble Eightfold Path and what makes them want to do so.

In a doctrinal talk given by the Buddha to King Pasenadi of Kosala, as recorded in the Saṃyutta Nikāya, the Buddha classified human beings into four groups:

1. Born to "darkness" and ending in "darkness";
2. Born to "darkness" and ending in "light";
3. Born to "light" and ending in "darkness";
4. Born to "light" and ending in "light".

This classification is applicable even today and will be so in the future too. We shall use this classification for our discussion without necessarily conforming to the descriptive characteristics of each group as given by the Buddha.

Group I refers to those beings who are born into a miserable environment, perhaps handicapped physically and sometimes mentally, and live in poverty and want. In spite of these conditions, or maybe because of them, not being able to understand the causes of their plight, they commit unwholesome acts by deed, speech and thought and due to this, these unfavourable conditions will continue. These conditions exemplify the manner in which the impersonal law of *kamma* and *vipāka* (action and reaction) operates. When the results of unwholesome kamma are exhausted, better conditions will prevail. There is no being, human or divine, who can alter this lawful situation here. All that we, who are not in this group, can do, is to show the greatest amount of compassion, give whatever relief possible, and not make their miseries any worse.

Group II refers to those who are born into unfavourable conditions, both personal and environmental. Due to exhaustion of their unwholesome kamma results, for one reason or the other, good sense prevails and their actions by deed, word and thought are wholesome, and favourable results are experienced even in this existence. Here again it gives some idea as to how the law of kamma operates. It is convincing evidence to give strength to those who are handicapped and stands opposed to a belief in eternal damnation for even one single act of wrongdoing.

Group III refers to those beings who due to past wholesome kamma are born into favourable conditions, both personal and environmental. Perhaps a large proportion of mankind belongs to this group, enjoying normal health, unimpaired faculties and a reasonable standard of living. Some even assume positions of influence and authority over fellow beings. However, they do not know why they are favoured in this manner and, in ignorance of the law of kamma, they commit unwholesome acts by deed, word and thought, and the evil consequences are experienced even in this existence not to speak of future ones. Striking examples are those who seek their pleasure in fox-hunts and big-game safaris, those who seek to increase their wealth by trading in destructive weapons, intoxicating drinks and drugs, and those who abuse their authority and power by inflicting cruelty and hardship on fellow beings.

Group IV refers to a very fortunate class of beings. Their wholesome past kamma has given them favourable conditions. Maintaining the same wholesome trend they act wisely by deed, word and thought. They are assets to humanity anywhere and at all times. The most outstanding example in this group is the Blessed One himself. Since his time there have been many more and some exist even today.

It is expected that those in group II can do with all the help available to follow the Noble Eightfold Path and it is hoped that those in Group III will pause for a while in their unwholesome trend, make a sensible appraisal of their favourable conditions and the causes thereof, and will be fortunate enough to come to the teachings of the Enlightened One. They too will then welcome whatever assistance they can get for spiritual advancement. Group IV, as implied above acting wisely, will always heed good advice and continue with their spiritual progress.

Beings come to the Teachings of the Blessed One in different ways

On account of past wholesome kamma a being is born to a family where the environment is conducive to spiritual advancement. The parents will guide the newcomer to the family in accordance with the teachings of the Blessed One; preceptors and good friends are at hand. As a result it is expected that such a person will not deviate easily from the Buddhist way of life. There are those who are born to families where Buddhist principles are alien but they are gifted with that rare intuition which makes them look at the world around them. They see so many facets of life which puzzle them and to which they find no satisfying answers in the doctrines handed down to them by their forebears; so they search elsewhere and are fortunate enough to arrive at the Buddha's doctrine. Such types are increasing in numbers particularly in the traditionally Christian countries.

There are those who "accidentally" come across a book on Buddhism, or happen to listen to a talk on Buddhism or meet someone who is already leading a Buddhist way of life. These encounters spark a gush of insight and they pursue their interest in the doctrine of the Buddha. These are no accidents; nothing happens by accident. It is wholesome kamma result coming into play. There are those who at some stage personally experience the bitter impact of the vicissitudes of life, call a halt to their erratic ways and seek comfort in the teachings of the Buddha.

The purpose of following the Noble Eightfold Path is to attain Nibbāna, which is the cessation of suffering. Most of us will probably not attain this supreme goal in this existence, but if one strives to become a Stream Enterer it will be quite an achievement. A Stream Enterer is one who has entered the first stage of the supramundane path by severing the first three of the ten fetters that bind one down to the repeated rounds of birth, death and re-birth. These three fetters are belief in a self or soul, sceptical doubt and belief in the efficacy of rites and rituals. The Stream Enterer will never be born in the lower planes of existence, will have seven re-births at the most and is destined to full enlightenment. Even if one cannot become a Stream Enterer there are other benefits to be experienced in this life by following the code outlined in the Noble Eightfold path. There will be an increasing measure of contentment and equanimity which will help one to overcome the tribulations of life. Such a person is no danger to any form of sentient life and, in fact, will be an asset to any society. Finally, when death says, "leave everything and come with me," there should be no bewilderment or confusion because one trains oneself to prepare for this moment. However, for many of us householders, especially if the environment is not conducive to a Buddhist way of life, there will be many difficulties as we try to go along this path. These obstacles may be our own personal ones or they may be from outside.

First we shall mention some of the difficulties in a general way and later in relation to the factors of the path and how we can refer these difficulties to quotations from the Dhammapada. By recalling to mind these words of wisdom in the Dhammapada, over and over again at the right time, there is no doubt that we can get much sustenance and encouragement.

Companionship

Traditionally, by Buddhist standards, a good companion is said to "have faith, be virtuous, learned and wise." It is, indeed, very rare in this day and age to find such a companion. The disciple who is earnestly trying to follow the path will have a strong desire to meet and converse with others having the same interests. Dhamma discussions are beneficial and stimulating. In the Kindred Sayings on Elements (*Dhātu Saṃyutta*) we find the Buddha's discourse on how beings of similar "tastes" flow together and meet together. In today's common parlance we would say "birds of a feather flock together." But, for the householder, keen on spiritual progress, especially in countries where the Buddha Dhamma is not yet established, the opportunity to "flock together" with another of similar interest may arise only rarely. Here we shall make a distinction between a companion and an acquaintance.

A companion is a person with whom one associates frequently, wants to do so and enjoys doing so. On the other hand, an acquaintance is a person whom one knows but with whom there is no degree of intimacy. It is inevitable that in the society in which the householder lives there will be acquaintances. The disciple, keen on making progress on the path, has to exercise caution when there is contact with these acquaintances. Some of them may be strongly motivated by greed, hatred and delusion, and an insidious influence is always a possibility. Hence one should say that, if unavoidable, the body may move with them but the mind must be outside their influence. We will have to conduct ourselves in this manner without conceit. Conceit can be overcome by practising loving-kindness (*mettā*) and compassion (*karuṇā*) towards all beings. Therefore, the following two verses from the Dhammapada have to be taken in the context of good companions as defined above, and when we are denied the privilege of meeting such persons, instead of becoming despondent, let us call to mind the following:

Faring along, should one not find
a better or an equal to oneself,
let firmly him pursue a solitary life.
There is with fools no fellowship.[1]

Associate not with evil friends,
associate not with mean men.
Associate with good friends,
associate with noble men.[2]

Reaction of Others

When one has decided to follow this path and is making a diligent effort to do so, the reactions of some with whom one comes in contact could, at the start, have a disturbing influence. As one's practice along the path is progressing, there is likely to be a change in one's demeanour which may become manifest in bodily actions,

1. Dhp 61. All translations are by the Venerable Nārada Mahāthera of Vajirārāma, Colombo, Sri Lanka unless indicated otherwise.
2. Dhp 78.

speech and composure. The bodily actions will be guarded and one will not wish to inflict the slightest harm on the smallest form of sentient life. If mindfulness in relation to the body is being practised, the bodily movements will be under control and purposeful. Speech too will be guarded; it will be truthful and not harsh, but gentle and kind, and there will be no inclination to indulge in gossip, slander or frivolous "small talk." The composure will show a change as one begins to see aspects of life in a different light which will lay bare the general unsatisfactoriness of this world around us. The misfortunes and tragedies that befall fellow beings will have an impact on one as they never did before. These changes in one's personality are not cultivated to give a "holier than thou" impression, but they occur as a natural response when the general pervasiveness of *dukkha* (unsatisfactoriness) dawns on one. But the purpose of following the path is not to go through life with this burden on one's head, but to come to know the real nature of this existence, lay down this burden, and emerge as a victor with a cheerful countenance. This is the priceless reward that awaits anyone who follows the Noble Eightfold Path with diligence. However, at the start, in some instances, the reactions of associates, friends and even members of one's family to these changing attitudes may result in the disciple's being the target of various epithets. On their part they stem from the three unwholesome roots of greed, hate and delusion, and, on the part of the one who is following the path, they are the results of one's own past unwholesome kamma. Understanding this, it is hoped that the disciple will not be deterred by those temporary obstacles but will forge ahead practising *mettā* and *karuṇā* to all living beings and recalling to mind these verses from the Dhammapada:

> *Many folk are ill-behaved*
> *but their abuse I shall endure,*
> *as an elephant in battlefield*
> *bears arrows shot from bow.*[3]

> *From old it has been, Atula—*
> *this is not only of today;*
> *sitting silent, him they blame;*

3. Dhp 320, translated by Phra Khantipālo.

speaking often, him they blame;
they blame him saying little too—
there's no one in the world unblamed.[4]

There never was and never will be
nor at present does exist
a person who is wholly blamed
or one who's wholly praised.[5]

Finding Fault

Though this occurs at all levels from the international to the individual, we are concerned here with the person following the path. Criticism may be constructive or destructive. Constructive criticism derives from good motives and is done for the welfare of the person criticized. The Buddha criticized his disciples, sometimes in no uncertain terms, when he found them lapsing into ways not conducive to spiritual advancement. A teacher will criticize a pupil with good intentions and so will a parent a child or one good friend another. A person neglecting his own welfare resents wholesome advice. The disciple following this path should be amenable to correction and accept good advice in the spirit in which it is given. In this context we have two verses:

Let him advise, let him instruct,
and from evil things restrain.
To the good, indeed, he's dear,
but not so pleasing to the bad.[6]

Should one a man of wisdom see,
who points out faults and gives reproof,
as though revealing treasure hidden
one should consort with such a sage,
for while one lives with one like him
better it is and never worse.[7]

---

4. Dhp 227, translated by Phra Khantipālo.
5. Dhp 228.
6. Dhp 77.
7. Dhp 76, translated by Phra Khantipālo.

Destructive criticism, on the other hand, bears the signs of malice, greed and delusions, all unwholesome. The Buddha has said that one who is always seeking faults in others is a long way from the destruction of his own defilements. Regarding a monk who had this habit the Buddha uttered this verse:

He who looks for others' faults
and is forever irritable,
his corruptions ever grow,
far is he from cankers' end.[8]

Since this habit of finding others' faults with malicious intent is quite prevalent and easy to indulge in, and since the purpose of following the path is to get rid of defilements, when we are tempted to look for faults in others, just for the sake of doing so, it will be salutary to pause for a moment and remember these two verses from the Dhammapada:

Not concerned with faults of others,
what they did or left undone;
but one's own faults should one look at:
what one did or left undone.[9]

Easily seen are faults of others,
though one's own are hardly seen.
So one winnows just like chaff
the faults that other people have.
But yet one's own one likes to hide
just like a cheat behind a losing throw of dice.[10]

Ill-Will and Anger

In ordinary parlance we say one "bears" ill-will and one "shows" anger or "gets" angry. A person could harbour considerable ill-will towards fellow beings and this may not be noticeable to others. Some of the most sordid crimes have been committed with a smile on the face. All worldlings have some form of ill-will in some kind or the other and in varying degrees. Ill-will is one of

8. Dhp 253.
9. Dhp 50.
10. Dhp 252.

the five hindrances and one of the "lower" five fetters that tie us to the sensuous world. Ill-will is temporarily repressed during the absorptions (the *jhānas*). It is radically and permanently eliminated when the fruits of the supramundane path are attained. At first it is weakened when one becomes a Once-Returner (*sakadāgāmi*) and then disappears forever when one becomes a Non-Returner (*anāgāmi*). On the other hand, anger is something that manifests itself rather crudely either by bodily action or by speech. It is there for all to observe. If one who is earnestly trying to follow the path unwittingly gives vent to anger, it acts as a setback even for a short time because it disturbs the mental calm one is trying to cultivate and also interferes with progress in meditation. As worldlings we can and should, by being mindful at all times, control and finally put an end to anger overcoming us. The stage at which the anger has to be checked is the moment when the thought of anger arises and before it leads to uncontrolled speech and bodily action. The mere awareness of the arising of the "thought with anger" will, with regular practice, suffice to make that thought impotent. In this respect the following verse is relevant:

Who can arisen anger curb,
like holding back a chariot:
Him a true charioteer I call—
mere rein-holders are other folk.[11]

On the other hand, the person who is bent on spiritual advancement, may be accosted by someone who is giving vent to anger. It may be difficult at the start, but it is important not to retaliate with anger. The power of *mettā* is unlimited and the truth of this can be verified by anyone who earnestly cultivates this sublime virtue. Any attempt to subdue anger with anger will never be successful in the final analysis. In this connection the Buddha uttered the following verse:

Not by hatred, hatred ceases
in this world of tooth and claw.
Love alone from hate releases.
This is an eternal law.[12]

11. Dhp 222.
12. Dhp 5, translated by Francis Story.

Sensual Temptation

This could be quite a problem for the average person who is making an effort to follow this path. Much effort will be required especially by the householder who is assailed in many ways from all sides by objects designed to titillate the senses. In the scriptural texts five "cords of sensuality" (*kāmaguṇa*) are described. They are visible objects, sounds, smells, tastes and bodily contact. Their existence is known to the sentient being through the respective sense organ. In addition, the mind is taken as the sixth sense organ receiving stimuli from mental objects which may be related to the past, present or future, and may be real or imaginary. Thus there are six sense organs and six kinds of sense objects. Dependent on each sense organ and its appropriate object the relevant consciousness arises. The coming together of these three, i.e. organ, object and consciousness is referred to as contact (*phassa*). Dependent on this contact feeling (*vedanā*) arises. This feeling may be pleasant, unpleasant or neutral. This feeling arises at every single occasion when the threefold contact occurs. It is a very important event to recognise because it is at this stage that mindfulness must be alert and sensual temptation can be overcome. This feeling arises and perishes in a moment signifying the transitory nature of the process (*anicca*); it is also a purely impersonal process signifying the no-self nature (*anattā*); these two features account for the unsatisfactoriness of what has taken place so far (*dukkha*). This feeling is followed by perception (*saññā*), that is, the being becomes aware of the distinctive marks of the particular object. Since we are here concerned with sensual temptation we shall confine ourselves to pleasant feeling. The worldling who is not conversant with the Buddha doctrine will not recognise the momentariness of the feeling, will be under the wrong impression that it is a "self" that is feeling, and the unsatisfactoriness due to these two features will not be comprehended. There will thus be an erroneous perception of the impermanent as permanent, the no-self as self and the unsatisfactory as satisfactory. In such a case the perception will be followed by thoughts, desires and yearnings. Therefore, when exposed to sensual temptations, perception must conform to reality, which is impermanent, without a self and unsatisfactory. If this is done there will not follow thoughts, desires and the subsequent train of events. There is no doubt that some sense objects produce pleasant feelings, otherwise beings will not seek satisfaction in them. There is also no doubt that this satisfaction is not lasting, otherwise beings will not be flitting from one object to another like the monkey in the jungle who grabs hold of one branch with one paw and then releases that after he has grabbed hold of another branch with the other paw. For the disciple intent on spiritual advancement, any yielding to sensual temptation will be a hindrance to progress and may even cause "defeat." The worthlessness of all sensual pleasures, not only in this world, but even in the heavenly existences, is brought out by the following utterances of the Buddha:

Not by a rain of golden coins
can one content in sensual pleasures find.
Desires give pain, but little joy.

When knowing this, the man who's wise,
not even in celestial joys will pleasure find.
In craving's end he will delight
the perfect Buddha's true disciple.[13]

Doubts (*vicikicchā*)

While attempting to follow the Noble Eightfold Path sceptical doubts may arise in the mind of the disciple. There may be doubts about the teachings of the Buddha, about the past and future, about the conditionality of existence, and whether there is any purpose served by leading a virtuous, wholesome life. These doubts form the fifth of the five mental hindrances to spiritual progress and the second of the ten fetters that bind beings to the wheel of existence. These doubts arise from time to time, in varying degrees, in all worldlings regardless of the faith (*saddhā*) in the threefold gem, because the faith is still shakeable and it becomes unshakeable only when the first stage of the supramundane path is attained. It is only then that sceptical doubt is eliminated forever. Until we reach this stage we should always be mindful when there is doubt and when doubts are not present. Furthermore, the moment doubt arises it

13. Dhammapada verses 186 and 187.

should be mindfully noted. Otherwise a train of unwholesome thoughts will follow. The mere awareness of the arising of doubt, the moment it arises, will dispel the doubt because the awareness thought has now replaced the doubt thought and only one thought can exist at a time. With this practice of mindfulness, supported by wise attention, investigation of reality, noble friendship and suitable conversation, fewer and fewer doubts will arise less and less frequently. The householder in a non-Buddhist environment, where suitable friendship and conversation are not available, can overcome lack of these blessings by resorting to quiet contemplation and reading of the Buddhist texts. If the disciple, living in accordance with Buddhist principles, gets the feeling of being different because all the others around are conducting themselves in ways contrary to the Buddha's teachings, it would, perhaps, help to remember the following verse:

Few are those among all men
who to the Further shore will go.
The rest of mankind truly,
just runs along this hither shore.[14]

There may be times when the disciple, who is leading a virtuous way of life in accordance with the path, will experience rather bitterly the vicissitudes of this existence. At the same time the disciple may find others who are not leading wholesome lives being spared these harsh experiences. They are enjoying comforts and are apparently happy. These seeming injustices could have a disturbing influence on the disciple in the earlier stages. In situations like this, while cultivating the four sublime virtues of loving-kindness, compassion, sympathetic joy end equanimity, one should recall to mind the following two verses which in themselves lend strong support for the belief in kamma and rebirth:

Even an evil-doer meets with good
as long as evil ripens not.
But when that evil bears its fruit
the evil-doer will with the evil meet.[15]

---

14. Dhp 85.
15. Dhp 119.

Even a good man meets with evil,
as long as goodness ripens not.
But when his goodness bears its fruit,
the good man reaps the good result.[16]

At all times when we need encouragement the following verse will provide just that. In this context the word "Bhikkhu" which is the Pali for a monk, is applicable to one who is dedicated to the practice of the Teaching.

He who dwells in Dhamma *and delights in it,*
on Dhamma *thinks again and again.*
Remembering the Dhamma *well,*
such Bhikkhu will not fall away from Dhamma.[17]

Remorse and Regret (*kukkucca*)

In the texts this is described as "repentance over wrong things done and right things neglected." This "uneasiness of conscience" (together with restlessness) forms the fourth of the five mental hindrances to spiritual progress. It is because we did what we should not have done and did not do what we should have that we are still here. Brooding over these deficiencies will, most probably, occur in the early stages. It is understandable but it will interfere with spiritual advancement. Therefore, the sooner we can give up this brooding the better it will be for us. Unlike in other doctrines there is no need for a self-tormenting feeling of guilt nor is it possible in Buddhist practice to seek redemption from "sins" by confession. Any confession of a transgression, according to Buddhist practice, is to serve as a restraint against that transgression being committed again and it is not for absolution. The first of the following two verses tells us that we alone are responsible for our evil actions and defilements and that we alone have to put an end to evil ways and get rid of defilements.

By oneself, indeed, is evil done,
by oneself is one defiled.

16. Dhp 120.
17. Dhp 364.

by oneself is evil left undone,
by oneself, is one purified.

Pure and impure on oneself depend
no one can purify another.[18]

The next verse indicates the results that ensue, even in this existence, when evil ways are abandoned and wholesome ways are cultivated.

Whoso with wholesome act
can compensate his evil deeds,
will shine and illumine this world
as does the moon, when free from clouds.[19]

Avarice (*macchariya*)

This is considered as one of the evil passions and it certainly retards spiritual advancement. In the texts five kinds of avarice are mentioned. They are in relation to dwellings, families, gains, recognition and mental things. Two of the three unwholesome roots, namely inborn greed and the delusion of a self, are responsible for avarice. The third, hate, is ready to step in when any threat to these objects of avarice is imminent. When hate enters the scene there could be all kinds of conflicts, from a fight between two villagers to a war between two nations. The fault lies not in any of these objects, but in one's attitude towards them. If one is endowed with material possessions there could be a desire to increase them or, at least, to hold on to them at any cost. If one is born to the so called "super-races" or "high-caste" families there could be some contempt for all the others and in some instances even the basic human rights have been denied to them. If recognition and honour are bestowed on one, it is best if these are graciously received without elation or a feeling of superiority. Regarding mental things, the "closed fist" of the teacher was mentioned by the Buddha. This is the tendency for one with knowledge to hold it back without imparting it to others. Realising that these possessions and positions are the results of one's kamma, liberality must be cultivated and *mettā* and *karuṇā*

18. Dhp 165.
19. Dhp 173.

practised towards all beings. As progress is made along the path and the three characteristics of existence begin to dawn on one, the "important self" begins to shrink and also the possessions and positions which lent themselves to avarice gradually lose their grip. The Buddha has extolled the virtues of liberality. It constitutes the first of the three kinds of meritorious activity, the other two being morality and mental development. In liberality it is the intention and volition that count and not the outward deed. As regards acquiring possessions, fame and honour, the Buddha has uttered this verse:

One way leads to worldly gain,
another to Nibbāna goes.
Clearly comprehending this,
the Bhikkhu, following the Buddha,
should not delight in gain and honour,
but should detachment cultivate.[20]

Patience (*khanti*)

Most people are impatient. The one who is trying to follow the path may find progress slow and difficult. The rate of spiritual advancement will depend on personal factors and on the environment in which the disciple lives. Regarding personal factors, some have more defilements than others. These have, since time immemorial, been lurking in the subconscious mind, the subliminal life continuum (*bhavaṅga-sota*) and, from time to time, been surfacing to conscious level where they have influenced our volitional actions by thought, word and deed. When they came to the surface they were not recognised as such. After having played their part they immediately sank back to their dark recesses awaiting the next opportunity to play their evil role. There are ten such defilements (*kilesas*): greed, hate, delusion, conceit, speculative views, sceptical doubt, mental torpor, restlessness, shamelessness and lack of conscience. When the disciple progresses in meditation and is mindful at all times, the defilements are recognised the moment they reach a conscious level. With repeated recognition of these defilements they lose

20. Dhp 75, translated by Phra Khantipālo.

their malevolent influence. In the initial stages, when we get to know what a considerable amount of defilements we do possess, we may find ourselves getting rather embarrassed or disturbed or even discouraged. However, we do not need to despair but may get fortitude from the following:

By degrees, and from time to time,
little by little let a prudent man
remove the stains from his own mind,
just as a smith the silver purifies.[21]

The environmental factors that can adversely affect spiritual progress are mainly lack of suitable companionship and opportunities for Dhamma discussions; also, getting too involved in worldly affairs can have the same effect. Living a virtuous life is by no means easy, especially for the householder who may have to cope with many distractions. We have to remind ourselves that what is wholesome and is for the welfare of the individual is difficult to practise and maintain. Hence the Buddha said:

Easy to do are things that are bad
and only harmful to oneself.
But good and beneficial acts
are difficult to do, indeed.[22]

Attitude to Other Religions

This is important, especially for the disciple who lives in a non-Buddhist environment. Any argument with followers of other doctrines, on matters of religious differences, is best avoided. It will only hurt their sentiments and foster one's own defilements, like hate and conceit. It is futile to try to thrust down another's throat the Buddha Doctrine. The Dhamma is beyond sophistry and has to be experienced individually "in one's own heart." However, if there is a sincere inquiry about the Doctrine of the Buddha it behoves the disciple to provide what is solicited. It we are inclined to be envious of the prosperity of other religious establishments it is time to remind ourselves of the following verse:

21. Dhp 239.
22. Dhp 163.

People give according to their faith
and also as it pleases them.
He whom envy makes perturbed
concerning others' food and drink,
will not find peace and concentration
be it daytime or at night.[23]

From here on, some verses of the Dhammapada will be quoted in reference to the different factors of the Noble Eightfold Path. These factors as stated earlier, are grouped together into three divisions which are morality (*sīla*), concentration (*samādhi*) and wisdom or insight (*pañña*).

Morality

This is an essential prerequisite for progress along the path. The disciple will, as progress is made, feel the disturbing effect of even the slightest lapse in *sīla*. Until we have reached the higher stages of spiritual development there will be lapses in *sīla* mostly in speech, less in bodily action. Each of these will be noted mindfully as they occur and every effort made to avoid their repetition. The less frequently these lapses occur the greater the encouragement to continue along the path. For one who is following the path the code of morality extends beyond the five Basic Precepts, namely abstention from killing any living being, taking what is not given, unlawful sexual intercourse, lying and the use of intoxicants. As regards speech, it is not only abstention from uttering falsehoods but also abstention from slander and gossip, harsh words and useless "small talk." It will be noted that the fifth basic precept, namely abstention from the use of intoxicants, is not specifically mentioned in the three factors of the path that comprise *sīla*. This has been taken as an excuse by some who claim to be leading a Buddhist way of life to "take a little drink." But even a little drink leads to moral carelessness and can be habit-forming. Rightly has it been said: "First a man takes a drink; then the drink takes a drink; then the drink takes the man." The Buddha has said that right livelihood is abstaining from any livelihood that brings harm to other beings and one of these, he said, is trading in

23. Dhp 249.

intoxicants. Therefore, nothing more need be said here regarding the necessity to abstain completely from intoxicants if *sīla* is to be perfect. In connection with *sīla* the following verses of the Dhammapada are quoted:

He who living things destroys,
who falsehood speaks,
and takes what is not given,
who to the wives of others goes
and is to alcoholic drinks addicted,
such a one, here in this very world,
the roots of his own welfare kills.

Know this, you worthy man:
hard to control are evil thoughts;
let not greed and wickedness
drag you down to misery.[24]

Concentration

The three factors of the path that are grouped together under this heading, namely right effort, right mindfulness and right concentration, are related to development of the mind. In order to develop the mind it is first necessary to know the mind, then how it can be protected, and then how it can be used for spiritual advancement. There are many verses in the Dhammapada which describe the nature of the mind. It is described as being fickle, fluttering, subtle, faring far and wide, hard to understand since it goes where it pleases, as it pleases and when it pleases, hard to check, and extremely swift. Two verses are quoted below to illustrate some of these qualities of the mind:

This flickering, wayward mind, is hard
to bring under control and guard.
The wise man straightens, just as do
skilled fletchers make their arrows true.[25]

24. Dhammapada verses 246, 247 & 248.
25. Dhp 33, translated by Francis Story.

The mind is hard to know and very subtle;
it settles where it pleases.
Let the wise man guard the mind:
a guarded mind brings happiness.[26]

The three links grouped under right concentration not only support each other, but also, one is more or less a precondition for the other two. Right effort is right mental effort, not physical. It is effort to prevent the arising of unarisen and to dispel arisen unwholesome thoughts, and to promote the arising of unarisen and to maintain and develop to maturity arisen wholesome thoughts. If there is no right effort directed towards these aims the mind could be occupied with unwholesome thoughts and it will not be possible to practise right mindfulness nor will it be possible to lead the mind to tranquillity. Right mindfulness comprises the four contemplations: body, feelings, states of consciousness and mind-objects. These four contemplations cover the five aggregates and the practice leads to insight into the three characteristics of existence. Without right mindfulness it in not possible to practise right effort as mindfulness is necessary to know whether the thoughts arisen, or not arisen, are wholesome or not, and whether they are acting as hindrances or not. Right mindfulness is also necessary to develop tranquillity because before tranquillity can be attained it is necessary to get rid of disturbing thoughts by bare attention, which is mindfulness. Right concentration is *samādhi*. This means fixing the mind on a single object. This may be for a brief moment or it may be for a prolonged period of time. In the Noble Eightfold Path, right concentration refers to the four absorptions (the *jhānas*). These are attained by fixing the mind on a single object over a prolonged period of time. However, to practise right effort and right mindfulness also, concentration is required as it is necessary to fix the mind on that particular object for a brief moment otherwise the object will not be noticed. The interdependence of these three links may, therefore, be summarised as follows:

26. Dhp 36.

Right effort:	Needed for right mindfulness and right concentration.
Right mindfulness:	Needed for right effort and right concentration.
Right concentration:	Needed for right effort end right mindfulness.

Mental development is of two kinds: development of tranquillity and development of insight. Both are extolled in the texts and in relation to these two end results of *bhāvanā* (mind development) the following two verses are respectively quoted:

Superhuman is the bliss of him
who, with his mind at peace,
has entered a secluded place,
and insight into Dhamma *wins.*

When he then fully comprehends
the rise and fall of the five groups,
he wins to rapture and to joy—
the deathless, this, for those who understand.[27]

Wisdom

Wisdom is also called insight and comprises right view or right understanding and right thoughts.

Right view is the understanding of the Four Noble Truths, that is, the universality of suffering, its origin, its cessation and the path leading to its cessation. This understanding will be gained only by one who goes for refuge to the Buddha, the Dhamma and the Saṅgha. This is clearly stated in the following two verses:

Who to the Buddha and the Dhamma
and to the Saṅgha goes for refuge,
sees with right knowledge
the fourfold teaching of the Noble Truths.[28]

He sees the suffering and its cause,
where suffering is overcome,

27. Dhammapada verses 373 and 374.
28. Dhp 190.

and sees the Eightfold Path
which to the stilling of all suffering leads.[29]

Right thoughts pertain to thoughts free from sensuous desires, free from ill-will and free from cruelty.

Sensuous Desires

There will be a growing realisation of the futility of trying to obtain any worthwhile or enduring satisfaction from attempting to hold on to any object whatsoever, be it animate or inanimate, because there is inevitable separation, sooner or later, of subject and object. The firmer the grasping, which is motivated by none other than selfish craving, the greater the suffering when the separation occurs. There is also a less obvious suffering when trying to get that object in the fear of not getting it and when holding on to it the fear of losing it. As worldlings we are always trying to hold on to something. If we can only make that hold less gluey then the inevitable separation will be less traumatic either when we part company from that object or the object leaves us. It is also true that if one does not have this grasping tendency there will be a greater appreciation of the object, purely on account of its own inherent properties rather than on the misguided notion that the object is one's very own possession. The Enlightened One and the Arahants, who had utterly destroyed the roots of craving, did, however, not live like computers. The Buddha appreciated the beauties of the countryside and often commented on it as he did with Vesāli, for example. Knowing that his *Parinibbāna* was to be in three months he turned to gaze at Vesāli and told the Venerable Ānanda: "This will be the Perfect One's last sight of Vesāli." The Buddha admired and extolled the virtues of his disciples. Yet, when the Venerable Ānanda informed the Buddha that the Venerable Sāriputta had finally attained Nibbāna the Buddha did not show lament or sorrow but said "How could it be that what is born, come to being, formed and bound to fall, should not fall?" Five verses in the Dhammapada, 212 to 216, illustrate the grief and fear that spring from endearment, affection, attachment, lust and craving. One is reproduced here:

29. Dhp 191.

From attachment springs grief,
from attachment springs fear.
For him wholly attachment-free
there is neither grief nor fear.[30]

Ill-will

As has been mentioned earlier, ill-will is given up completely only when the third stage of the supramundane path is attained. However, as one follows the Noble Eightfold Path an understanding of the toxicity of harbouring ill-will towards any sentient being begins to grow and this poison is gradually removed from the system. The less ill-will one feels towards fellow beings the easier will be the conscience and the smoother the journey we have to make. The Buddha was able to say the following about himself and his disciples who had reached spiritual advancement:

Ah! Happily we dwell, from hatred free
amid the hating, free from hate are we![31]

Cruelty

Thoughts of being cruel in any way to any form of sentient life will fade away as one follows the path. In this world today there is a considerable amount of cruelty inflicted on humans and non-humans. We hear about the gruesome tortures practised on political prisoners; we are aware of the pain and suffering animals have to undergo for the purpose of scientific investigations; we are told how tender seal pups are clubbed on the head and skinned even before they are dead. There are also other not-so-obvious forms of cruelty like keeping animals in captivity for the purpose of exhibiting them to satisfy man's curiosity, or compelling them to perform acts not at all natural to them for the purpose of satisfying man's thirst for excitement. The disciple knows that every sentient being has its own right to live without fear of pain or of death. Hence these two verses:

30. Dhp 214.
31. Dhp 197 (F. St)

All tremble before violence,
all are afraid of death.
Comparing others with oneself,
kill not, nor cause to kill.[32]

Whoso, desiring happiness himself,
inflicts on beings harm
who likewise happiness desire,
will gain no happiness in after-life.[33]

It is hoped that by reproducing these verses from the Dhammapada and relating them to specific situations, readers will appreciate the beauty, the practicality and the timelessness of the Buddha's utterances. They are not about fanciful and imaginary ideas. What was uttered more than 2500 years ago is applicable without any change even today and will be so in the future too. There has been no need, with the passage of time, to give different twists to suit the changing attitudes of man and to conform with the results of scientific research. In fact, changing scientific ideas are beginning to conform with what the Buddha said so many years ago. There is a trend to talk of "Western Buddhism" and "Scientific Buddhism." There is no need for this. What the Buddha taught is applicable, without alteration, universally. Science will have to catch up with the Buddha Doctrine. Any attempt to treat the Dhamma as a cold abstract philosophy must fail because there is a thread of loving kindness, compassion and altruistic joy running through the whole Doctrine. What we should do is have confidence which is "reasoned and rooted in understanding." With this confidence and the other four spiritual faculties, namely energy, mindfulness, concentration and wisdom, we should try to attain to at least the Stage of Stream Entry. The following verse explains why this should be done:

Better than being the earth's sole ruler,
better than going to heavenly realms,
better than lordship of all the worlds,
is the fruition of the Stream-Winner's state.[34]

---

32. Dhp 129.
33. Dhp 131.
34. Dhp 178.

We have to bear constantly in mind that Māra, the personification of evil and passion, is lurking round the corner, in various guises, waiting for an opportunity to catch us in his snare. For six years Māra shadowed the Bodhisatta trying to prevent his attainment of enlightenment. Even after enlightenment Māra followed the Buddha looking for any weakness, but in vain. Therefore, it is not surprising that we worldlings can be easy prey to Māra unless we are forever mindful of the wiles of Māra and his three daughters, namely *taṇhā* (craving), *arati* (discontent) and *rāga* (passion). Regarding Māra and *taṇhā* the following verse is quoted:

This I say to you: Good luck to you,
to all who are assembled here!
Dig up the root of craving
like the sweet root of Bīrana!
Let not, like the flood a reed,
Māra break you again, again![35]

35. Dhp 337.

Acknowledgements

The translations of the Dhammapada verses included here, are mostly based on those of the Venerable Nārada Mahāthera of Vajirārāma. Colombo, Sri Lanka. Some changes, however, have been made in them, but not such as to affect the meaning. A few verses have been taken, or adapted, from the translations by Francis Story and Phra Khantipālo. The translations by the latter appeared under the title *The Dhammapada: The Path of the Truth.* This book includes two introductory essays which are recommended to the reader as they present valuable additional material on the topic.

For the expositions given here, grateful use has been made of the following two books: *The Buddha's Ancient Path*, by Ven. Piyadassi Mahāthera and *Buddhist Dictionary: Manual of Buddhist Terms and Doctrines*, by Ven. Nyanatiloka Mahāthera (both issued by the Buddhist Publication Society, Kandy).

The Position of Women in Buddhism

by

Dr. (Mrs.) L.S. Dewaraja
Associate Professor in History
University of Colombo Sri Lanka

WHEEL PUBLICATION NO. 280

The Position of Women in Buddhism

Today, when the role of Women in Society is an issue of worldwide interest it is opportune that we should pause to look at it from a Buddhist perspective. In the recent past, a number of books have been written on the changing status of women in Hindu and Islamic societies, but with regard to women in Buddhism, ever since the distinguished Pali scholar, Miss I.B. Horner, wrote her book on *Women under Primitive Buddhism* as far back as 1930, very little interest has been taken in the subject.

It seems, therefore, justified to raise again the question whether the position of women in Buddhist societies was better than that in non-Buddhist societies of Asia. We will look briefly into the position in Sri Lanka, Thailand, Burma and Tibet, at a time before the impact of the West was ever felt.

Hugh Boyd who came as an envoy to the Kandyan Court in 1782 writes,[1]

> "The Cingalese women exhibit a striking contrast to those of all other Oriental Nations in some of the most prominent and distinctive features of their character. Instead of that lazy apathy, insipid modesty and sour austerity, which have characterised the sex throughout the Asiatick world, in every period of its history, in this island they possess that active sensibility, winning bashfulness and amicable ease, for which the women of modern Europe are peculiarly famed. The Cingalese women are not merely the slaves and mistresses, but in many respects the companions and friends of their husbands; for though the men be authorized by law to hold their wives and daughters in tyrannical subjection, yet their sociable and placable dispositions, soften the rigour of their domestic policy. And polygamy being unknown and divorce permitted among the Cingalese, the men have none of that constitutional jealousy, which has given birth

1. *The Miscellaneous Works of Hugh Boyd, with an account of his Life and Writings* by L.D. Campbell (London 1800), 54–56. Boyd was sent in 1782 as an envoy to the Kandyan court by the British Governor at Madras.

to the voluptuous and unmanly despotism that is practised over the weaker sex in the most enlightened nations, and sanctioned by the various religions of Asia. The Cingalese neither keep their women in confinement nor impose on them any humiliating restraints."

The above quotation is just one selected from a series of comments which European observers have made on the women of Sri Lanka. Many of these European visitors to our shores came during the 17th, 18th and early 19th centuries. There were among them, envoys, missionaries, administrators, soldiers, physicians and ship-wrecked mariners. They had first-hand knowledge of the women in Europe and many of them came through India having observed the women in Hindu and Islamic societies. Hence their evidence is all the more valuable. The recurring comments made by these widely travelled visitors on the women of Sri Lanka have evoked our curiosity to conduct this inquiry. The discussion that follows will deal with conditions that prevailed up to the middle of the nineteenth century. Prior to this our sources are so meagre that we cannot detect any major social changes. After this, due to the impact of Western imperialism, commercial enterprise and Christian missionary activity, incipient changes in the traditional structures become perceptible.

It is only in European writings that one finds lengthy accounts of the social conditions prevailing in the island. The indigenous literature, being mainly religious, lacks information regarding mundane topics like women. But from circumstantial evidence one could surmise that the liberal attitude towards women in Sri Lanka is a trend that has continued from the remote past. When one thinks of women in the traditional East, the picture that comes to our minds is that of the veiled women of Islamic societies, the zenanas where high class Indian ladies lived in seclusion, the harems of Imperial China where lived thousands of royal concubines guarded by eunuchs, the *devadasis* who in the name of God were forced into a life of religious prostitution; all manifesting different aspects of the exploitation of women in the East. It is little known that there were societies in Asia where the position of women was a favourable one, judging even from modern standards. Thailand and Burma too belong to this category. In those instances also we have based our conclusions mainly on the observations of

Europeans who lived in these two countries in various capacities in the 19th and early 20th centuries. R. Grant Brown, who was a revenue officer for 28 years in Burma (1889–1917) has remarked, "Every writer on Burma has commented on the remarkable degree of independence attained by the women. Their position is more surprising in view of the subjection and seclusion of wives and daughters in the neighbouring countries of India and China ..."[2]

A British envoy to the Court of Ava was struck by the equal treatment accorded even to royal ladies. "The queen sat with the king on the throne to receive the embassy. They are referred to as 'the two sovereign Lords'. It is not extraordinary to the Burmans for with them, generally speaking, women are more nearly upon an equality with the stronger sex than among any other Eastern people of consideration."[3]

Lieutenant General Albert Fytche, Late Chief Commissioner of British Burma and Agent to the Viceroy and Governor General of India, wrote in 1878, "Unlike the distrustful and suspicious Hindus and Mohammedans, woman holds among them a position of perfect freedom and independence. She is, with them, not the mere slave of passion, but has equal rights and is the recognised and duly honoured helpmate of man, and in fact bears a more prominent share in the transactions of the more ordinary affairs of life than is the case perhaps with any other people, either eastern or western."[4]

Further inquiries have revealed that in Thailand too, though not to the same extent, the women enjoyed considerable liberty. For instance, J.G.D. Campbell,[5] Educational Adviser to the

2. R. Grant Brown, *Burma as I saw it 1889–1917* (London 1926). Grant, who was a member of the Indian Civil Service, was a magistrate and revenue officer in Burma for 28 years.

3. *Journal of an Embassy from the Governor General of India to the Court of Ava* by John Crawfurd, 2nd ed. in 2 vols. (London 1834), Vol. I, 243.

4. *Burma Past and Present,* Lt. General Albert Fytche, 2 vols. Vol. II (London 1878).

5. *Siam in the Twentieth Century, Being the Experiences and Impressions of a British Officer,* by J.G.D. Campbell (London 1902) 112–113. Campbell was Inspector of Schools and later Educational Adviser to the Siamese Government.

Government of Siam wrote in 1902, "In Siam at any rate whatever be the causes, the position of women is on the whole a healthy one, and contrasts favourably with that among most other Oriental people. No one can have been many days in Bangkok without being struck by the robust physique and erect bearing of the ordinary woman ... It can be said of Buddhism that its influence has at least been all on the right side; and when we remember the thousand arguments that have been advanced in the name of both religion and morality to degrade and debase the weaker sex, this is indeed saying much to its credit."

Sir Charles Bell, British Political Representative in Tibet, Bhutan and Sikkim, writes in 1928, "When a traveller enters Tibet from the neighbouring nations of India and China few things impress him more vigorously or more deeply than the position of the Tibetan woman. They are not kept in seclusion as are Indian women. Accustomed to mix with the other sex throughout their lives, they are at ease with men and can hold their own as well as any women in the world." Bell continues, "And the solid fact remains that in Buddhist countries women hold a remarkably good position. Burma, Ceylon and Tibet exhibit the same picture."[6]

These comments on the freedom and independence enjoyed by the women in certain pre-industrialised and sometimes isolated Asian societies are startling. It is not suggested that in any of these countries, Sri Lanka, Burma and Thailand, the women are on a par with the men both in theory and practice. But they have been favourably compared with the women of the neighbouring countries of India and China, where Hindu, Confucian and Islamic doctrines held sway. This statement may appear contradictory for Burma and Thailand were products of a synthesis of Indic and Sinic civilisations. In Sri Lanka too the impact of Hinduism was very strong. The question arises as to how the situation with regard to women in those three societies should be different from the major cultures of Asia. The common feature predominating in those countries is that they are intensely Buddhist. It is tempting therefore to conclude that Buddhism has helped to better the position of women in Sri Lanka, Burma and Thailand.

6. *The People of Tibet*, Charles Bell (Oxford 1928), p. 147.

This conclusion would take us back to the question of the Buddhist attitude towards women and how it differs from that of other religions. Examining the position in ancient India it is clear from the evidence in the Rigveda, the earliest literature of the Indo-Aryans, that women held an honourable place in early Indian society. There were a few Rigvedic hymns composed by women. Women had access to the highest knowledge and could participate in all religious ceremonies. In domestic life too she was respected and there is no suggestion of seclusion of women and child marriage. Later when the priestly caste of Brahmins dominated society and religion lost its spontaneity and became a mass of ritual, we see a downward trend in the position accorded to women. The most relentless of the Brahmin law givers was Manu whose Code of Laws[7] is the most anti-feminist literature one could find. At the outset, Manu deprived women of their religious rights and spiritual life. "Sudras, slaves and women" were prohibited from reading the Vedas. A woman could not attain heaven through any merit of her own. She could not worship or perform a sacrifice by herself. She could reach heaven only through implicit obedience to her husband, be he debauched or devoid of all virtues.

Having thus denied her any kind of spiritual and intellectual nourishment, Manu elaborated the myth that all women were sinful and prone to evil. "Neither shame nor decorum, nor honesty, nor timidity," says Manu, "is the cause of a woman's chastity, but the want of a suitor alone".[8] She should therefore be kept under constant vigilance: and the best way to do it was to keep her occupied in the endless tasks of motherhood and domestic duties so that she has no time for mischief. Despite this denigration there was always in Indian thought an idealisation of motherhood and a glorification of the feminine concept. But in actual practice, it could be said by and large, Manu's reputed Code of Laws did influence social attitudes towards women, at least in the higher rungs of society.

It is against this background that one has to view the impact of Buddhism in the 5th century B.C. It is not suggested that

7. *Laws of Manu*, trans. G. Buhler, *Sacred Books of the East*, Vol. XXV (Oxford 1866).

8. *Ibid.*, IX, 10.

the Buddha inaugurated a campaign for the liberation of Indian womanhood. But he did succeed in creating a minor stir against Brahmin dogma and superstition. He condemned the caste structure dominated by the Brahmin, excessive ritualism and sacrifice. He denied the existence of a Godhead and emphasised emancipation by individual effort. The basic doctrine of Buddhism, salvation by one's own effort, presupposes the spiritual equality of all beings, male and female. This should mitigate against the exclusive supremacy of the male. It needed a man of considerable courage and a rebellious spirit to pronounce a way of life that placed woman on a level of near equality to man. The Buddha saw the spiritual potential of both men and women and founded (after considerable hesitation) the Order of Bhikkhunīs or Nuns, one of the earliest organisations for women. The Sāsana or Church consisted of the Bhikkhus (Monks), Bhikkhunīs (Nuns), laymen and laywomen so that the women were not left out of any sphere of religious activity. The highest spiritual states were within the reach of both men and women and the latter needed no masculine assistance or priestly intermediary to achieve them. We could therefore agree with I.B. Horner when she says that Buddhism accorded to women a position approximating to equality.[9]

Moving from the sphere of philosophy to domestic life one notices a change of attitude when we come to Buddhist times. In all patriarchal societies the desire for male offspring is very strong for the continuance of the patrilineage and, in the case of Hindus, for the due performance of funeral rites for only a son could carry out the funeral rites of his father and thus ensure the future happiness of the deceased. This was so crucial to the Hindu that the law allowed a sonless wife to be superseded by a second or a third one or even turned out of the house.[10] It is said "through a son he conquers the world and through a son's son he attains immortality."[11] As a result of this belief the birth of a daughter was the cause for lamentation. In Buddhism future happiness does not depend on funeral rites but on the actions of the deceased.

9. I.B. Horner, *Women under Primitive Buddhism: Laywomen and Alsmwomen* (London 1930), XXIV.

10. *Laws of Manu,* IX, 81.

11. Ibid., IX, 137.

The Buddhist funeral ceremony is a very simple one which could be performed by the widow, daughter or any one on the spot, and the presence of a son is not compulsory. There is no ritual or ceremonial need for a son and the birth of a daughter need not be a cause for grief. It is well known that the Buddha consoled King Pasenadi who came to him grieving that his queen, Mallikā, had given birth to a daughter. "A female offspring, O king, may prove even nobler than a male ..."[12] a revolutionary statement for his time. Despite the spiritual equality of the sexes and the fact that a son is not an absolute necessity in securing happiness in the after life, yet even in Buddhist societies there is a preference for male offspring even today, so potent is the ideology of male superiority.

Marriage and family are basic institutions in all societies whether primitive or modern and the position of woman in a particular society is influenced by and expressed in the status she holds within these institutions. Has she got the right to own property and dispose of it as she pleases without reference to her husband? Has she got the same rights as her husband to dissolve the marriage bond? Has she the right to remarry or is this a man's privilege? The answers to these questions will undoubtedly determine the position accorded to women in any society. Let us examine the Buddhist attitude to the question. In Buddhism, unlike Christianity and Hinduism, marriage is not a sacrament. It is purely a secular affair and the monks do not participate in it. In Sri Lanka, Thailand and Burma there is a good deal of ceremony, feasting and merry-making connected with the event but these are not of a religious nature. Sometimes monks are invited to partake of alms and they in turn bless the couple. Although there are no vows or ritual involved in the event of a marriage, the Buddha has laid down in the Sigālovāda Sutta the duties of a husband and wife:

> "In five ways should a wife as Western quarter, be ministered to by her husband: by respect, by courtesy, by faithfulness, by handing over authority to her, by providing her with ornaments. In these five ways does the wife ministered to by her husband as the Western quarter, love him: her duties are

12. Quoted by I.B. Horner in *Women in Early Buddhist Literature*, The Wheel Publication, No. 30 (Colombo 1961), 8–9.

well-performed by hospitality to kin of both, by faithfulness, by watching over the goods he brings and by skill and industry in discharging all business."[13]

The significant point here is that the Buddha's injunctions are bilateral; the marital relationship is a reciprocal one with mutual rights and obligations. This was a momentous departure from ideas prevailing at the time. For instance Manu says, "Offspring, the due performance of religious rites, faithful service, highest conjugal happiness and heavenly bliss for one's ancestors and oneself depends on one's wife alone."[14] Confucius, an older contemporary of the Buddha, spoke in the same tone: "In this way when the deferential obedience of the wife was complete, the internal harmony was secured, and a long continuance of the family could be reckoned with."[15] Confucius gives in detail the duties of the son to the father, the wife to the husband and the daughter-in-law to the mother-in-law but never vice-versa; so that the wife had only duties and obligations and the husband only rights and privileges. According to the injunctions of the Buddha as given in the Sigālovāda Sutta, which deals with domestic duties, every relationship was a reciprocal one whether it be between husband and wife, parent and child, or master and servant. Ideally, therefore, among Buddhists, marriage is a contract between equals.

However, it does not necessarily follow that social practice conforms to theory. The egalitarian ideals of Buddhism appear to have been impotent against the universal ideology of masculine superiority. The doctrine of Karma and Rebirth, one of the fundamental tenets of Buddhism, has been interpreted to prove the inherent superiority of the male. According to the law of Karma, one's actions in the past will determine one's position, wealth, power, talent and even sex in future births. One is reborn a woman because of one's bad Karma. Thus the subordination of women is given a religious sanction. It is not unusual even in Sri Lanka for women, after doing a meritorious deed, to aspire to be redeemed from womanhood and be reborn as a man in future.

13. *Dialogues of the Buddha,* trans. C.A.F Rhys Davids, part III, 181–182.

14. Laws of Manu, IX, 28.

15. *The Sacred Books of China: The Texts of Confucianism,* trans. James Legge (Oxford 1879) *Sacred Books of the East,* Vol. XXVIII, 431.

Despite the remarkable degree of sexual equality in Burmese society, all women recite as a part of their Buddhist devotions the following prayer: "I pray that I may be reborn as a male in a future existence."[16] In Thailand in 1399 A.D., the Queen Mother founded a monastery and commemorated the event in an inscription in which she requested, "By the power of my merit, may I be reborn as a male ..."[17]

Several examples could be quoted from the popular parlance of all three societies to show that even women, whatever their station, have accepted the idea of female inferiority and this has influenced the husband-wife relationship in varying degrees in the societies concerned. In Sri Lanka where this idea is least perceptible, it is considered becoming even in modern times to maintain a facade of husband domination. The wifely control is unobtrusive and subtle. This ambivalent attitude is more pronounced in Burma where women are a specially privileged lot. They control the family economy; socially, politically and legally they are on a par with men. But the wife makes a show of deference to the husband which in itself is no measure of male dominance but an adaptation to a cultural norm. On the other hand, the fact that men could have multiple spouses, whereas the women were restricted to one, placed the husband in a privileged position. The reverse was true in Sri Lanka where polygamy was unknown except in the royal family, but polyandry was practised (though not widespread) till recent times.

In traditional Thailand the subordination of the wife in the family hierarchy was sanctioned by law. Till 1935 polyandry was legally recognised. As stated by Reynolds, "Fundamental to the family law in the Law Code of 1805 was the conjugal power of the husband, which meant that he managed the property held jointly by the spouses, that he could sell his wife or give her away and that he could administer bodily punishment to her, provided the

16. Quoted by Melford E. Spiro in *Kinship and Marriage in Burma: A Cultural and Psychodynamic Analysis* (London 1977), 260.

17. Quoted by C.J. Reynolds in "A Nineteenth Century Thai Buddhist Defence of Polygamy and some Remarks on the Social History of Women in Thailand," a Paper prepared for the Seventh Conference International Association of Historians of Asia, Bangkok, 22–26 August 1977, 3.

degree of punishment was in proportion to the misdeed."[18] The Royal Decrees of 1854, 1868 and 1874 removed some of the legal disabilities of women, but still in Thailand female subordination seems to be more a reality than in Sri Lanka or Burma.

From the nature of the marriage contract one passes on to the question whether both parties had the same facilities for terminating the contract. It is seen that in most cultures the woman is irretrievably bound by the chains of matrimony while the man can shed his shackles with ease. The Confucian code of discipline provides the husband with several grounds for divorce. Not only leprosy and sterility, even disobedience and garrulity, were valid reasons to get rid of a wife. Among the Hindus marriage was an indissoluble sacrament for the woman, while the man had the right to remarry even when the first wife was alive. Says Manu, "A barren wife may be superseded in the 8th year. She whose children all die in the 10th, she who bears only daughters in the 11th, but she who is quarrelsome without delay."[19] In addition a man could abandon a blemished, diseased or deflowered wife.[20] Under Islamic law the marriage contract may be dissolved by the husband at his will without the intervention of a court and without assigning any cause. But a wife cannot divorce herself from her husband without his consent except under a contract made before or after marriage. If the conditions of the contract are not opposed to Muslim law then the divorce will take effect.[21]

In Buddhism marriage received no religious sanction and in the absence of a Buddhist legal code comparable to the Laws of Manu or the Sharia Law of the Muslims, the dissolution of the marriage contract was settled by the individuals concerned or their families. With regard to Sri Lanka, there is a document dated 1769 which gives an orthodox and official view on the subject. The Dutch who were ruling the maritime provinces of Sri Lanka wished to codify the laws and customs of the island. The Dutch Governor I.W. Falck sent a series of questions to the eminent monks of Kandy and the answers to these are given in

18. *Ibid.*, 6–7.
19. *Laws of Manu*, IX, 81.
20. *Laws of Manu*, IX, 72.
21. D.F. Mulla, Principles of Muhammedan Law (Calcutta 1955), 264.

the document known as the *Lakrajalosirita.* The governor raised the question whether divorce was permitted among the Sinhalese. The reply was:

> "A man and a woman who have been united in marriage with the knowledge of their parents and relations and according to the Sinhala custom cannot become separated at their own pleasure. If a man wishes to obtain a divorce it must be by proving that his wife, failing in the reverence and respect due to a husband, has spoken to him in an unbecoming manner; or that she has lavished her affection on another and spends his earning on him, and if her improper conduct is proved before a court of justice he will be permitted to abandon her."

The next question is for what faults on the part of the husband may the wife sue for and obtain a divorce from him. The Bhikkhus reply:

> "If being destitute of love and affection for his wife, he withholds from her the wearing apparel and ornaments suitable to her rank; if he does not provide her with food of such a quality as she has a right to; if he neglects to acquire money by agriculture, commerce and other honourable means; if associating with other women, he squanders his property upon them; if he makes a practice of committing other improper and degrading acts such as stealing, lying or drinking intoxicating liquors, if he treats his wife as a slave and at the same times behaves respectfully to other women, on proof of his delinquency before the above mentioned court, the wife may obtain a divorce."[22]

The significant point is that even in theory the Sinhala laws were equally applicable and binding to both husband and wife. One clearly sees the influence of the injunctions of the Sigālovāda Sutta in the development of these institutions. However, litigation being a tedious process then as now, it is unlikely that the average Sinhalese of the 18th century resorted to this lengthy judicial procedure. The *Lakrajalosirita* was written by Buddhist

22. *Lakrajalosirita,* ed. and trans. Bishop Edmund Pieris, Published by the Ceylon Historical Manuscripts Commission, 10 and 11.

monks for the information of a foreigner, and judging from the rest of the document they tried to depict ideal conditions. Only the very well-to-do could afford the luxury of a court case. A more realistic account has been left by Robert Knox who spent 19 years in the company of poor peasants: "But their marriages are but of little force and validity for if they disagree and mislike one another they part without disgrace. Yet it stands firmer for the Man than for the Woman: howbeit they do leave one the other at their pleasure."[23]

According to Sinhala laws of the 18th century the wife was treated very liberally at the time of divorce. She got back all the wealth that her parents gave her at the time of marriage and half of all the property acquired by the couple after marriage. Also she was given a sum of money sufficient to cover her expenses for the next six months. It is worthy of note that in Sri Lanka prior to European occupation both sexes had equal facilities for divorce, both in theory and in practice. The situation changed, however, with the impact of Christianity and the introduction of Roman Dutch Law by the Hollanders in the areas under their control.

In traditional Burma too a code of divorce provided for ill assorted unions. Where there was a mutual desire for separation due to incompatibility or other causes, parties can divorce each other by an equal division of property. If one is unwilling the other is free to go provided all property is left behind. A woman can demand a divorce if her husband ill-treats her or if he cannot maintain her; and a man in case of sterility or infidelity of the wife. Another method, not uncommon, is for the aggrieved party to seek refuge in monastic life; for this would at once dissolve the marriage bond. This easy availability of divorce in Burma has been condemned by Father Bigandet, the Roman Catholic Bishop of Rangoon as "damnable laxity". Despite this censure, it is said that this easy and equal facility for divorce has rendered the Burmese spouses more forbearing and that serious connubial quarrels are rare among them.[24]

---

23. Robert Knox, *An Historical Relation of Ceylon* (Glasgow 1911), 149. Knox was a ship-wrecked British sailor who spent 19 years from 1660 to 1679 as a prisoner in the Kandyan Kingdom.

24. Fytche, Vol. II, 75.

In Thailand although women had legal disabilities, they could initiate divorce proceedings which enabled them to escape from a tyrannous husband. As far back as 1687 the French envoy to the Siamese court observed, "The Husband is naturally the Master of Divorce but he never refuseth it to his wife when she absolutely desires it. He restores her portion to her and their children are divided among them in this manner ..."[25] Although the conjugal power of the husband was fundamental to the 1805 Code, yet the wife's right to divorce was preserved and she was treated generously when the marriage was annulled.

Moving on to the question of the remarriage of widows and divorcees, one notices that in certain societies the wives were regarded as the personal property of their husbands. As such the custom of slaying, sacrificing or burying women alive to accompany their deceased husbands along with their belongings has been found in many lands as far removed as America, Africa and India. The best known example is the *sati pūja* or self immolation of high-caste Hindu widows. This custom which was unknown in the Rig-Veda, developed later; it was never very widespread but there were isolated instances continuing even up to early British times. The British had to introduce legislation to prevent it. Among the Hindus a widow was expected to lead a life of severe austerity and strict celibacy for she was bonded to her dead husband. Further she lost her social and religious status and was considered an unlucky person. The question of the remarriage of divorcees did not arise because a Hindu wife could not repudiate her husband; even if she was rejected by the latter she had to remain celibate.

In Buddhism death is considered a natural and inevitable end. As a result a woman suffers no moral degradation on account of her widowhood. Her social status is not altered in any way. In Buddhist societies she does not have to advertise her widowhood by shaving her head and relinquishing her ornaments. She is not forced to fast on specific days and sleep on hard floors for self-mortification has no place in Buddhism. Nor does she have to

25. Simon de la Loubere, *The Kingdom of Siam, With an Introduction by David K. Wyatt* (London 1968), 53. De la Loubere was an envoy sent to Siam by Louis XIV of France in 1687. He was in Siam for four months only.

absent herself from ceremonies and auspicious events. Above all there is no religious barrier to her remarriage.[26] The remarriage of rejected wives is also known in Buddhist literature.

Women whose marriages break up were free to remarry with no stigma attached, ..."But if they chance to mislike one another and part asunder ... then she is fit for another man, being as they account never the worse for wearing."[27] Even the *Lakrajalosirita,* which gives an orthodox Buddhist view, permits the remarriage of women after separation from their spouses. It was common even in the highest rungs of society. In Burma and Thailand too women had the right to remarry after divorce. As far back as 1687, La Loubere the French envoy noticed that in Thailand, "After the Divorce both can remarry and the woman can remarry on the very day of the Divorce."[28]

It is clear, therefore, that Buddhism has saved the daughter from indignity, elevated the wife to a position approximating to equality and retrieved the widow from abject misery.

The social freedom that women enjoyed in Buddhist societies, above everything else, has evoked from Western observers the comments that we have quoted earlier in this paper. It is not so much the equality of status but the complete desegregation of the sexes, that has distinguished the women in Buddhist societies from those of the Middle East, the Far East and the Indian subcontinent. Segregation of the sexes only leads to the seclusion and confinement of women behind veils and walls. The Confucian code lays down detailed rules on how men and women should behave in each other's presence. Manu went to the furthest extreme of segregation by warning that one should not remain in a lonely place even with one's own mother and sister. Sexual segregation pervades all aspects of life in Islamic societies.

In early Buddhist literature one sees a free intermingling of the sexes. The celibate monks and nuns had separate quarters, yet the cloister was not cut off from the rest of the world. It is recorded that the Buddha had long conversations with his female disciples. The devout benefactress Visākhā frequented the monastery decked

26. I.B. Horner, *Women under Primitive Buddhism,* 72 sqq.
27. Knox, 149.
28. De la Loubere, 53.

in all her finery and, accompanied by a maid servant, she attended to the needs of the monks. Her clothes and ornaments were the talk of the town, yet neither the Buddha nor the monks dissuaded her from wearing them. It was after she developed in insight and asceticism that she voluntarily relinquished her ornaments.

This free and liberal attitude certainly had its impact on the behaviour of both men and women in Buddhist societies. In Sri Lanka in the 17th century, "the Men are not Jealous of their Wives for the greatest Ladies in the land will frequently talk and discourse with any Men they please, although their Husbands be in presence."[29] It has been remarked that the women visited places of worship always dressed in their best attire. This is quite a contrast to the stand taken by Manu according to whom the love of ornamentation was an evil attribute of women; and the Koranic injunction that the pious woman should hide all beauty and ornamentation behind the veil. Burmese women of all ranks went unveiled and ornamented and added colour to all occasions, though flanked by India and China where customs such as purdah and foot binding prevailed. In Thailand it has been noticed that the women of the upper classes, though by no means confined to lives of strict seclusion, did not appear much in public.

In conclusion we could say that the secular nature of the marriage contract, the facility to divorce, the right to remarry, the desegregation of the sexes and above all else the right to inherit, own and dispose of property without let or hindrance from the husband, have all contributed to the alleviation of the lot of women in Buddhist societies. Conflicting with the Buddhist ethos and negating its effects in varying degrees is the universal ideology of masculine superiority. So that in all three societies— Sri Lanka, Thailand, Burma—there is an ambivalence in the attitudes towards women. Yet their position is certainly better than in any of the major cultures of Asia.

29. Knox, 104.

ABOUT PARIYATTI

Pariyatti is dedicated to providing affordable access to authentic teachings of the Buddha about the Dhamma theory (*pariyatti*) and practice (*paṭipatti*) of Vipassana meditation. A 501(c)(3) nonprofit charitable organization since 2002, Pariyatti is sustained by contributions from individuals who appreciate and want to share the incalculable value of the Dhamma teachings. We invite you to visit www.pariyatti.org to learn about our programs, services, and ways to support publishing and other undertakings.

Pariyatti Publishing Imprints

Vipassana Research Publications (focus on Vipassana as taught by S.N. Goenka in the tradition of Sayagyi U Ba Khin)

BPS Pariyatti Editions (selected titles from the Buddhist Publication Society, copublished by Pariyatti)

MPA Pariyatti Editions (selected titles from the Myanmar Pitaka Association, copublished by Pariyatti)

Pariyatti Digital Editions (audio and video titles, including discourses)

Pariyatti Press (classic titles returned to print and inspirational writing by contemporary authors)

Pariyatti enriches the world by

- disseminating the words of the Buddha,
- providing sustenance for the seeker's journey,
- illuminating the meditator's path.

www.ingramcontent.com/pod-product-compliance
Lightning Source LLC
Chambersburg PA
CBHW020348170426
43200CB00005B/95
* 9 7 8 1 6 8 1 7 2 1 9 2 7 *